THE McCABE READER

THE McCABE READER

EDITED AND INTRODUCED BY BRIAN DAVIES AND PAUL KUCHARSKI

Bloomsbury T&T Clark
An imprint of Bloomsbury Publishing Plc

B L O O M S B U R Y
LONDON · OXFORD · NEW YORK · NEW DELHI · SYDNEY

Bloomsbury T&T Clark

An imprint of Bloomsbury Publishing Plc

Imprint previously known as T&T Clark

50 Bedford Square	1385 Broadway
London	New York
WC1B 3DP	NY 10018
UK	USA

www.bloomsbury.com

Bloomsbury, T&T Clark and the Diana logo are trademarks of Bloomsbury Publishing Plc

First published 2016

British Library Cataloguing-in-Publication Data
A catalogue record for this book is available from the British Library.

ISBN:	HB:	978-0-56766-889-9
	PB:	978-0-56766-888-2
	ePDF:	978-0-56766-890-5
	ePub:	978-0-56766-891-2

Library of Congress Cataloging-in-Publication Data
Names: McCabe, Herbert, 1926-2001, author. | Davies, Brian, 1951- editor.
Title: The McCabe reader / edited by Brian Davies and Paul Kucharski.
Description: 1st [edition]. | New York : Bloomsbury T&T Clark, 2016. |
Includes bibliographical references.
Identifiers: LCCN 2015050509| ISBN 9780567668899 (hbk) | ISBN 9780567668882 (pbk)
Subjects: LCSH: Catholic Church--Doctrines.
Classification: LCC BX4705.M1775 A25 2016 | DDC 230/.2--dc23 LC record available at http://lccn.loc.gov/2015050509

Cover design: Terry Woodley
Cover image © Getty Images

Typeset by Fakenham Prepress Solutions, Fakenham, Norfolk NR21 8NN
Printed and bound in India

CONTENTS

PREFACE

Herbert McCabe was one of the most gifted English-speaking theologians and philosophers of the twentieth century. He had a profound grasp both of the history of Christian thinking and of secular philosophy. In an illuminating way, he especially brought together ideas coming from Thomas Aquinas and Ludwig Wittgenstein while presenting and defending his religious beliefs in a manner that few have equalled. And his influence on thinkers in the United Kingdom and the United States has been notable, especially since his death in 2001 and the subsequent appearance of six posthumously published volumes of his writings. As someone quipped at an Oxford colloquium on McCabe in 2011, 'Since his death, Herbert has been not so much decomposing as composing'.

Many reviews of McCabe's work have appeared. And his praises have been sung by a number of distinguished authors: literary figures such as Terry Eagleton and Seamus Heaney; theologians such as Stanley Hauerwas, Fergus Kerr and Rowan Williams; and philosophers such as Anthony Kenny and Alasdair MacIntyre. To date, however, there has been no single book that allows readers to find the best of McCabe's writings in one place.

The present work aims to address that need. Following an introduction to McCabe's life and works, it comprises a selection of some of his best essays drawn from almost everything by him that has now appeared in print. Of necessity, its contents represent but a fraction of his literary output, a tip of the proverbial iceberg. But we hope that they will provide a useful presentation of McCabe at his finest, both for those who know little about him and for those already familiar with his ideas and his inimitable way of presenting them.

One commentator has said that 'the best thing to knowing Herbert

McCabe is to read him'. In what follows, we aim to present a helpful opportunity to read McCabe on his greatest and most lucid form. As an aid to
anyone wanting to study his writings in detail, we also provide a list of his
major publications, though this does not cite the many, often brilliant, editorials that he wrote on a monthly basis for *New Blackfriars* during his time as
editor of that journal.

We have divided the following text into sections: 'Philosophy of God and
Christian Doctrine', 'Ethics and Moral Theology', 'Essays on Aquinas' and
'Sermons'. Readers of this volume should, however, recognize that the sections
that we employ are, to some extent, arbitrary. That is because, like Aquinas,
McCabe had a habit of touching on more than one topic in things that he
wrote. Thus, for example, when he writes about God, he often has things to
say about ethics, and when he writes about ethics, he often has things to say
about God. And the thought of Aquinas is ever present in his sermons and
most of his other writings. So, in the sense that many of Aquinas's texts often
cannot be easily listed as dealing with particular matters, such is the case with
the writings of McCabe. We trust, though, that the sections we provide will
prove helpful to some extent.

We should note that in what follows we have sometimes edited previously
published essays by McCabe with an eye to matters of punctuation and so
as to delete some cross-references by McCabe that appear in his book *God
Matters*.

Chapter 1 below originally appeared in *New Blackfriars*, 94 (1052), July
2013. It is reprinted by kind permission of Wiley-Blackwell. The other
chapters appeared in the following books by McCabe: *God Matters* (London:
Geoffrey Chapman [subsequently Continuum], 1987: Chs 3, 4 and 20); *God
Still Matters* (London and New York: Continuum, 2002: Chs 2, 7, 8, 9, 13,
16, 17, 18 and 22); *God, Christ and Us* (London and New York: Continuum,
2003: Chs 19, 21, 23, 24 and 25); *Law, Love and Language* (London and New
York: Continuum, 2003: Ch. 12); *The Good Life* (London and New York:

Continuum, 2005: Chs 10 and 11); *Faith Within Reason* (London and New York: Continuum, 2007: Chs 5, 6, 14 and 15).

For encouragement on this project we thank Robin Baird Smith and Anna Turton at Bloomsbury.

Brian Davies and Paul Kucharski

Introduction

I

Herbert McCabe was born on 2 August 1926 in Middlesbrough, UK. He died in Oxford on 28 June 2001.[1] His baptismal name was 'John Ignatius'. He applied to join the Order of Preachers (better known as the Dominicans) in 1949 and was a novice at its priory at Woodchester in Gloucestershire, where he was given the name 'Herbert'. Aspirants to the Dominicans when McCabe joined them were obliged to accept a religious name on their reception of the habit, and McCabe was surprised to find himself suddenly called 'Herbert'. In 1953, just before his solemn profession as a Dominican, he asked permission to be known as 'Fabian', but the English Dominican provincial of the day refused the request.

Before becoming a Dominican, McCabe was an undergraduate at Manchester University.[2] He went there in 1944 to study chemistry, but ended up switching to philosophy and was taught by Dorothy Emmet (1904–2000), who once said that McCabe was a student she could never forget. In Manchester McCabe also interacted with Alasdair MacIntyre, now one of the best-read authors on moral philosophy. MacIntyre did not much overlap with McCabe at Manchester. They first met when MacIntyre arrived there just before McCabe joined the Dominicans. However, MacIntyre's graduate student friends at Manchester were people for whom McCabe, even as absent, was a living presence, one which stayed with him over the years. In time, said MacIntyre, McCabe played 'a key part' in his own acceptance of the Catholic faith.[3]

McCabe became a priest in 1955 and was subsequently sent to work at St Dominic's church in Newcastle-upon-Tyne from 1958 to 1960. He was then assigned to St Sebastian's parish in Salford, from which he was deputed to look for a house in Manchester where Dominicans could establish themselves.[4] This turned out to be 33 Alan Road in the suburb of Withington. McCabe lived there until 1965. From Alan Road he travelled to give lectures on philosophy and theology to student societies at various British universities. He also worked on what came to be the third volume of the monumental Blackfriars edition of the *Summa Theologiae* published by Eyre and Spottiswoode between 1964 and 1981.[5]

McCabe was happy in his Manchester assignation. After a few years, though, he was transferred to the Dominican priory in Cambridge. The English Dominican records have him noted as being posted there from 1966/1967. Unlike his time at Alan Road, however, McCabe's period in Cambridge proved to be difficult and, indeed, traumatic for him.

Everything began on quite a high note, for McCabe was moved to Cambridge so as to become editor of *New Blackfriars*, a journal of theology, philosophy and related matters published under the auspices of the English Dominicans. His appointment to this position must have been perceived by himself and others as a mark of approval from his religious superiors, and it left him with room to exercise his talents on behalf of his order and with an eye on a readership of something close to two thousand subscribers, mostly in the United Kingdom and the United States.[6] In particular it allowed him to publish monthly editorials in *New Blackfriars*. This editorial licence, however, led to an unfortunate sequence of occurrences early in 1967, ones sparked off by events in the life of Charles Davis (1923–99).

By 1967 Davis, a Catholic priest, was the best-known Roman Catholic theologian in Britain. Ordained in 1946, he was Professor of Dogmatic Theology at St Edmund's Seminary, Ware, from 1952–65, Professor of Theology at Heythrop University College (then in Oxfordshire) from 1965–6 and editor of

The Clergy Review. Davis was also a theological adviser (*peritus*) at the Second Vatican Council and was much reported by British and American newspapers for his comments at press conferences as the council met. In December 1966, however, Davis announced his decision to leave the priesthood and the Catholic Church, and on 1 January 1967 he provided an explanation of himself in the British newspaper the *Observer*.[7] In the February 1967 issue of *New Blackfriars*, McCabe published an editorial concerning Davis and his departure from the Church. In it, and picking up terminologically on an article by Brian Wicker in the *Guardian* newspaper, he said: 'The Church is quite plainly corrupt'.[8] As a result of this editorial McCabe was dismissed from his editorial position and was also, though very briefly, suspended from his priestly functions.[9]

In 1967 the Apostolic Delegate to the United Kingdom was Archbishop Hyginus E. Cardinale (1916–83), who in an interview reported in the English *Catholic Herald* said that McCabe's editorial displayed 'considerable immaturity', 'ignorance' and 'lack of pastoral concern'. This verdict might be thought to have been premature, since there is reason to think that Cardinale had not actually read McCabe's editorial before commenting on it.[10] Be that as it may, the editorial is anything but the product of an immature thinker, displays only a little ignorance, is full of pastoral concern and aims to explain why Charles Davis should *not* have left the Church. It can be best described as an essay in bridge-building.

It begins by lamenting and expressing shock that Davis should have acted as he did. Davis, says McCabe, is no 'lightweight' theologian, so Catholics ought to worry about his departure. Why would someone like Davis walk away? Having suggested that Vatican II might have left many Catholics victims of a dubious 'liberal' or 'progressive' kind of 'orthodoxy' promoted by 'a new elite of "right-thinking people"', McCabe goes on to say that what is needed is a willingness on the part of Christians with different views to learn from each other and live together. Such willingness, says McCabe, is not much in evidence in the 'official' Catholic Church which is 'racked by fear, insecurity and anxiety, with a consequent intolerance and lack of love'. There is 'a concern for authority at the expense of truth' – something, says McCabe, notably lacking in great figures like Pope John XXIII, Cardinal Bea and Bishop Bekkers.[11]

According to McCabe, the purpose of his 1967 editorial was, as he says in it, 'to defend a position which is that of many Catholics who would ordinarily have been thought more "radical" than Charles Davis and who have no intention of leaving the Church'. The editorial was a sympathetic critique of Davis, not an endorsement of his departure.[12] Its argument was that what Davis found unbearable in the Church was not a reason for cutting himself off from it. We should, said McCabe, realize that 'a dialectical tension between the framework of the Church and its points of growth seems to be a condition of Christian existence'. To be sure, he adds, 'what does not need to be endured indefinitely is the special irrelevance of so much of the behaviour of Church officials' seemingly smitten with 'directives and prohibitions', with the playing of 'domination games' and a demand for 'docility' and obedience to orders. *And yet*, McCabe insists, all of this can be tolerated as Church officials speak with 'the real authority that comes with understanding and concern and listening to others; the authority that sees itself not in terms of power but as a service to the community, the channel of communication by which each part of the community is kept in touch with the whole, a whole that extends through time as well as space'. It is, concludes McCabe, 'because we believe that the hierarchical institutions of the Roman Catholic Church, with all their decadence, their corruption and their sheer silliness, do in fact link us to areas of Christian truth beyond their own particular experience and ultimately to truths beyond any experience, that we remain, and see our lives in terms of remaining, members of this Church'.

In retrospect, one might now think that McCabe's February 1967 comments were somewhat old-fashioned, but they led the then Dominican Master

General, Fr Aniceto Fernandez, to sack him from his editorship. In a letter of 15 February 1967 to the English Dominican Provincial, Fr Ian Hislop, Fernandez explains that, with regret, he felt himself to have no option concerning this 'severe action'. Referring to McCabe's February editorial, Fernandez says that 'all that he has written … is subversive not only of ecclesiastical authority but indeed of the very constitution of the Church'. Fr Fernandez did not speak English, so his letter to Fr Hislop presumably came in the form of a translation by an English speaker to hand at the Dominican headquarters (*Curia Generalizia*) at Santa Sabina in Rome.[13] Also, presumably, Fr Fernandez never did read McCabe's editorial in the language in which it was published. Anyway, McCabe's suspension as editor of *New Blackfriars* remained in effect until he was reappointed to the position in 1970. His first editorial upon reinstatement began with the words: 'As I was saying before I was so oddly interrupted …'.

By this time McCabe had been assigned to Blackfriars, Oxford, which then housed the novitiate of the English Dominicans as well as their centre for theology and philosophy, the English Dominican *Studium*. McCabe lived at Blackfriars from 1968 until his death. During this time he taught Dominicans in formation and lectured regularly at Bristol University and the University of Malta. He also travelled widely as a visiting lecturer and preacher. He continued to edit *New Blackfriars* until October 1979, when he voluntarily resigned and gave way as editor to Fr Alban Weston, whom he admired. In 1981 he became the English Dominican Novice Master, a position he retained until 1988, and in 1989 he was awarded the highest academic degree given by the Dominican Order – the STM (Master of Sacred Theology). McCabe never held a full-time academic position outside the Dominican Order. However, as is evident from a 1965 letter to him from C. J. F. Williams (1930–97), there was a desire on the part of people at the University of Hull to have him appointed to a job in its theology department. In later years, Anthony Kenny advised the University of Bristol to appoint McCabe to its Chair of Theology, though McCabe never applied for the position and it was given to someone else.

McCabe's assignment as Novice Master and his being given the STM indicate the respect that he came to enjoy among Dominicans following the stormy business of 1967. This is not to say that all of his brethren found him personally congenial. Some did not, largely because he could sometimes be extremely acerbic, not to say bellicose, especially when under the influence of alcohol. But his Catholic orthodoxy and loyalty to Dominican ideals were recognized by everyone in his province. Even those Dominicans who found McCabe difficult to tolerate in certain ways would never have denied that he was an exceptionally talented preacher. His sermons, always delivered from a carefully prepared typescript from which he read while not appearing to be reading at all, were consistently lively and packed with arresting theological insights presented in a way that only the best communicators can manage. They were models of clarity and incisiveness. The same can be said of everything published under his name.

II

McCabe was a cautious author and not much given to the publishing of books. He produced numerous editorials in *New Blackfriars* and a number of articles both in that journal and in others, but he personally saw only three books into press: *The New Creation* (1964), *Law, Love and Language* (1968) and *God Matters* (1987). In 1985 and at the instigation of Maurice Couve de Murville, then Archbishop of Birmingham, McCabe published *The Teaching of the Catholic Church: A New Catechism of Christian Doctrine*, which was more a pamphlet than a book. This text was republished by Darton, Longman and Todd in 2000 and comes with a Foreword by Timothy Radcliffe, then Master General of the Dominican Order. If Fr Fernandez was not a fan of McCabe in 1967, Fr Radcliffe clearly is these days. Alasdair MacIntyre says of McCabe's *Catechism* that it 'is as remarkable for its questions as for its answers, since it not only includes questions that we ought to ask, but may not have asked, but also – to an extent that is unusual in catechisms – the questions that many of us do actually ask'.[14]

Why did McCabe publish relatively few books in his lifetime? A perfectionist element in him was probably partly responsible. McCabe often, and understandably, struck people as hugely self-confident, but he was really very self-doubting and nervous of not getting things right when speaking and writing. For an example of this tendency in him, one can cite the large number of corrections to be found in the typescripts of sermons that he ended up delivering. One might also cite the extreme care he went through when composing his 1985 Catechism. This is a short text running to only 78 small pages in its latest edition, but McCabe spent an enormous amount of time on it. Then again, McCabe was just someone who liked to recycle. His literary remains show that he often drew on the same sermon or lecture several times for different preaching or teaching engagements.

At the time of his death, however, McCabe left behind a considerable amount of material in a set of filing cabinets, and a fair amount of it has now been edited and published in a series of well-received and influential volumes. These are *God Still Matters* (London and New York: Continuum, 2002), *God, Christ and Us* (London and New York: Continuum, 2003), *The Good Life: Ethics and the Pursuit of Happiness* (London and New York: Continuum, 2005), *Faith Within Reason* (London and New York: Continuum, 2007), *On Aquinas* (London and New York: Continuum, 2008) and *God and Evil in the Theology of St Thomas Aquinas* (London and New York: Continuum, 2010).

III

Central to McCabe's thinking is the claim that we have philosophical reason to suppose both that God exists and that we do not know what God is. This, of course, might seem an odd conclusion to arrive at. If one does not know what something is, then how can one produce arguments for the thing existing? Must not such arguments rely on a knowledge of what the thing would be if it existed? McCabe, however, takes the view that our *very reason* for believing that God exists effectively *implies* that we are seriously ignorant concerning God's nature.

When it comes to arguing for God's existence, McCabe embraces a form of what is usually called 'the cosmological argument'. He holds that God exists because the existence of the universe at any time has to be accounted for causally and with reference to what is not part of the universe. Some philosophers have held that God must exist since the concept of God entails the existence of God or since the world shows evidence of being designed.[15] According to McCabe, however, we cannot know that X exists just because X is definable in some way. He also insists that since God accounts for the existence of everything other than God, God's characteristic effect is that things should exist, period, not that they should have some particular feature.[16] For McCabe, we do not come to see that God exists because of any logical contradiction involved in denying God's existence or because something or other displays certain characteristics. We recognize, or should recognize, that God exists because there is something rather than *nothing*.

This idea can be found in many of McCabe's writings but it comes explicitly to the foreground in Chapter 1 of *God Matters* and Chapter 2 of *God Still Matters*.[17] Here McCabe notes how we might follow our noses when wondering why something is the case. We might, he says, wonder why some particular thing exists, and we would be right to suppose that there is something that accounts for it existing. So, it is proper to think that, for example, some particular dog exists because of the activity of other dogs. Should we not, however, equally wonder why there are *any* dogs or any members of other kinds that one cares to mention? Should we not, for instance, wonder how there come to be any dogs? McCabe thinks that we should and that we actually do so, and, he adds, we can legitimately keep asking 'How come?' so as to aim for a final account of what in the world accounts for anything at all in it. In other words, McCabe's view is that we should always seek for scientific explanations. Yet what accounts for there being a world in which different things account for other ones? Should not our natural tendency to wonder 'How come?' lead us to the question 'How come the universe at all?' McCabe thinks that it should. He is, however, quite clear that the question here is not a scientific one with a scientific answer. He does not take it to be asking why something in particular exists. He thinks of it as asking why there is *anything* that we might take to be part of the spatio-temporal world, as asking why there is anything at all. McCabe agrees that this question is not as easy to understand as 'How come' questions raised with a view to particular things or classes of things. Yet, he maintains, it is a pressing one. He goes on to say:

> Now of course it is always possible to stop the questioning at any point; a man may refuse to ask why there are dogs. He may say there just *are* dogs and perhaps it is impious to enquire how come – there were people who actually said that to Darwin. Similarly it is possible to refuse to ask this ultimate question, to say as Russell once did: the universe is just there. This seems to me just as arbitrary as to say: dogs are just there. The difference is that we now know by hindsight that Darwin's critics were irrational because we have familiarised ourselves with an *answer* to the question, how come there are dogs? We have not familiarised ourselves with the answer to the question, how come the world instead of nothing? But that does not make it any less arbitrary to refuse to ask it. To ask it is to enter on an exploration which Russell was simply refusing to do, as it seems to me. It is of course perfectly right to point out the mysteriousness of a question about *everything*, to point to the fact that we have no way of answering it, but that is by no means the same as saying it is an unaskable question. [18]

Why does McCabe think that we have no way of answering the question 'Why is there something rather than nothing?', since it seems that he has already given an answer to that question? It is because he thinks that we arrive at understandable answers to causal questions only when we can examine the cause or causes to which they lead. We understand 'John has flu' as an answer to 'Why is John exhibiting symptoms x, y and z?' because we know what it is that causes people to have symptoms x, y, z. Again, we understand 'John Smith' as an answer to 'Who murdered Jane Jones?' because we know who and what John Smith is. But do we have a comparable understanding when it comes to the answer to 'How come something rather than nothing?' McCabe thinks not because he holds that the answer to this question cannot be an item in the universe around which we can get our minds so as to arrive at a comprehensive knowledge of its nature. Having argued in the *Summa Theologiae* that God exists, Aquinas immediately goes on to say 'We do not know what God is'.[19] He means that we lack a knowledge of God comparable to the scientific knowledge we can, with luck, gain of what exists in the world, and he thinks that this is so because God is not an item in the world. McCabe is of the same mind as Aquinas here and therefore, like Aquinas, stresses the need to think about what God *cannot* be. So, he writes:

It is clear that we reach out to, but do not reach, an answer to our ultimate question, how come anything instead of nothing? But we are able to exclude some answers. If God is whatever answers our question 'How come everything?', then evidently he is not to be included amongst everything. God cannot be a thing, an existent among others. It is not possible that God and the universe should add up to make two. Again, if we are to speak of God causing the existence of everything, it is clear that we must not mean that he makes the universe out of anything. Whatever creation means it is not a process of making. Again it is clear that God cannot *interfere* in the universe, not because he has not the power but because, so to speak, he has too much; to interfere you have to be an alternative to, or alongside, what you are interfering with. If God is the cause of everything, there is nothing that he is alongside … And I should add, I suppose, that it cannot be possible to ask of him, how come God instead of nothing? Not just in the sense that God must be imperishable, but that it must make no sense to consider that God might not be.[20]

Cosmological arguments for God's existence are frequently attacked on the ground that they inconsistently hold that God needs no causal explanation while supposing that everything else does. McCabe's account of God, however, is immune from this criticism. He is not saying that everything that exists has a cause, and yet God, who exists, somehow lacks a cause. Without taking himself to have any prior knowledge of God, he is saying that the universe raises a critical, though unusual, causal question to which there must be an answer even if we cannot fully understand it, and that the answer to this question cannot be something that raises the same question. Aquinas makes the same point by saying that if God accounts for the fact that things have *esse* (being or existence) as received from God, then God cannot be like them in this respect but must rather be thought of as *ipsum esse subsistens* (subsisting being itself).[21] McCabe makes this point by saying: 'Only in the uncreated is there no potentiality in any sense at all, not even a distinction of essence and existence; only the Uncreated exists without *having* existence.'[22] Elsewhere he writes:

To say that we have a valid question [sc. 'Why something rather than nothing?'] … is to say that God exists; for what we mean by 'God' is just whatever answers the question. Apart from knowing this … All we can do is point, as systematically as we can, to several kinds or categories of things that the answer *could not be*. For one thing, whatever would answer our question could not itself be subject to the question – otherwise we are left as we were, with the same question still to answer. Whatever we mean by 'God' cannot be whatever it is that makes us ask the question in the first place.[23]

The idea here, roughly, is that (a) I *have* existence since I might never have existed, since my existing does not follow from what I am by nature, since my existing at all *from moment to moment* derives from what is not me, while (b) if God accounts for things having existence, then God does not have existence as *receiving* it and must exist *by nature*.[24]

This notion of God as transcending the world of created things permeates McCabe's writings, as it does those of Aquinas.[25] But some critics of what people like McCabe and Aquinas say about God argue that they are defending belief in something different from what Christians take God to be. In particular, they claim that people like McCabe and Aquinas make God into something remote and uninvolved with creatures. The God of McCabe and Aquinas is unable to be conceptualized and is not an inhabitant of space and time. Yet, so it has been suggested, this is a philosophical or pagan notion of divinity, not the Christian one. Why so? Because, it has been said, the Christian God as revealed in the Bible engages with us, is a 'who' not an 'it', is something that experiences change and exists in time, and is even something that undergoes voluntary suffering on our behalf. By contrast, so the argument continues, the Thomistic God is a static and abstract entity, a product of 'Greek' thinking rather than of what we find in Scripture.

How does McCabe react to this criticism? He does so basically by saying that it badly misrepresents what people like he and Aquinas are driving at in their talk about divinity. For one thing, he notes, it is wrong to suppose that to say, for example, 'God is not something that undergoes change or suffering' is equivalent to saying 'God is static or apathetic or even callous'. 'It is almost as though if Aquinas had said that God could not be a supporter of Glasgow Celtic, we supposed he was claiming God as a Rangers fan.'[26] If I am not Belgian, it does not follow that I am Irish or Australian. So, we should not construe 'God is not changeable or able to suffer' as implying that God is inert or unrelated to suffering. Again, argues McCabe, if we take our stand on the thoroughly biblical idea that God is the creator, to suggest that God is not a spatio-temporal object, with all that this implies, is only to tease out what the Bible is loudly proclaiming. Ancient Greek philosophers, notes McCabe, 'did not, of course, have any notion of creation'.[27] That is to say they did not ask the typically Jewish (and thus Christian) question about the *esse* (existence) of things, the ultimately radical question that, for Aquinas, points us towards the unknown God.'

As for the suffering of God, McCabe recognizes that talk about God suffering owes its impetus to the claim that Christ was God and that Christ died on a cross, a teaching that McCabe wholeheartedly accepts in deference to the Council of Chalcedon (AD 451).[28] On the other hand, however, he thinks that it needs to be interpreted in the light of the fact that, as he puts it, 'the "creation" question has to be prior to the fullest understanding we can have of Jesus'. Our use for the word 'God', he observes, 'does not begin with christology' since, 'to put it at its simplest, we cannot ask the question: "In what sense is Jesus to be called Son of God?" without some prior use for the word "God". And, of course, the New Testament did have such a prior use. The NT is unintelligible except as the flowering of the Hebrew tradition and the asking of the creation question that became central to the Jewish Bible'.[29] In McCabe's view, the God whose existence he is at pains to defend is indeed the God of the Bible, 'the God of Abraham, Isaac and Jacob, the God who is not a god, not a powerful inhabitant of the universe, but the creator, the answer to the question "What does it all mean?", "Why anything anyway?"'.[30]

What, though, of the suggestion that the God whose existence McCabe defends is distant from creatures and in this sense uninvolved with any of them? McCabe responds to it by stressing two points. First, he argues that, in view of what the Council of Chalcedon teaches about Christ, God is involved with human beings as one of them. He writes: 'Chalcedon, then, does allow us to say that God suffered quite literally (and not even analogically) as we do. It is the doctrine that God is involved in the whole human condition not simply as creator but as having a created nature.' He adds: 'I think it is the loss of this doctrine by those who fear that to confess the divinity of Jesus would be to diminish his humanity that has led some of them to attribute suffering to God as such.'[31] Second, McCabe notes that the fact that God is the creator means that God is more intimately involved with creatures than any creature can be with another since God makes all of them to exist. Even in our most intimate moments together we are present to each other while still being outside each other. But, McCabe reasons, God is never outside us but is always in us as making all that is real in us. He writes:

> Our only way of being present to another's suffering is by being affected by it, because we are outside the other person. We speak of 'sympathy' or 'compassion' just because we want to say that it is *almost* as though we were not outside the other, but living his or her life, experiencing his or her suffering. A component of pity is frustration at having, in the end, to remain outside. Now, the creator cannot in this way ever be outside his creature; a person's act of being as well as every action done has to be an act of the creator. If the creator is the reason for everything that is, there can be no actual being which does not have the creator at its centre holding it in being. In our compassion we, in our feeble way, are seeking to be what God is all the time: united with and within the life of our friend. We can say in the psalm 'The Lord is compassion' but a sign that this is metaphorical language is that we can also say that the Lord has no need of compassion; he has something more wonderful, he has his creative act in which he is 'closer to the sufferer than she is to herself'.[32]

IV

Following through on this thought in different places, McCabe endorses a rarely found position on the topic of God and evil. How can there be evil if God exists? Does not evil show that God cannot exist? Here, in a nutshell, is the famous philosophical 'problem of evil'. Can it be solved? Many have argued that part of the solution lies in something called the 'Free Will Defence'. According to this, God should be thought of as rightly putting up with the evil that people choose to bring about or engage in since he has made us to be freely acting creatures and since it is good that he has done so. We may lament the awfulness and the consequences of actions that people choose to perform, but we should rejoice that God has given them the ability to choose and has not manufactured a race of robots always acting in accordance with a divine blueprint for doing good built into them. Yet McCabe rejects this line of thinking. Indeed, he holds, it conflicts with the idea that God is the creator.

Why so? Because, says McCabe, if God is the maker of all things, God must be as creatively at work in my free choices as in the existence of anything else. The Free Will Defence asks us to think of God as able to stand back so as to allow us to do our own thing. It presents God as being like parents with sense who let their children make their own decisions when they have come to a certain age. It encourages us to think of God as taking risks in a good cause: the cause of freedom. Yet, says McCabe (again echoing Aquinas), human free actions must be brought about by God if God accounts for there being something rather than nothing. It makes no sense to think of them existing independently of God. They are what they are, and, since they *are*, they are created by God. With respect to the Free Will Defence, therefore, McCabe observes:

> I hope it will be clear that this whole position involves a false and idolatrous picture of God. The 'God' here is an inhabitant of the universe, existing

alongside his creatures, interfering with some of them but not with others. If what I have been saying is true then we must conclude (I) that since everything that exists owes its existence to God, since he is the source of anything being rather than nothing, he must also be the source of my free actions, since these are instead of not being: there can be no such thing as being independent of God, whatever my freedom means it cannot mean not depending (in the creative sense) on God, but (II) this kind of dependence on God is not such as to make me an automaton ... God brings about all my free actions and ... this does not make them any less free. Failure to grasp this difficult truth has, I think, accounted for a very great deal of the muddle that western theology has got itself into during the last few centuries.[33]

In saying all this, of course, McCabe is striving to strike a balance. Holding to his view of God as creator, he wants to say that our free actions are creatively caused by God. On the other hand, he denies that we are, therefore, determined to act as we do and is not saying that we never act freely. Can he, however, consistently embrace both of these positions?

There is a well-known philosophical theory that readers of McCabe have taken him to subscribe to, one which, if true, would readily allow us to answer the question we have just raised in the affirmative. According to this theory, known as Compatibilism, someone's action can be free even if it is causally determined by outside causes since it springs from what the outside causes have made the acting person to be and, in this sense, springs from the person. Yet McCabe does not subscribe to Compatibilism understood in this way. 'An action of Fred', he says, 'is free when it is caused by Fred and not caused by any other thing. I mean that if Fred goes berserk and slays twelve, a question might arise as to whether he did this freely or not. If it can be shown that he acted under the influence of the drug that I put in his coffee then to this extent we would say that his action was not free. It is free if *he* did it and nothing *made* him do it.'[34] If all of our activity is determined by forces in the world working on us, McCabe holds, 'it would be impossible to argue a case with anyone'. Why? Because 'if your words come from your mouth as automatically as sounds come from a tape recorder, then two people apparently engaged in discussion are in no different position from two tape-recorders playing simultaneously'.[35] McCabe does not believe in determinism at all. For him, an action is free only insofar as it is caused by the person whose action it is, only insofar as it is an action for which the person has a reason or motive.

In that case, however, how can a human action be free if it is caused by God? According to McCabe, it can be free although caused by God since God is not an agent in the world acting alongside people and coercing them, since God directly and creatively makes us to be the freely acting creatures that we sometimes are – just as he creatively makes creatures that lack the ability to choose freely. The free/determined distinction, says McCabe, is a distinction to be drawn when it comes to ways in which various created things are in relation to other creatures. He therefore argues:

> God is not a separate and rival agent within the universe. The creative causal power of God does not operate on me from outside, as an alternative to me; it is the creative power of God that makes me *me* ... I am free in fact, not because God withdraws from me and leaves me my independence ... but just the other way round. I am free because God is in a sense *more directly* the cause of my actions than he is of the behaviour of unfree beings ... The creative act of God is there immediately in my freedom ... We are free not because God is absent or leaves us alone, we are free because God is more present ... God is not acting here by causing other things to cause this act, he is directly and simply himself causing it. So God is not an alternative to freedom, he is the direct cause of freedom. We are not free in spite of God but because of God.[36]

So, McCabe never invokes the Free Will Defence when writing about God and evil. Instead, his strategy is usually to emphasize: (a) that everything good is caused to exist by God; (b) that evil is a lack or privation of being and is, therefore, not creatively caused by God; (c) that in the case of naturally occurring evil there is always an explanation in terms of concomitant good; and (d) that attacks on belief in God which presume that God has some moral case to answer miss the point that God is not, like people, a moral agent subject to moral duties or obligations and is not something we can intelligibly think of as possessing human virtues and vices.[37] Again, we see the importance for McCabe of his notion of God as creator.

V

As interested as he was in God, however, McCabe was equally interested in people, in what they are and how they behave. So, his writings contain a lot of material on philosophy of the human person and on ethics. Or perhaps one should say that a lot of them contain material bringing these two subjects together since, for McCabe, our thinking about ethics will significantly depend on what we take people to be.

When it comes to human nature, McCabe was resolutely opposed to the Platonic-Cartesian idea that people are essentially immaterial centres of consciousness. We are, he says, essentially material things even though we have powers that lift us above what is material. In other words, McCabe on human nature resolutely echoes what Aquinas, with Aristotle behind him, has to say about it. For both McCabe and Aquinas we are living, self-moving animals and, therefore, essentially physical. Yet McCabe and Aquinas also hold that we are animals with knowledge or intellect, that knowing and understanding cannot be a material process and that because of our knowing and understanding we can be at one with each other and, therefore, members of a community.

In McCabe's way of presenting this last point, the means of union between people is language, considered as the bearer of meaning and the necessary condition for intention, reflection, choosing and creativity.

We make meanings; we do not just find the world meaningful in certain ways. Nobody *inherits* the French language or even the Irish; instead of inheritance and evolution we have tradition and history. It is this creative capacity to make new ways of interpreting the world that constitutes our freedom. In the new system of meanings there is included the possibility of the interpretation having been different; human language is the system of meanings that includes negation. When we choose to act in one way we might have chosen not to.[38]

Intention, says McCabe, is the stuff of which biographies or life-stories, as opposed to lifetimes, are made. 'It is essential to a story that the course of events depends on the fulfilled or unfulfilled intentions of the protagonists. The protagonists have to be the kind of animals that are able to tell themselves the story in which they are engaged. Human living is enacted narrative – this is what differentiates the human animal from others.'[39] For writers like Descartes, I am my mind and my mind is sharply to be distinguished from my body which is not at all needed for me to exist. For McCabe, the truth is that my mind and body are parts of or aspects of one thing. So, he says:

For the Cartesian, consciousness is a way of being private; it belongs to an essentially hidden interior life; for the Aristotelian, thinking belongs to a world more social, in the sense of more *shared*, than any other. So long as, like other animals, I am restricted to sensual experience my life is private. No one can have *my* sensations; everyone can have my thoughts. If they could not they would not be thoughts. There is a special kind of conversation that we call discussion or argument which is a way of testing whether what I take to be my thoughts really are thoughts – they are not unless they can be shared by others. The use of language, then, is what frees us from imprisonment in the isolated self; it is a way of transcending my individuality; to use the old jargon, it is a way of being 'immaterial'. The highest kind of auto-mobility of being spontaneous and self-originating is to transcend oneself, one's individuation, and this is what language consists in.[40]

It is with thoughts like these in mind that McCabe turns to ethics or moral philosophy, the purpose of which he takes to be not the construction of a set of rules governing behaviour but reflection on what might lead us to be happy, virtuous and, therefore, good. Some philosophers have taken ethical judgements to be nothing but the expression of a personal preference, but McCabe thinks otherwise since he takes praising and blaming to be sensible activities and since, as he puts it, 'if all you want to do is express your rage or delight it seems to me sensible to do it with four-letter words or whoops of joy rather than disguising it misleadingly in what look like statements of truth'.[41]

According to McCabe, 'good' is what Peter Geach (1916–2013) calls a logically attributive adjective, one which contains descriptive content grounded in what certain things are with the result that 'good' in 'good X' or 'good Y' can signify the possession of different properties.[42] So McCabe takes good people to be ones matching up to certain descriptions, ones which pick out certain aspects of a human being so as to note that they are truly virtuous *as people*. They are good at living well. They are good at being human, meaning that they have a grasp of sound practical reasoning and can make decisions on that basis for their benefit and for that of others. McCabe is clear that to think as he does about ethics is to think within a tradition, this being a basically Aristotelian one according to which there are virtues that help us to flourish, even though, like the virtue of justice, we might be killed for having them.

Why pay attention to this tradition, however? McCabe's basic answer is: 'Because fulfilment and happiness is to be gained by doing so since virtues are things we need to be good people.' Yet McCabe does not think that the happiness in question here is to be acquired by just learning about the Aristotelian tradition. It is to be acquired by growing into that tradition rather in the way that we grow to love others, by becoming people of a certain kind with certain tastes and dispositions – which is why McCabe always sees ethics as having a serious political dimension. The good life, he stresses, 'is not handed down simply in words. It is handed down in institutions and practices within society (all of which involve words). Our critical reception of the tradition is not, then, simply a matter of changing our words and ideas but of changing fundamental structures of human living. It is a political matter. What is done with, for example, a society's health resources, or its police force, amounts to a series of ethical statements concerning the good life.'[43]

If we embrace the good life, then, thinks McCabe, that is because we are instinctively good people, not armchair moral philosophers or intellectual historians. In particular, McCabe argues, we are people who have acquired what Aquinas called *prudentia*: not a tendency to be cautious or to save money, but a disposition to recognize what needs to be said or done in particular situations, many of them wildly different from each other and few of them able to be regulated for by a moral manual containing a list of moral impera-tives. In one of his essays McCabe suggests that the best way to understand what Aquinas means by *prudentia* is to think of it as equivalent to what Jane Austen calls 'good sense'.[44] *Prudentia*, for McCabe, is a skill acquired over time. On the other hand, however, he does not deny that absolute prohibitions have a place in ethical discussions. Indeed, he thinks that they are essential since, as he often puts it, boundaries have to be drawn when it comes to what counts as loving behaviour. It is not his view that 'anything goes', and in *Law, Love and Language* we find a withering critique of situation ethics. This was a conse-quentialist approach to ethics popular in some quarters when McCabe was writing that book. Situation ethicists argued that moral rules are not absolutes but rules of thumb to be rejected in the name of loving action.[45] McCabe, however, takes a different view. 'We cannot be sure beforehand what might turn out to be loving behaviour,' he writes, 'but if we can't say of any behaviour at all that it is definitely *not* loving behaviour, then I think that the word "love" would be hopelessly vague.'[46] In one place, and thinking of absolute prohibitions, McCabe, somewhat jokingly though with utter seriousness, speaks of it being 'very decent of God to help us out by giving us an outline of what it is to live in friendship: this is the Ten Commandments'.

> God thought that we *might*, after some thought, come to the conclusion that friends would not kill each other or seduce each other's husbands or wives or get them falsely convicted of crimes or kidnap or enslave them or seek to defraud them of their possessions; yes, we might come to work that out, but all the same it would be a good idea to get all this down in black and white, or better still, on tablets of stone. Well, it wasn't quite like that: but the Decalogue *is* part of God's summons to Israel to be *his* people, to share in his life and his righteousness. God is telling them that the first step to being God's people is to be human people, and that means living in friendship. This use of human means is a minimal requirement for living beyond our means, living in the divine friendship which is God … [though] it is important to see that what is provided by such a document as the Decalogue is precisely an *outline* of friendship. That is to say, it draws a boundary around friendship to show where it stops: beyond these limits friendship does not exist.[47]

Notice the idea in this last quotation that living well finally amounts to sharing in the life of God, in becoming like God. It indicates that McCabe, like Aquinas, was not just a secular moral philosopher like Aristotle but was a Christian thinker ultimately concerned about ethics with uniquely Christian notions in mind. Like Aquinas, who commonly refers to Aristotle as 'the philosopher', McCabe wrote texts that he thought could be read with profit even by people with no religious belief. Yet he also constantly bears in mind that, as well as being able to acquire Aristotelian virtues by their own efforts, people can be objects of God's grace, which is given, unearned and not acquired by training.

Aquinas has two words that can be translated into English as 'happiness'. One is *felicitas*, by which he means happiness in the present life. The other is *beatitudo*, which he takes to be perfect union with God established by God. Aquinas takes *felicitas* to be happiness which we can set about obtaining, especially by attending to the virtues discussed by Aristotle. *Beatitudo*, however, is, for Aquinas, entirely God's work. In his view there is a happiness which only God can bring about, and McCabe shares this belief, which he often elaborates on when talking about the life and death of Christ and on what he takes the incarnation to be about. For McCabe, the good life finally turns out to involve being drawn into the being of the Trinity. He writes:

> Friendship is both the aim of all the virtues and also the necessary means by which virtues are cultivated, sustained, and developed. Virtues can only be taught by friends. Friendship can only be sustained by virtues ... That's moral *philosophy*, but from the point of view of moral *theology* the *philia* [love] which defines the game is *agape* or *caritas*, the friendship which God shares with us and enables us to share with each other ... Virtues which enable us to live the life of *caritas*, which is the life of God, life in the Spirit, although they encourage us to more intensive practice, are rooted not in our efforts but in the initiative of God – this is what we mean by God sharing his life with us. This is what is traditionally called 'infused' as distinct from 'acquired' virtue. The divine, or so-called 'theological' virtues of faith, hope, and charity can only be infused through the grace of God, but this grace also gives a new dimension to, and indeed transforms, our acquired virtues. As Aquinas puts it, the charity we *have* becomes the *form of all our virtues*, and our whole life becomes a sharing in divinity.[48]

This conclusion is fleshed out many times over in McCabe's writings. It is there, for example, in what he says about penance, the Eucharist and the

Trinity in *God Matters* and *God Still Matters*. It is there in what he says about prayer and the sacraments in general. It is there in his treatments of sin and redemption. It is all over the sermons in *God, Christ and Us* and is as much a part of McCabe's thinking as is any of the philosophical argumentation that he offers.

VI

McCabe did not claim to be very original. In the Preface to *God Matters* he says: 'In the end, I suppose, I am only trying to say two not very original things: that the only God who matters is an unfathomable mystery of love because of which there is being and meaning to anything that is; and that we are united with God in matter, in our flesh and his flesh.' Again, in the Preface to *The Good Life* we find: 'If readers discover any new truths in the course of reading this book, they should not attribute it to any originality of mine. That will be exhibited only in my mistakes. For my aim in what follows is simply to expound, as faithfully and sympathetically as I can, a certain tradition of ethical thinking, one which is particularly well expressed in the *philosophical* account that Thomas Aquinas gives of human behaviour.'

In a sense, McCabe was right to disclaim originality since he was a conservative theologian and not a theological liberal.[49] Hence the respect he accords to Aquinas and the criticisms he often makes of people who ignore or misunderstand what Aquinas has to say. McCabe did not like to be called a 'Thomist', but that was because he thought that, given what most people who use the word 'Thomist' seem to have in mind, Aquinas himself was not a Thomist.[50] Yet McCabe was undoubtedly a disciple of Aquinas, than whom no more orthodox theologian can be conceived. He also owed much to the thinking of Ludwig Wittgenstein (1889–1951). As Alasdair MacIntyre observes, by the time McCabe began writing 'it had become impossible to avoid reckoning with Wittgenstein ... So good work in philosophy required Herbert to learn how to address both Thomas's questions and Wittgenstein's within a single enquiry.'[51]

Originality, however, is very much context-dependent and can also consist in style and presentation. In the Preface to *God Matters*, McCabe speaks of there being thoughts that 'bear repetition because they are perennially forgotten', and many of his thoughts were presented to a world that had largely forgotten them and continues to forget them. Much of the ink that has been spilled defending what is now called 'new atheism' provides ample illustration of this.[52] The same can be said of much that is currently written by philosophers of religion aiming to defend belief in God.[53] It can also, for various reasons, be said of much that currently passes for theology in some quarters.[54]

So, McCabe stood out in his time rather as Old Testament prophets did in theirs, and when it comes to the matter of style and presentation, McCabe was exceptional. As many readers have testified, he had a skill in expounding Aquinas that makes him come alive as a contemporary interlocutor, a skill that a number of writers on Aquinas have noticeably lacked. And all of his writings are crisp, incisive, carefully reasoned, jargon-free, often very humorous and frequently abounding in positively memorable and profound sentences. Thus, for example: 'Christian love implies equality; it is distinct from philanthropy, it is different from being kindly, affectionate, caring.'[55] 'Our praying is as much God's gift as is the answer to it.'[56] 'If you *are* good, it is because God's love has already made you so; if you *want to try* to be good, that is because God is loving you; if you *want* to be forgiven, that is because God is forgiving you.'[57] 'Loving yourself is the way you love God. I mean that loving yourself is, in a way, more important than loving your neighbour because, without loving yourself, it is quite impossible to love your neighbour.'[58] 'Easter is not a cancellation of the cross. It does not, in any important sense, celebrate anything different from the cross.'[59] 'Serving God does not mean that we do not try to succeed, to exercise power, to achieve what is good and necessary. It means that, whether we succeed or fail, we search into our life to detect in it the love of God which is sustaining us both in success and failure.'[60] 'The story of Jesus is nothing other than the triune life of God projected onto our history, or enacted sacramentally in our history, so that it becomes story.'[61]

Make of these sentences what you will, but they are typical of what McCabe had to say and they indicate his genius very well.[62]

Notes

1   McCabe's death certificate lists 'peritonitis, caecal infarction, and severe aortic atheroma' as the 'cause of death'.

2   McCabe was never a postgraduate student in a UK university.

3   This information derives from correspondence from MacIntyre to Brian Davies dated November 2000.

4   After nearly seventy years in St Sebastian's parish, the English Dominicans decided to give it up in 1961, having worked there since 1892. They did so because of increased demands on them coming from houses they had in South Africa and the West Indies.

5   The Blackfriars edition of the *Summa Theologiae* is now reprinted and published by Cambridge University Press. For its third volume McCabe provided the English translation of *Summa Theologiae*, 1,12–13 together with four illuminating appendices. The Introduction to the volume came from Fr Thomas Gilby OP, the general editor of the Blackfriars edition.

6   *New Blackfriars* came into being in 1964 from an amalgamation of the Dominican journals *Blackfriars* and *Life in the Spirit*. Entirely produced by the English Dominicans for many years, it is now published by Wiley-Blackwell, though it remains a Dominican journal with a Dominican editor.

7   Davis was Professor of Religious Studies, University of Alberta, Edmonton from 1967 to 1970 and Professor of Religious Studies at Concordia University, Montreal, from 1970 to 1991.

8   Brian Wicker, formerly Principal of Fircroft College, Birmingham, and Chairman of *Pax Christi*, is a British Catholic author who has specialized in issues to do with the ethics of war. In the 5 January 1967 edition of the *Guardian* Wicker said of Davis that his leaving the Catholic Church was an act of witness since 'in him the Church looks at itself from the outside, and understands from that perspective the depth of its own corruption'. McCabe quotes this line from Wicker in his 1967 editorial before himself saying that the Catholic Church is corrupt.

9   The suspension, which was canonically irregular, was lifted after only a few days.

10   For this see p. 22 of Simon Clements and Monica Lawlor, *The McCabe Affair*
     (London and Melbourne: Sheed and Ward, 1967). This volume is indispensable
     reading for anyone concerned with what was happening with McCabe in 1967.
     With respect to Archbishop Cardinale, however, some words of praise might be
     in order. In 1967 he was accused of being an instigator in McCabe's suspension as
     editor of *New Blackfriars*. But he was no such thing and was basically an innocent
     bystander in the wrong place at the wrong time. In a very polite letter to the English
     Dominican Provincial dated 16 February 1967, Cardinale confesses himself to be
     somewhat ignorant as to what was going on with McCabe following his dismissal as
     editor of *New Blackfriars*, while asking the Provincial 'to convey to Fr McCabe my
     esteem for his silence following the Master General's decision'. In another letter to
     the English Dominican Provincial, Cardinale elaborates on his reasons for objecting
     to McCabe's editorial. He begins by expressing appreciation for the ideas conveyed
     to him by various individuals who wrote to him in protest concerning McCabe's
     dismissal. He goes on to say that he strongly believes in the right to free speech
     but not in the right to make 'unsubstantial allegations', and he goes on to note that
     McCabe was wrong to say, as he did in his editorial, that the Congregation of Rites
     'has just asserted (*Times*, 5 January 1967) that a family communion celebrated in a
     private home and followed by a meal is a practice "alien to the Catholic religion"'.
     Cardinale goes on to make a good case for his position here while showing that
     McCabe should have paid more attention than he did to the article in *The Times*
     and on what it was reporting. That said, however, Cardinale did not seem to have
     entirely appreciated the 'big picture' that McCabe had in mind when writing his
     editorial.

11   Augustin Bea (1881–1968) was a biblical scholar and ecumenist. He was the first
     president of the Secretariat for Promoting Christian Unity and was highly influential
     at the Second Vatican Council. Bishop Wilhelmus Marinus Bekkers (1908–66) was a
     Dutch prelate who was much respected in the Netherlands and well known because
     of his many television appearances. His catch phrase was 'Caritas Pro Armis' ('With
     Love as a Weapon'). He aimed to promote an approach to Catholicism emphasizing
     consensus between clergy and lay people. McCabe's reference to John XXIII, Bea
     and Bekkers provides a sense of what he admired in the Catholic Church of the
     twentieth century.

12   Five weeks after his article in the *Observer* Davis got married in an Anglican
     church. There were eighty or so people in attendance, one of whom was McCabe.
     His presence at Davis's wedding has sometimes been taken to indicate that he
     thoroughly approved of Davis's decision to leave the Church. But it is evident from
     his 1967 editorial why he thought that Davis was wrong to make this decision.

13   This might have been Fr Hilary Carpenter, who in 1967 was Assistant General for
     the English Dominican Province.

14   The quotations here come from personal correspondence from MacIntyre to Brian
     Davies.

15   The first line of thinking here usually goes by the name 'the ontological argument',
     versions of which can be found in the writings of St Anselm of Canterbury and
     René Descartes. The second line of thinking is commonly called 'the argument from

design', a famous version of which can be found in William Paley's *Natural Theology* (1802).

16 Cf. *God Matters*, p. 6: 'Obviously God makes no difference to the universe; I mean by this that we do not appeal specifically to God to explain why the universe is this way rather than that, for this we need only appeal to explanations within the universe. For this reason there can, it seems to me, be no feature of the universe which indicates that it is God-made. What God accounts for is that the universe is there instead of nothing.' Here, of course, McCabe is thinking of God as the Creator, as accounting for the sheer existence of things in distinction from processes that occur in the world.

17 The first item here originally appeared as an article in *New Blackfriars* published in October 1980. The second was originally a lecture delivered at the Royal Institute of Philosophy in London and first appeared in print in Martin Warner (ed.), *Religion and Philosophy* (Royal Institute of Philosophy Supplements 30, Cambridge University Press, 1992).

18 *God Matters*, p. 5.

19 Prologue to *Summa Theologiae*, 1a,3.

20 *God Matters*, p. 6. McCabe is conscious that Aquinas does not, as he does, treat thinking as more or less synonymous with talking. He holds, though, that to speak of thinking as he does helps one to see what Aquinas is driving at in his talk about thinking. Cf. *The Good Life*, p. 1.

21 Cf. *Summa Theologiae*, 1a,3,4 and 1a,13,11.

22 *God Still Matters*, p. 20.

23 *God Still Matters*, p. 41.

24 Note the phrase 'from moment to moment' in this sentence. Like Aquinas, McCabe is *not* arguing that God must exist since the universe must have been caused to exist some time in the past. His idea is that God accounts for the existence of things not only as they begin to exist but *as they continue to do so*. For this reason, McCabe was always utterly uninterested in debates about the existence of God which turn on the truth or falsity of the view that the universe sprang into being at some time that we think we can record.

25 It is presented with especial force and clarity in 'God and Creation' (*New Blackfriars*, Volume 94, July 2013).

26 *God Matters*, p. 41.

27 This is certainly true of Aristotle (384–322 BC), who is often taken to be a major influence on Aquinas. In more than one place in his writings McCabe labours the fact that, in a serious sense, Aquinas is no Aristotelian.

28 In *God Matters* McCabe defends the Chalcedonian account of the incarnation against criticisms of it to be found in John Hick (ed.), *The Myth of God Incarnate* (London: SCM Press, 1977). He also engages in a debate on the incarnation with Maurice Wiles (1923–2005), then Regius Professor of Divinity at Oxford University.

In Chapter 10 of *God Still Matters* McCabe, drawing on Aquinas, tries to explain what the Chalcedonian account of the incarnation amounts to and why it can be defended from the charge of being logically contradictory.

29 *God Matters*, p. 42.

30 *God Matters*, p. 42.

31 *God Matters*, p. 48. The point of the allusion to attributing suffering to God 'as such' lies in the fact that, like Aquinas, McCabe distinguishes between what can be said of Jesus *as a human being* and what can be said of him *as God*. McCabe, insisting that Jesus was one subject with two distinct natures, wants to assert that he suffered *as man* but not *as God*, even though he was truly God. Cf. *God Matters*, Ch. 10.

32 *God Matters*, pp. 44–5.

33 *God Matters*, p. 11.

34 *God Matters*, p. 11.

35 *God Matters*, p. 12.

36 *God Matters*, pp. 13–15. Cf. *God Matters*, p. 241, and *God and Evil in the Theology of St Thomas Aquinas*, pp. 10, 120–7. For Aquinas saying the same kind of thing on God and human freedom as McCabe does, see his commentary on Aristotle's *Peri Hermeneias*, 1, 14. Also see *Summa Theologiae*, 1a,19,8.

37 See Chapter 3 of *God Matters*, Chapter 6 of *Faith Within Reason* and most of *God and Evil in the Theology of St Thomas Aquinas*.

38 *The Good Life*, p. 68.

39 *The Good Life*, p. 71.

40 *The Good Life*, pp. 72–3.

41 *The Good Life*, p. 5.

42 Cf. Peter Geach, 'Good and Evil' (*Analysis* 17, 1956).

43 *The Good Life*, p. 11.

44 *God Still Matters*, Ch. 14.

45 Cf. Joseph Fletcher, *Situation Ethics: The New Morality* (Philadelphia: Westminster Press, 1966).

46 *Law, Love and Language*, p. 20.

47 *On Aquinas*, p. 55.

48 *On Aquinas*, pp. 69–70.

49 In one place he writes: 'But I must not let myself be carried away by passionate conservatism.' See *God Still Matters*, p. 65.

50 Thomists are often taken to be people who think that Aquinas was infallible and should be studied and reported on that basis and with no reference to contemporary

philosophers and the questions and positions that they present. McCabe did not approach Aquinas in this way. He also believed that the teachings of Aquinas as presented by many self-styled Thomists are often not really those of Aquinas but something rather more like views to be found in the writings of Descartes, from which they need to be rescued.

51   Preface to *God Still Matters*.

52   Cf. Brian Davies, 'The New Atheism: Its Virtues and its Vices' (*New Blackfriars*, Volume 92, 2011).

53   Cf. Brian Davies, 'Letter from America' (*New Blackfriars*, Volume 84, 2003) and, in connection with this, D. Z. Phillips (ed.), *Whose God? Which Tradition? The Nature of Belief in God* (Aldershot and Burlington: Ashgate, VT, 2008).

54   Cf. Brian Davies, 'Is God Beyond Reason?' (*Philosophical Investigations*, Volume 32, 2009).

55   *God Still Matters*, p. 4.

56   *God, Christ and Us*, p. 7.

57   *God, Christ and Us*, p. 27.

58   *God, Christ and Us*, p. 69.

59   *God, Christ and Us*, p. 89.

60   *God, Christ and Us*, p. 137.

61   *God Matters*, p. 48.

62   We are very grateful to Fr John Farrell, who, as Provincial of the English Dominicans, kindly gave us access to materials that we drew on for the biographical section of this Introduction.

PART ONE

PHILOSOPHY OF GOD AND CHRISTIAN DOCTRINE

1

God and Creation

To put things in some kind of perspective, let me begin with the geography and history and sociology of America. Consider the enormous sweep of that continent, the vast central plains, the Rockies and the difference between Southern California and Cape Cod. Spare a thought for the human race's first experiment in wholesale democracy, and the attempt to bring together people of startlingly different traditions. Think of Melville, Faulkner, Flannery O'Connor and James Hadley Chase. Think of the vast expansion of capitalism in the United States and the growth of its technology. Think of what you can remember of the war between the States, the Mexican wars, General Motors, and the United Fruit Company. Meditate on the part that America has played in the world during and since the Second World War. Remember the civil rights movement, McCarthyism, Mayor Daly and the Chicago Convention. There is a lot to think about, isn't there?

Now imagine some child who has just overheard someone say 'If it were not for America we would have no Kentucky Fried Chicken'. Suppose s/he has heard nothing else whatever about America. Suppose s/he doesn't even know whether 'America' means a person or a place or a sum of money or a cooking technique. This child, I want to say, would know enormously more about the intricacies of American politics, economics, history, geography and way of life than we know about God from knowing that God is Creator of the world. By comparison with theologians and philosophers who talk about

God, this child would be a learned and scholarly expert on America. After all, a certain amount might be deduced about America from the fact that without it there would be no Kentucky Fried Chicken (at least there are several intelligent guesses and alternative scenarios one might construct), whereas we can deduce nothing we can understand about God from the fact that if it were not for God there would be nothing at all. We can, of course, know some things that could not possibly be true of God, and we are able to say things about God, to make statements which are not all negative in form. Unfortunately, though, we do not really know what these statements mean. They do not convey to us any information as to what God is like.

All this is what Thomas Aquinas meant when he said that because creation is an effect which is not adequate to its cause it does not tell us anything about what this cause is, only that it is. It is the knowledge or belief that there is *That-without-which-there-would-be-nothing-at-all* that permits us to speak of God. In other words, it is the content of this conviction that controls our use of the word 'God'.

We can use the word 'God' correctly or incorrectly, but the criterion for correct and incorrect use is not something we know about the nature of God. It is something that is thought to be true of our world. In other words, God's being creator of the world is what gives us our meaning for the word 'God'. I have in the past, even in print, I'm afraid, permitted myself to say that 'What Christians mean by God is: "He who raised Jesus from the dead"'. But I was wrong to say this. Christians believe that it was God and not anything else that raised Jesus from the dead. We cannot formulate our beliefs concerning Jesus without a prior knowledge of what the word 'God' means. As Edward Schillebeeckx says (I reproduce selections from a 128-word sentence): It has to be 'reasonably demonstrated that in and through [certain] experiences and identifications of "salvation", belonging to a particular human community, we really are in contact with the reality to which we human beings in the course of our history have ascribed the name of God, the Creator of all that is and is to be ... that in this person, Jesus of Nazareth, we actually have to do with the One who liberates and yet at the same time – however incomprehensibly – is the final arbiter of meaning, the "Creator of heaven and earth"'.[1] '*Et hoc omnes intelligunt Deum*', as Aquinas puts it. The notion of God as creating is basic to our use of the word. It does not, of course, follow that creation is basic to God. On the contrary, it is just because it isn't, just because it does not belong to the nature of God that God is a world maker, a Creator. It is just because of this that God's having happened to create the world doesn't tell us anything about God's nature.

The quotation from Schillebeeckx, however, indicates two, on the face of it, different determinants for the meaning of the word 'God': one is 'Creator of all that is' and the other is 'final arbiter of meaning'. The last phrase is a bit obscure, but you could see that someone might sensibly say 'without God the world would have no ultimate meaning' or 'ultimately no meaning' (two different but perhaps related phrases.) I myself do not see how God could be said to give meaning to the world, or to be the final meaning or purpose of the world, unless God were the one who made it in some sense. But it is not unimaginable that some people might have a word meaning 'what it's all about', or 'the point of everything', or 'what makes the world not meaningless', and yet never have reflected on the world as created or made. And I think we might very reasonably say they were nonetheless talking about God.

However, in our culture at any rate, the use of the word 'God' is heavily conditioned by Genesis 1 and the sentence 'In the beginning God made the heavens and the earth'. In speaking of God the creator we are approaching the mystery through the notion of making. As we should expect, the notion gets badly mauled in the process. We end up saying 'God made the world', but not in the sense of 'making' that we ordinarily understand (and not, in fact, in any sense we can understand). But at least we do not end up saying 'God made the world but also God did not make the world'. In other words, I should say that we use the word 'make' here analogically and not just metaphorically.

Metaphors can be inconsistent ('the still small voice'/'the shaking cedars'). They can also be simultaneously denied ('God is a warrior'/'God is not a warrior'). We cannot have the same inconsistency with literal usage, and analogy is a form of literal usage. As Aquinas sometimes put it, the difference between words used analogically is not that they differ in literal meaning but in their way of meaning (*modus significandi*).

When you say 'God is a warrior' and 'Goliath is a warrior' the word warrior is being used in exactly the same sense. What makes 'God is a warrior' metaphorical is not a variation in either the meaning or the *modus significandi* (way of meaning) of 'warrior' but the whole role of the sentence in which it occurs. I mean that the sentence (taken at random from *Pride and Prejudice*) 'But Elizabeth was not formed for ill humour' differs from the statement I might now make: 'But Peter was not formed for ill humour'. But it does not differ because of any differences in the meaning of the words. It is just that one is fiction and the other fact. The difference between 'God is a warrior' and 'Goliath is a warrior' is more like the difference between fiction and fact than it is like the difference between, say, 'This curry is very good' and 'The weather is very good': a case of analogy. The word 'create' then, when used of God, has just the same meaning as the word 'make', but we use the special word 'create' in order to indicate a new *modus significandi*, a new way of meaning-making. Now how does that work?

To say that 'creation' is 'making' with-a-new-mode-of-meaning is to talk, I think, about the whole intellectual process by which you get to the word: the whole process and not just the end of it. I mean: you start by saying 'God made the world' and then you add various qualifications, all qualifications of a certain systematic kind, all qualifications, if you like, in a definite direction. And by the time you have finished, the notion of making has been whittled away. It has, as Antony Flew put it, 'died the death of a thousand qualifications'.[2] Flew was right about this. But he was wrong to conclude that the whole process was therefore nugatory. It is the intellectual process itself that matters, that points us towards what we cannot say. There is no short cut. You yourself have to go through the slow killing of the verb 'to make'. There is no separable end product, no finally refined concept, which is the meaning of the verb 'to create'. The death of the verb 'to make' is consummated in a resurrection as elusive as that of Christ. It does not simply come back to life. Just as the only way to get at the resurrection is to go through the crucifixion, so the only way to 'understand' creation is to attend to the whittling away and death of 'making'. We cannot just use an analogical term of this kind as we can use the word 'cat'. Every time we use it, or at least every time we use it with any understanding at all, we have to go again through the whole process of starting with a word used in one way and then taking away the *modus significandi*, qualifying the way it means until it disappears. Most theological mistakes come from carelessly thinking that we have now 'grasped' what our terms mean, that we no longer need to work them out again for ourselves. Theological understanding, such as it is, comes just as the meanings elude our grasp.

'God made everything' or 'God makes everything' sounds harmless enough at first, but let us look at some of the implications. In the first place, if God made everything, God cannot be included in everything. God can't be one of the beings that go to make up everything. So everything-plus-God is not any greater than everything just by itself (or themselves). If this is paradoxical it is because we have illegitimately used the phrase 'everything-plus-God'. You can only add together things that share some common nature or at least belong to some common class. You could add another egg to the clutch because they are all eggs. You could add in three wasps because they are all things in the basket. You could add a bicycle and twelve people because they are all things Fred noticed and thought about on Friday. And so on. But you can only add if you can find some way in which the items have something in common. What we have to do is to say that God has nothing in common with things, so that there isn't any sense to 'everything-plus-God', so that the paradox 'everything plus God is the same as everything' doesn't arise.

Do I hear you say that there is at least *this much* common between God and things: that they all exist, that they all have being? N things + God would be N + 1 beings or existents. But not so. To be existent is not a nature. An existent is not a kind of thing. 'Fido exists' means 'There is an X such that X is a dog (called Fido)'. 'Jumbo exists' means 'There is an X such that X is an elephant (called Jumbo)'. If you say 'There is an X such that X is', you haven't said anything yet, because you have simply not finished your sentence.

The famous doctrine of Aquinas that 'in God there is no distinction between essence and existence'[3] does not mean that in God's case uniquely you can say 'There is an X such that X is'. It does not mean that existence stands to God in the way that dogness stands to Fido or elephantineity (-itude?) stands to Jumbo. What it does mean we shall shortly see. For now, though, my point is that the fact that God exists and that everything exists does not imply that they have 'existence' in common, as Fido and Rover have dogness in common. There is not enough common ground between them for you to add God to everything. God is not part of everything. If God made everything, God is not a thing.

Next, if God made everything, then God did not make it out of anything, or at least there are some things that God did not make out of anything (for, of course, besides creating things, God might also make bubbles out of chewing gum just as we do). So creation is making, but not making out of anything. When X is created there is not anything that is changed into X. Creation is *ex nihilo* (not out of anything). Creation, then, is not a change in anything; there was nothing to be changed. There was nothing to suffer an alteration when things were created, and similarly it does not make any difference to a thing that it is created. A created giraffe is just the same as a giraffe. Being created does not add any difference to being a giraffe in the way that being spotted or being hungry does. This is fortunate, for otherwise it would be impossible for God to create a giraffe. However hard God tried the result would always be a created giraffe, and that would be something different. It follows from this, of course, that you cannot deduce the activity of the Creator from the fact that things have the property of being created. There is no such property as the property of being created. The fact that things are created does not make the slightest detectable or undetectable difference to them, any more than being thought about makes a difference to things.

Let us now compare being created with being born or conceived or whenever you count as my coming into existence. Being born also clearly makes no difference to me. Until I was born I was not there to have a difference made to me. But in this case a difference was made all the same, though not to me. A great change came over the world in 1926: hitherto it had been lacking Herbert; henceforth it contained Herbert. I do not say the lack of Herbert was a deprivation for the world before 1926. I do not usually see the first quarter of the twentieth century groaning in expectation, labouring and yearning until Herbert was brought forth. It was simply that Herbert could have been made and was not yet made. In other words, before I came into existence I was potential in the world. I was possible, in the real sense that there were agents in the world which could bring me about. Let us forget for the moment complications such as that my soul is directly created by God and not simply caused by creatures. For what I am saying I could have used the example of Fido instead. So let me use Fido to be on the safe side. Before Fido began to exist there was a potentiality, a capability, a possibility, for his existence which had two aspects. On the active side, there were causes which were capable of bringing him into existence. On the passive side there were things that could be made into him. When the time came these active causes acted upon these passive things and changed them into Fido. This is the sense in which Fido was potential before he existed. When he came into existence by being born he did not, of course, change. But these active causes probably changed and these passive materials certainly changed. So in these two ways, actively and passively, the world was potential to Fido.

There is a third sense in which Fido was possible before he came into existence. This is sometimes called 'logical possibility'. While the real potentiality of which I have been speaking is a matter of the physical existence of real causes and real materials which can result in Fido, logical possibility is thought to be independent of any such vulgar facts. Fido is thought to be logically possible quite independently of any state of affairs; logical possibility is, so to speak, eternal. It was from eternity in some timeless sense possible that there would be a Fido. I think it is very important to see that this is a mistake. The so-called 'logical possibility' of Fido simply consists in the possibility of framing sentences concerning 'Fido' in some language. Logical possibility resides, not in eternity, but in the rules, semantic and syntactical, of the actual language that can speak of Fido, just as real potentiality resides in the actual causes that can produce Fido. As Aquinas says, potentiality, possibility, always resides in some actuality. Act is prior to potency. The logical possibility of Fido only seems eternal because language gives us the illusion that it is eternal and necessary.

The making of Fido, then, by birth (or generation, to use the conventional term) demands the pre-existence of a world which, actively and passively, is ready for him to be produced, and which changes in producing him. You may say that Fido, in being born, fills a Fido-shaped gap in the world. It is because things came into existence by generation that Aristotle thought that the whole world could not have come into existence. Evidently before there was any world there could not be a world-shaped gap in anything. There would be no world for the gap to be in. The whole world could not be potential or possible, only particular things within the world. It is nonsense to think of the world being generated from 'possible worlds', and hence, thought Aristotle, since it is here, it must always have been here. And if the only sense in which things can be said to come into existence were by generation, then this would be a perfectly valid argument. If the only thinkable sense in which things come into existence were generation, then a beginning of the whole world would be unthinkable. This is quite probably the case. Creation does seem unthinkable. Étienne Gilson thought that Aquinas was constrained by his belief that God made the world out of nothing (a belief he derived from the Hebrew-Christian tradition) to reflect on the possibility of a coming into existence which is not a generation but a coming into existence which not only makes no difference to the thing itself but even makes no difference to a world, which amounts to no difference at all. For Aristotle, potentiality has to be residing in an actual presupposed world. The sense in which Fido was potential, the sense in which Fido might not have been, is that this presupposed world might not have generated him. We can call this precariousness of Fido's existence his contingency. Fido's existence is contingent upon certain causes operating to bring him about. 'Fido might not have existed' means 'The world might not have resulted in Fido'. Yet Aquinas speaks of a different dimension of potentiality. Not now simple contingency, a potentiality which is Fido-over-against-a-world which might not have contained Fido, but the potentiality which is *Fido-over-against-nothing-at-all* (the possibility that Fido might not have been *created*). Aristotle dealt with the quite intelligible possibility that Fido might not have been generated, the possibility of a world empty of Fido. Aquinas invites us to look at the mysterious possibility that Fido might not have been created. He invites us to the vertiginous thought of just nothing at all. In technical language familiar to readers of Aquinas, when we contemplate (or try to contemplate) the possibility that Fido might not have been created, we should say that Fido's essence (nature) is potential with respect to *esse* (existence). And here we have a very strange kind of possibility, one which does not reside in an actuality being potential with respect to Fido, a potentiality without any actuality for it to be in. The temptation is always to confuse this possibility (which does not reside in any actual world) with what we called logical possibility (which seems not to reside in any actual world). The temptation is to think that the distinction between *esse* and essence in creatures is just the fact that you can have a concept of a dodo even though there aren't any dodos.

But the fact that you can think of something not existing does not mean that its essence and existence are distinct; it is merely a fact about the way our language works. The distinction of essence and existence in a thing means that it might not have been created, and the only reason why we mention this is in order to deny it of God. To say that there is no distinction of essence and existence in God is not to say that God's essence is existence in the sense that Fido's essence is dogness. It is simply to say that God is uncreated. It is to say that there is no possibility that God might not have been in the common-or-garden sense of contingency (as Fido is contingent in that he might not have been generated). But it is also to say that there is no possibility that God might not have been in the sense of createdness. It is important to be clear about this, for even Aquinas himself in a very early work, *De ente et essentia*, seems to treat the fact that you can think of X without knowing or caring whether X exists as a reason for saying that its essence and existence are distinct. But this is a mistake: it does not follow from the fact that you can think of dodos although there are no dodos (the fact that dodos are logically possible) that the essence of a dodo is distinct from its existence.

There are three main things to consider:

1   Fido might not exist, and might not have existed.

2   You can think of Fido without knowing or caring whether he exists.

3   Fido might not have been created.

The first refers to the ordinary contingency, potentiality, of Fido, to what Aquinas calls the composition of matter and form in Fido, or if you like, the fact that what it is to be Fido includes the factor of matter as well as form, of potentiality as well as actuality. This means that although Fido has his form he can lose it and be turned into something else (he can perish) and that similarly he acquired this form (although he might not have done so) by something else happening to be turned into him. Things that are composed of matter and of form are material things and are the only things that can be made (generated) and can perish. If you had a non-material thing in which the essence were simply form without matter (an angel) it could not be made out of anything else nor could it perish by turning into something else. When an angel does not exist it is not really potential (there is no world with an angel-shaped gap; there is nothing that can be turned into the angel). In this sense there is no such thing as a possible angel. Nor is there such a thing as a logically possible angel, for, since we have no concept of angels, we cannot deal with them in language, and so-called logical possibility is nothing but the capability of a language to generate sentences. The only sense in which angels are 'possible' is that they are created and might not have been created. Their essences are potential with respect to their existence. Material things have two sorts of possibility: with respect to the causes in the world which brought them about but might not have done, and with respect to God who created them but might not have done. Angels only have this second kind of possibility. This means that while, given a sufficiently developed biology, the meaning of the word 'cat' might correspond to and represent the essence of a cat, the meaning of the word 'angel' or the word 'Gabriel' never represents the essence. We know how to use the word 'Gabriel' (just as with the word 'God') not because we have even the beginnings of a hazy notion of what Gabriel is, but because of what we know of other things. (We only have the beginnings of a hazy notion of what a cat is, but it is one of the tasks of biology to make this understanding more precise. There is no way we could even begin to know what Gabriel is.) If, *per impossibile*, we did know what an angel is, if we knew the essence of an angel, we would know that it existed (because there could be no such notion as the notion of a possible angel).

With material things it is like this: to know a thing's essence is to know the meaning of its name, but not conversely (we may be a little hazy about both). To know what a horse is, is to know what 'horse' means, how to use the word 'horse'. When all the horses die, although there is now of course no essence, we can go on understanding the meaning of the word 'horse'. It is not that the essence of any horse has been separated from its existence (that can never occur); it is just that the act of understanding by which we understand the essence is now an act of understanding of the meaning of a word. It is only material things that go out of existence in this way, leaving their names behind them like ghosts. But then it is only material things that have names. If, *per impossibile*, we had a name for an angel, that is, if we had a word whose meaning was the essence of the angel (as the meaning of 'horse' is [an approximation to] the essence of a horse), then to know that meaning and to know that essence would also be to know the existence of the angel. This would have no tendency to show that essence and existence are identical in the angel. Certainly, if an angel has, or rather is, an essence, then it has existence. But this is true of a horse too, for all essences must exist (that's what the word 'essence' means). It is just that with the horse the ghost of essence (the meaning of the name) carries on when the existence and essence have gone.

Our language is the way we have of making sense of (making intelligible) our material world. This means that: (a) the only thing we understand, as Aquinas puts it, is the nature of material things; and (b) the grammar of our language is the grammar of the material world. What I mean by this latter remark is that the contingency of material things shows up in our language as the logical contingency of sentences, but their createdness does not. It is a contingent fact that Fido is brown (it may or may not be the case), and, correspondingly, the sentence 'Fido is brown' is logically contingent. 'Fido is not brown' makes just as much sense. We can construct non-contingent, necessary sentences in our language, but they turn out to be statements of the grammar of the language itself. Amongst statements about the grammar of our language I include such statements as 'A human being is a linguistic animal', which (if there is a human being) is true and non-contingently true. ('A human being is not a linguistic animal' does not make sense.) What Aquinas called definitions, which state the essence of things, are statements of the grammar of the language. This correspondence between mode of being (contingency) and logical form (logical contingency) breaks down when we try to use words to speak of angels or God. Thus, although God exists necessarily, the proposition 'God exists' is not a logically necessary one. Conversely, to show that some equivalent of the sentence 'God exists' is logically necessary (as in the Ontological Argument) has no tendency to show that God exists necessarily, or indeed exists at all. See Aquinas's brilliantly laconic refutation of Anselm in *Summa Theologiae*, 1a,2,1,ad.2. The aim of an argument for the existence of God is of course to show not that 'God exists' is logically necessary, but that it is necessary that it is true, and this is shown not by what we know of God or the meaning of the word 'God' but by what we know of the world: that there might have been nothing at all.

What we know of the world is that it bears a relation to a Creator. The relationship is not, of course, real in God (just as the relationship of being looked at is not real in what you are looking at), but it is a reality in the creature. This reality is not, however, one which makes a difference to the creature. It is in fact the distinction of *esse* and essence, the fact that the essence of the creature is in potency to its *esse*. This relationship, then, between the creature, which is, but might have been nothing (not merely potential), and God, which cannot in any sense not be, the relationship of the creature in which essence and *esse* are distinct and God in whom they are not distinct, is what creation is. It is clear how far away we are by now from the original idea of making.

If this is what is meant by creation then the created world may well have always existed. Aquinas thought that the Bible tells us otherwise, but this seems to me to be rather dubious exegesis. It is also clear that creation is not something that can be investigated by the physicist. The notion of creation is entirely neutral as between theories as to the physical origin of our universe. Finally, may I remind you that what I have called the 'notion of creation' is not intelligible to us. We do not understand what creation means. We merely point towards it in the process of qualifying to death the notion of

God-making-the-world. For the world to be created is for it to exist instead of nothing. And we can have no concept of nothing. We can have no concept of creation (any more than of God), but this will not, I trust, prevent us from talking about them.

Notes

1   Edward Schillebeeckx, *Jesus: An Experiment in Christology*, trans. Hubert Hoskins (New York: The Seabury Press, 1979), p. 31.

2   Antony Flew and Alasdair MacIntyre (eds), *New Essays in Philosophical Theology* (London: SCM Press, 1955), p. 97.

3   Cf. *Summa Theologiae*, 1a,3,4.

2

The Logic of Mysticism

This title represents, I suppose, a kind of challenge; for there seems at first sight some incompatibility between the practice of logic and mysticism, a contrast between the rational and the intuitive, the tough-minded and the tender-minded. In taking up this challenge, I propose to argue with the help of two thinkers commonly admired for their attention to logic and its rights. I shall refer for the most part to St Thomas Aquinas but with occasional reference to Wittgenstein. Whatever may be said of the latter, it seems to me quite clear that St Thomas was a mystical thinker in that he was centrally concerned with the unknown and, in one sense, ineffable mystery of God and that he devoted a great deal of thought and writing to the problems associated with speaking of what is, in this sense, ineffable. I want to argue that in what is sometimes misunderstood as his dryly rational approach, even in his arguments for the existence of God, he is in fact engaged in, and inviting the reader to be engaged in, a mystical exploration, which is not at all the same thing as a mystical experience. Here the key notion is that of what he refers to as *esse*.

Perhaps I should say right away that for St Thomas we come to see the need for the particular use he has for the word *esse* (which is, after all, only the Latin infinitive of the verb 'to be') as the result of an argument, not as the result of an experience – not even the experience of being convinced by an argument. It is a central thesis of his that we grasp the use of this word not as we grasp other meanings – by what he calls *simplex apprehensio*, the having of a concept or the understanding of a meaning, such as having learnt and not forgotten the meaning of, say, *'fatwah'* – but as we deploy such concepts in the making of true or false judgements which issue not in meanings, but in statements. It is not simply in our capacity to use signs, our ability, for example, to understand words, but in our actual use of them to say what is the case that we have need of and lay hold on the *esse* of things. It is only by analogy that we can speak of the 'concept' of *esse*; we do not have a concept of existence as we have a concept of greenness or prevarication or polar bears.

In order to make sense of this use of *esse* I shall need to begin with our familiar understanding of things existing and not existing. It is generally believed that there are no dodos any more. If, however, the rumour arose that some had survived in the remote interior of Mauritius, an expedition might set forth for these parts to inquire into the matter. Whatever else these explorers brought with them, an essential piece of equipment would be some understanding of what distinguishes dodos from parrots and ptarmigans. They would have to grasp the meaning of the word 'dodo' sufficiently to be able, in that geographical context, to pick out dodos from other things. They would then hope to discover something that fitted their formula: some X, such that X was a dodo. It is in just such a context that the conventional account of what it is to say that something exists is at home. Philosophers have been anxious to point out that when we want to know whether dodos exist we do not go and look at dodos to see whether they have existence or not; we go to see whether there is anything at all that would count as a dodo. It was a point familiar to Aristotle and to medieval thinkers: to ask *an sit?* (whether it is) you have to start with at least some meaning for a word.

Suppose, then, to everyone's surprise, we are successful and we find some dodos. We shall then have answered the question *an sit*. Having done so we shall be able to settle down with them in their proper habitat, and by living amongst them over the years we may come slowly to some *scientia*, some scientific understanding of what is essential to being a dodo, what it takes for it to exist at all, and what is merely adventitious, as, for example, living exclusively in Mauritius or looking slightly ridiculous to slightly ridiculous European observers. This will ordinarily involve the elaboration of a new section of language or a jargon. What first struck people about dodos was their apparent foolishness and clumsiness, hence the original Portuguese name 'doudo', meaning awkward, and the international term 'didus ineptus'. As we came to understand more clearly the nature of the dodo, its essence or substance, we should probably devise some quite new name to signify this nature. In this way chemists devised the sign H_2O, the meaning of which (that is, its relationship to such other signs as HCl, CO_2, etc.) expresses, on the one hand, the essential structure common to such apparently quite diverse objects as those called 'ice', 'water' and 'steam', and, on the other hand, the natural physical relationships of such substances to what used to be called 'muriatic acid' and 'carbonic acid gas'. We should, in fact, try to devise a jargon with a structure of meanings reflecting the actual structures of the physical, chemical, biological world. If we should get closer to what an Aristotelian would call a definition expressing the essence of the thing, we would be closer to answering the new question: *quid sit*? – what does it take for such a thing to exist? If, as Aristotle remarked, there is nothing corresponding to our definition, nothing with this essence, then what looks like a definition of the essence is, in fact, nothing more than an explanation of the meaning of a word.

Understanding of what a dodo is would come ordinarily from a lengthy process of observation and experiment, a process I have called 'living with' the object of our study, and for this to take place there obviously have to be such objects. So, to repeat, we start with the common meaning of the name, sufficient for picking out the object in a particular context; we can then answer the question *an sit*, and if we answer that in the affirmative we can go on by investigation to get clearer about *quid sit*. Despite what nominalist philosophers may say, this is what ordinary working scientists such as chemists and botanists think they are sometimes engaged in. Our conventional account of what it is to say that tame tigers exist or that yetis do not exist is at home in just this context. Of course not all, in fact rather little, of our rational discourse is like doing chemistry – not even for chemists. One way of understanding our rational discourse concerning God is to see how radically it differs from this.

In seeking to show that we can prove the existence of God, that God's existence is *demonstrabile*, St Thomas faces a technical objection. In a true demonstration, as for example in the theorems of Euclid, we show not merely that something is the case but that it has to be the case. To demonstrate is to produce *scientia*, an understanding of how and why the world is as it is. Anyone may know that sugar, unlike marble, dissolves in water; it takes a physical chemist to show how this has to be the case given the molecular structure of the materials involved. His aim is to demonstrate that because of the nature of sugar, because of his definition of its essence, of course it dissolves.

The objector begins by stating that '*medium demonstrationis est quod quid est*': the central link of demonstration is the defined nature (*Summa Theologiae*, 1a,2,2). Then, he argues, to demonstrate that God exists must be to show that, given the definition of his nature, he has to exist; but since we do not know the definition of his nature, but only what he is not, we cannot have a demonstration that he exists. The objector is arguing that the only demonstration that God exists would have to be something like the Anselmian ontological argument in which the existence of God is thought to follow logically from something about God's nature. St Thomas in reply does not deny that we are ignorant of God's nature, but he points out that answering the question *an sit* is quite other than the kind of demonstration in which you show how some operation or effect has to flow from a thing the definition of whose nature you already know. Trying to find if there are any yetis is quite different from trying to show that sugar has to dissolve in water. We go looking for footprints in the snow and if we find them we argue that, given this evidence, it has to be the case that yetis exist; we do not seek to show that yetis have to exist, just that they do. We are arguing that an opponent necessarily has to accept the proposition, not that the proposition is a necessary one. In such an argument, then, we start not by knowing what God would be but only from features of the world we do know and which seem to be effects of God. It is our knowledge of these effects and not any knowledge of God's nature that gives us our rules for the use of the word 'God'. So you start by claiming that certain phenomena are effects, i.e. must have a cause. Not everything that is the case does have a cause: the stars in the night sky are arranged, it is alleged, in patterns reminiscent of various Greek gods and heroes, but it would be very odd to look for some power whose characteristic activity was the cause of this. But St Thomas, as is well known, thought that certain phenomena such as real change from mere potentiality to actuality, and the power of certain things to effect such change, did demand causal explanation. So he answers his objector here: 'When we argue from effect to cause, the effect will take the place of the definition of the cause in the proof that the cause exists; and this is especially so if the cause is God. For when proving anything to exist the central link is not what that thing is (we cannot even ask what it is [*quid est*] until we know that it exists [*an est*]) but rather what we are using the name of the thing to mean. Now when demonstrating from effects that God exists, we are able to use as link what the word "God" means, for, as we shall see, the names of God are derived from these effects' (*Summa Theologiae* 1a,2,2,ad.2). In this reply, as it seems to me, St Thomas is, as so often, simply saying enough to answer an objection; not, as it were, showing his whole hand. We should in fact be misled if we took it that his arguments for the existence of God start from a 'nominal definition' of God, as though he said: 'This is what people use the word "God" to mean, this is how we can at least pick out God from other things, now let us see if there is one.' It is, to my mind, of the greatest importance that his arguments end with, but certainly do not begin with: 'and this is what people call "God"'. The arguments do not presuppose any view of the nature of God, they simply begin with philosophical puzzles arising from features of the world that we understand and take us to what we do not understand. They start with questions we can answer and lead us to a question we cannot answer. St Thomas would accept Wittgenstein's statement: 'A question [can exist] only where there is an answer' (*Tractatus*: 6.51), but in this case we know that we cannot give the answer for that would be to know God's nature which is beyond the margins of our ways of grasping meanings. But of this more in a moment.

We need to take a brief look now at the kind of argument St Thomas has in mind. We may begin by noticing that there is some parallel between dependence in causality and dependence in information; indeed the latter is a particular case of the former. Some of the things I know I know because I am a witness to them, but most of what I know (and nearly all the interesting things) I do not know in that way but by hearsay. If I am to know by hearsay it is not, of course, sufficient merely to have been told. I must have been told by one who is reliable, and her reliability must be due either to her being herself a witness or else to her having had, in her turn, a reliable informant, and so on. Unless hearsay is finally anchored, as it were, in what is not hearsay but witness, there can be no reliable hearsay, only baseless rumour. I can really know what I am told only if there is or was someone who knows or knew without being told. Faith, which 'comes by hearing', has to depend on somebody's knowing.

This argument you will perhaps recognize as having the same logical structure as the one St Thomas sketches as the second of his Five Ways. If there are things that have to be brought from potentiality to existence by the power of another thing, there must be one or more things that are not under this condition: that exist actively and are not brought into existence and activity by another. Just as what I am told is only as reliable as the witness who did not need to be told, just as the truth I think I know on hearsay depends totally on the truth of what that witness says, so the existence of anything that has to be brought into existence by another depends totally on the existence and activity of one that does not have to be so brought into existence. Note that in each case the conclusion of the argument is to something that is known negatively, to something that does *not* have a dependency of some sort. There is no suggestion of what, positively, such a being might be. All the arguments lead to a power which is not of a kind we understand: to an unknown God. When I repeat what I know by reliable hearsay I am ultimately being the mouthpiece of the original reliable witness. In the same way every creature that exercises its power to bring things or features of things into being is ultimately the instrument of the power which is not the instrument of anything.

It seems (though I shall want to qualify this later in the case of God) that nothing exists except by being something, some kind of thing. What exists does so by having a particular form. 'No entity without identity' as Quine used to say; '*forma dat esse*' as St Thomas used to say. When a cause brings an effect into being it does so by providing the form by which this effect is and has its particular essence – though in the case of caused features of things (which, as St Thomas says, rather *insunt* than *sunt*) we should perhaps speak of an 'inessence'. A cause in nature does this by giving a new form to what previously existed by another form but was capable of losing this (perishing or changing) and being given a new one. When I was brought into existence by my parents they trans-formed material things of various kinds (the food they had eaten, the genes they had inherited) into a material thing of a new kind, existing by a new *human* form we call a human *life*. Before I existed there was already a natural world of material things that were potentially of my kind – not in the sense that they themselves had the power to become human, but simply in the sense that they could be made into, trans-formed into, a human being; and there were other material things with the power to effect this trans-formation. Before I existed there was already a natural world with a me-shaped hole in it waiting to be filled by the active power of a cause. Now natural causality is like hearsay: trans-formation is a genuine source of existence, as hearsay is a genuine source of truth. The possibility of receiving existence from a merely trans-forming cause (like the possibility of receiving truth from mere hearsay) depends on anchorage in a being which is more than a trans-forming cause, a being which is the source of existence as the original witness is the source of a truth. Such a being would not make by the trans-forming of what already has another form, a making 'out of' what already exists. Its bringing into existence must take place without the attendance of a background world, without any background at all, not even empty space.

Natural causes, operating as trans-formers, provide the answer to the question: Why did these things come to exist instead of those others that used to exist or instead of those others that might have existed? Answer: Because they were brought about by this cause that operates in this particular way because of its own particular form. (Explanation by appeal to the specific causal powers of things within the world – things with their own special natures – is the characteristically Aristotelian alternative to the Platonic appeal to participation in the eternal forms.) God, on the other hand, would provide the answer to the question: Why is there anything at all rather than nothing? The object of natural trans-forming causes is the existence of something that has this or that particular form. The object of the divine creative cause is the existence of everything that has existence. I say that God *would* provide the answer to that question (Why is there anything instead of nothing?) because, since we do not know what God is, we do not have an answer to our question.

Natural agents can only have the power to bring things into existence by trans-formation because they are instruments of God's causality – just as hearsay can only convey truth because it is from the mouthpiece of the original witness. We can certainly say that it is the fire that brings into being the boiling of the water (because that is its nature and natural power); we also say, in a different tone of voice, that God, using the instrumentality of the fire, boils the kettle. Everything that is brought about by natural causes is brought about by God; and there are some things, like human free decisions, that are not brought about by any natural causes but *only* by God.

The artist's colours are arranged in blobs on his palette and his brush moves them and puts them in a new arrangement on the canvas so that a painting is made. In this way the power of the brush to move the paint makes a work of art. But that it makes a work of art is because it is wielded by the artist. In this illustration we can for the artist read *God*, for the paint-brush read *the natural trans-forming cause*, for the new arrangement of the paint read *the new form* and for the work of art *the new thing* that exists by this form.

We refer to natural trans-forming causes when, given the world, we want to ask scientific questions: Was it the fire that boiled the water or was it the micro-wave? We refer to God when we are asking a more radical question: Why do explanations explain what they do? Why do trans-forming causes bring things into existence? – as we might ask: Why is this hearsay reliable?

Given the natural world, we understand the natures of things by contrast with what they are not. Given the world, we understand what it is for this to exist through its particular form by contrast with what exists by another form. The structuralist is surely right here to insist that meanings consist in oppositions of contraries. This at least seems right when we are allowed to take the world for granted. But suppose we try to understand not simply what it is to exist by this particular form – to see it as the expectable product of this power in the world and not that – but the existence of the world itself. This would be trying to understand the power upon which particular powers depend for their efficacy. If it be true that there has to be such a power, then the world we take for granted must be *granted* in a much richer and more mysterious sense.

It is this gratuitousness of things that St Thomas calls their *esse*: their existence not just over against the possibility that they might not have been a part of the world (if natural causes had operated differently – which is why the dodos do not exist), but their existence over against the possibility that there might not have been any world at all. In thinking of the *esse* of things we are trying to think of them not just in relation to their natural causes but in their relation to a creator. If we can simply take the world for granted then within this world to exist is just to be this kind of thing (there is an X such that X is a dodo), for things in the world that come into existence and perish (contingent things) there is a polarity of potential matter and actualizing form, but there is no demand for a polarity of essence and existence. It is only when we consider the world as created that we see that even non-contingent, 'necessary beings' (which would not, indeed, depend for their existence and meaning on other natural causes) would have a dependent existence in relation to God. So in all created things, and beyond the polarity belonging to contingency (based on the distinction of matter and form), there is the polarity of createdness (based on a distinction of essence and existence), which would belong to even 'necessary beings'. Only in the Uncreated is there no potentiality in any sense at all, not even a distinction of essence and existence; only the Uncreated exists without *having* existence. This distinction between contingency with respect to form and dependency with respect to existence is clearly spelled out in St Thomas's Third Way.

Put it like this: you may at some time have a very strong feeling of the gratuity of things, a quasi-religious experience as in nature-mysticism, which seems to contain or lead into a sense of gratitude for there being a world. In the Romantic tradition this was associated with the wilder countryside, especially Cumbria. The sense that we are here understanding some great truth is, however, vulnerable to recognizing the naturalness of nature, a scientific recognition of the complex causes by which the world just had to become the way it is. You may remember the story of the man expatiating on the wonders of Niagara Falls – all those thousands of tons of water cascading down every minute – and his friend, who remarked: 'But, after all, what is there to stop it?' It is understandable that Victorian scientific rationalists should have sought to replace such Romantic nature-mysticism with the 'wonders of science' which seemed less likely to threaten them with metaphysics. 'Wonder' is, however, not part of the vocabulary of science, any more than is 'existence' or 'God' or, indeed, 'science'.

But there remains the wonder that there is science at all, that there is a world of powers and action and new existents. This is not itself one of the wonders of science, and, however fascinating the work of physicists investigating the Big Bang, it is not relevant to this mystery of gratuitousness, the createdness, the *esse* of things.

When I speak of science I am not restricting the term to the mathematically governed 'physical sciences'; I mean any and every account of how what happens in the world 'has to happen' (necessarily or naturally or of course). What characterizes science in this sense is not just an appeal to mathematics but an appeal to an order of nature, to the essence and character of things such that they act in expectable ways. David Hume, for whose empiricist epistemology knowing was essentially a matter of having mental images, denied that things really have powers and tendencies and expectable behaviour, for while you may be able to make a picture of me balancing a billiard cue on my nose, you cannot in the same way make a picture of me being able or likely to perform this feat. However, knowing what things are capable of and likely to do is a large part of understanding what they are; a man who showed no surprise at all at seeing a rabbit chasing a wolf would show that he knew very little about the nature of rabbits and wolves. Our scientific understanding of what goes on around us is rooted in such expectations. But talk of *esse*, the gratuitousness of things, has no place, and ought to have no place, in such natural science.

When Wittgenstein in the *Tractatus* says 'Not *how* the world is, is the mystical, but *that* it is' (6.44), it seems to me that he is engaged with the same question as St Thomas is when he speaks of *esse*. As St Thomas distinguishes between the creative act of God (which we do not understand) and natural causality (which we do), between creation and trans-formation, Wittgenstein distinguishes the mystical from 'what can be said' (6.53).

Positivist interpretations of the *Tractatus* took this as a cheerful dismissal of all such metaphysical talk, but it now seems to be the general view that such was far from his intention and that the unease which is shown (but cannot be said) at the end of the work is an unease with the sharp dichotomy of *either* scientific language *or* silence, an unease which perhaps subsequently bore fruit in Wittgenstein's later stress on the multiplicity of language-games.

For St Thomas, then, the *esse* of things turns out to be their createdness, their gratuity; so that all talk of God has its foundation in the *esse* of creatures. This is not a reductionist view of God-talk (as though we were saying that all talk of God is 'really' about features of the world). It is not reductionist just because what is in question is their *esse*, and this is not a feature of things that, for example, distinguishes them from other things: clearly we cannot set the class of existents over against a class of non-existents – not even an empty class of non-existents. We can however, as St Thomas points out, distinguish between nouns and noun-phrases such as 'the power of seeing', which refer to something that is, and terms such as 'blindness', which refer to an absence of what might have been expected to be. In that sense we can say that blindness is a non-being. We can also distinguish the sense in which a dog is and the irreducibly distinct sense in which his barking is, or in which he is upside-down, or in Germany. We can distinguish, in fact, different categories of being. What we cannot do is set a class of existent things, activities or relations over-against a shadowy class of non-existent things, activities and relations. In a trivial sense you could say that what is common to absolutely everything is existence; but in saying this you would be conveying nothing at all: this Highest Common Factor is purchased at the cost of having no height at all. It is not in this way that *esse* is common to all – not, that is, as the asymptotic point at which specificity or determinateness vanishes altogether. No, *esse* is, in St Thomas's phrase, 'the actuality of every form', the determinately distinct actuality of every form.

For an Aristotelian, matter is what is relatively indeterminate and unstruc-tured, waiting to be determined by some form or structure, the wood that may be made into the table, the table that may become part of the dining room suite. Matter in one form, one actualization, is said to be potential with respect to being actualized by some other form. You never catch matter without some form or other. Form is the relatively determining factor giving being and intelligibility to a thing. With this in mind we can see that in a definition which is made by differentiating a genus (as the specific difference, rational, determines the genus, animal, in the classical definition of the human), the meaning of the genus word 'animal' is, in a sense, material, potential, open, waiting to be determined by the *differentia* word 'rational' which determines *in what sense* this is an animal. So to say that a human being is a rational animal is logically quite different from saying that a milkman is a man employed to deliver the milk: for men employed to deliver the milk and men not so employed are men in exactly the same sense; whereas rational and irrational animals are not animals in the same sense. Being rational is not an adventitious accidental feature of a general-purposes animal; it is having a certain (specific) kind of animality. However, being employed to deliver the milk is an adventitious accidental feature of a general-purposes human being and does not signify a special kind of humanity. You never catch anything that is simply generically an animal without being differentiated as this or that species, just as you never catch matter which is not actualized and determined by some form. So, to repeat, genus words are 'open' (material) words that need to have their meaning 'closed' (formally) by a specific difference.

Now it is an Aristotelian thesis that *esse*, being, is not simply the widest, most all-embracing, most 'open' or material of genus words; it is not a genus at all. Cornelius Ernst puts it well:

The community of the indefinite variety of all that is in *esse* is not only trans-generic in the sense that *ens* is found in all the genera (substance, quality, quantity and so on); it is trans-generic in the more fundamental sense that it is quite unlike the community of genus at all. For while the community of genus is subordinate and quasi-material, awaiting the formal determination of specific difference, the community of *esse* is superordinate and quasi-formal, the community of whatever has already achieved its appropriate differentiation as this or that discriminate individual: as [St Thomas] puts it in the *Summa Theologiae* (1a,4,1,ad.3): *ipsum esse est actualitas omnium rerum, et etiam ipsarum formarum* [*esse* is the actuality of all things including forms themselves]. Or again (1a,8,1): *Esse autem est illud quod est magis intimum cuilibet, et quod profundius omnibus inest, cum sit formale respectu omnium quae in re sunt* [*esse* is that which is most intimate to each thing and what is in them most profoundly, for it is formative (*formale*) with respect to all that is in them].[1]

To go back to the painter with his brush and his (and its) achievement: this achievement, that of being a work of art, is the ultimate actuality (cf. *esse*) which is the work of the painter in being the actuality of the paint-arranging (cf. trans-forming) achievement of the brush. The various works of Picasso may or may not have certain characteristic features in common, but when we say they are all Picasso's works we are not referring to these features or to any common feature, we are speaking simply of their common dependence on his action. The community of all things in *esse*, therefore, is their community as creatures of God, and it is this that is *das Mystische*.

The characteristic work of the paint-brush is to re-arrange paint, and simultaneously, in the same operation, the characteristic work of the artist wielding the brush is to make a painting: the work of the brush counts as painting because it is the work of the artist. It is thus the *esse* of things that leads us to speak of God – which for Wittgenstein in the *Tractatus* cannot be done. For him, we approach the mystical simply by recognizing the limits of what can be said. 'We feel that even if *all possible* scientific questions be answered, the problems of life have still not been touched at all. Of course there is then no question left, and just this is the answer' (6.52).

St Thomas does not give up so easily. He sets himself to understand how language is used in the biblical tradition to which he belonged. He whole-heartedly agrees that we cannot say what God is, and he sets himself the task of understanding how we could speak of what, being the source of *esse* itself, is outside the scope of the world of existents, of what could not be an inhab-itant of any world or subject to any of the intelligible limitations implied in being such an inhabitant, of what could not be one kind of thing rather than another, nor of course subject to the special limitations of material spatio-temporal beings, of what could not be *here* and *then*. We construct and learn the meanings of our language, and thus acquire our concepts, in coping with our world characterized by all these limitations, and intelligible precisely in terms of these limitations, in terms of forms which have their meanings as opposed to and distinct from other forms. No such concepts could possibly express what it means to be God.

Nevertheless, St Thomas concludes that there are two considerations which make it possible to give sense to the traditional biblical God-talk: first that we can understand what God is not, and second that we can use words not only to say what they mean but also to point beyond what we understand them to mean.

In listing just now the reasons for finding God unintelligible, I was pointing to just the negative knowledge which can form a basis not only for the negative statements I was making but for positive statements as well. Knowing what God is not can be a basis for saying (though not for understanding) what God is, or at least certain things about God. Let me give an example: God is intelligent (I think this may be what some people mean by saying that God is 'personal').

St Thomas regards both intelligence and intelligibility as a transcendence of material limitation. Sensation is necessarily subjective, rooted in this individual body with all its unique peculiarities. Because sensation is a kind of knowing, sensations are meanings. A meaning is always the role or function of some part in an organized structure – as, for instance, the meaning of a word is the part it plays in the language. The meaning which is a sensation is a bodily role, a meaning within the structure of my nervous system and brain. It is just in this way that sensing provides me with an interpretation of my world. Thus, for example, we determine whether a certain kind of animal has the sense of sight or not, not by looking to see if it has any eyes but by observing whether or not its behaviour (and hence its interpretation of the world) is any different when it is in the light or in the dark. It is because of this subjectivity of sensation that nobody else can have my sensations though, being the same kind of animal, they are likely to have similar ones. But with the advent of language we create a structure of meanings which is nobody's private domain. In principle nobody could have my sensation; but in principle everybody could have my thought. For the meanings of words are their roles not within the structure of any individual body but within the structure of language, which is in principle (in order to be language at all) shared by all. Because of the essential historicity of human language and human thought it may be impossibly difficult in practice to think the thoughts of Homer or Moses, but at least we would here be failing in a task; there is no such task as having the sensations of Homer or Moses or of the man next door. For St Thomas, what is bodily and material about me constitutes my privacy, my individuality; whereas my intellectual capacities liberate me from the prison of my subjectivity. My thought can never be just mine as my sensations are mine (there could scarcely be a greater contrast with the world of René Descartes). St Thomas did, however, think (and brilliantly argued in a little book called *De Unitate Intellectus*, which we may translate as *Is there only a Single Mind?*) that the act of thinking my thought is my own – because my capacity to think it is a capacity of my soul which is individuated as being the form of this individual material body: in this sense my thinking is mine just as my walking or digesting is mine. My thinking is my capacity to transcend my individuality; it is my thinking of meanings which are not just mine.

The point of that excursus was to make the connection between immateriality and understanding. For St Thomas's way of thinking, whatever is not subject to material limitation is intelligent. He thought rationality, our form of intelligence, was the lowest kind, being the activity of a being whose existence was as a material bodily being, though having a capacity to transcend purely bodily action. It is, however, the only kind of intelligence we are able partially to understand. Because intelligence belongs to the immaterial, if we deny materiality to God we must say he is intelligent. Because of a piece of negative knowledge, we can make this positive statement. But of course we are not saying that God has our kind of intelligence, that he is limited to rationality. We do not, in fact, understand the intelligence we are attributing to God. We can confidently assert that God is intelligent (or 'personal') while cheerfully admitting that we do not know what intelligence would be in God.

By similar processes of argument we can attribute to him goodness, justice, power and will without claiming to understand what these attributes would be in God. St Thomas, indeed, argues that having a multiplicity of attributes is itself a limitation that has to be denied of God. As they are in us, justice, mercy, intelligence and happiness are distinct characteristics: no such divisions could have place in God. God, indeed, could not have any characteristics as he does not have existence. The mystery of his intelligence and the mystery of his mercy and of his justice must be just the one mystery which is God. It cannot be one thing for him to exist and another for him to be wise and another for him to be good. The predicates we attach to the word 'God' have, indeed, different meanings in that their meaning is derived from our understanding of these things as properties in our world, but what they refer to in God is a single mystery which is quite unknown to us. We have some understanding of the wisdom that God creates in us, but when we say that God is wise we mean neither that he is the creator of wisdom in us, nor simply that he is not foolish; we mean that the quality we call wisdom in us exists in God in some higher and utterly mysterious way (cf. *Summa Theologiae*, 1a,13,5).

If we are surprised that we should use the same words to refer in God to something quite different from what we use them to refer to in our world, St Thomas refers us to the common phenomenon of the analogous use of words. I may say that I love wine, my mistress, my country and my God, but nobody supposes that the word 'love' here signifies the same thing in each case. Nor does anyone suppose that I am merely making puns. It is common enough for a word to be used in different contexts with systematically different senses, with what St Thomas would call a different *modus significandi*. St Thomas argues that this is just what happens with a great deal of our language about God, especially when we are doing theology: with, however, this special feature that in the case of God we do not (yet) understand the *modus significandi* of the words we use. That will have to wait for the beatific vision when we shall know God by sharing in his self-knowledge. St Thomas did also think that even in this life we may share, through faith, in that divine self-knowledge, but faith seems to us rather a darkness, an awareness of ignorance, than an intellectual clarity.

So for St Thomas, when we speak of God we do not know what we are talking about. We are simply taking language from the familiar context in which we understand it and using it to point beyond what we understand into the mystery that surrounds and sustains the world we do partially understand.

St Thomas, however, also insists that the greater part of our religious language is not, and should not be, understood in this way: most of the language we use in speaking of or to God is not even used analogically but metaphorically, by an appeal to images. What he calls *Sacra Doctrina* – meaning God's activity in teaching us in and through Scripture – requires, he says, such imaginative language. We need a great many images, preferably incompatible images (God is a mighty fortress, a still small voice, a vine-dresser, a mother eagle, he is wrathful and he is compassionate, he is faithful to his word but he repents of what he has done, and so on); moreover it is better to have many grotesque and base images (*sub figuris vilium corporum*), for all this preserves us from idolatry, from mistaking the image for God, from thinking of God as subject to the limitations of our imagery.

St Thomas distinguishes words like 'hearing', 'courageous', 'seeing' and 'wrathful', all of which have as part of their meaning a reference to what is material (you cannot be wrathful without the bodily emotions associated with aggression; you cannot see without eyes occupying a definite position in space), from words which, although we learn how to use them in bodily experience, do not have this physical reference as part of their meaning: as 'justice', for example, 'love' or 'goodness'. The former can only be used metaphorically, to provide images of the unknown God; the latter can be used to speak of him literally though only analogically, so leaving him still utterly mysterious to us.

For St Thomas, metaphor is the heart of religious language but it cannot be sufficient of itself. It needs to be underpinned by such non-metaphorical but analogical assertions as that God exists, that God is good, that God is the creative cause and sustainer of our world, that he is loving. It is these literal assertions that are subject to the caveat of analogy. Although we do not understand what they refer to in God, they are our way of asserting that the riches of religious imagery are more than the art-form of a particular culture (though, of course, they are that) but are part of our access to a mystery beyond our understanding which we do not create, but which rather creates us and our understanding and our whole world.

Note

1   *The Gospel of Grace*, vol. 30 of the Blackfriars edition of the *Summa Theologiae* (London and New York: Eyre and Spottiswoode and McGraw-Hill Book Company, 1972), pp. xx–xxi.

3

The Involvement of God

I have called this chapter 'The Involvement of God' because I want to take part
in a discussion about such questions as whether God suffers with the sufferings
of his creatures, in order to ask how far God is involved in his world. I shall
first try to defend what I take to be the classical doctrine of God derived from
Augustine and Aquinas: that it is not in the nature of God to be involved in the
suffering of the world as spectator, sympathizer or victim, but that it is in God's
nature nonetheless to be involved with his creatures more intimately than
any creature could be involved with any other. Secondly I shall argue that the
christology of Chalcedon does make sense of the notion that God suffers and
in fact was tortured to death; indeed, in large part it just *is* this notion. Thirdly,
and a bit more tentatively, I shall suggest that a sacramental interpretation of
Chalcedonian christology yields the whole of the doctrine of the Trinity.

* * *

The subject of God's suffering is so popular amongst theologians today that
I am quite incapable of even beginning to give a survey of recent literature.
This is partly because I haven't read enough and partly because I don't want
to misrepresent authors by isolated quotation. I shall quote very little: I am
concerned with certain ideas, how they hang together and how they fall apart.

There is, of course, today a strong and respectable tendency to criticize
what is taken to be the traditional notion of God, essentially on the grounds

that it fails to take the measure of the biblical revelation of God and fails because it is blinkered by what are thought of as 'static' Greek philosophical categories of thought. The God of metaphysics is a Greek intrusion on Hebrew revelation, it is claimed. This is not, of course, a modern idea (it was very familiar to Luther), but it has been given, I think, a new lease of life by the revival of process theology and especially by the arrival of liberation theology. (Don't get me wrong here, incidentally. The *praxis* of liberation theology, that unity of theory and practice taking place in base communities and elsewhere, especially in Latin America, seems to me clearly the most important thing going on anywhere in the Christian movement today – much too important to get entangled in an incoherent theology of God.)

In spite of all my good intentions I shall begin with a quotation, from Jürgen Moltmann. He is speaking of Aquinas's Five Ways:

> The cosmological proof of God was supposed by Thomas to answer the question *utrum Deus sit*, but he did not really prove the *existence* of God; what he proved was the nature of the divine … Aquinas answered the question 'What is the nature of the divine?', but not the question 'Who is God?'.[1]

This remark will seem very peculiar to those of us who remember that the next sentence but one after the Five Ways begins: 'But because concerning God *we cannot know what he is* but only what he is not …' (*scire non possumus quid sit*). It seems improbable that Aquinas had so quickly forgotten what he had just been doing or that he misinterpreted himself so radically. Readers of Aquinas, however, including some of those who see themselves as his disciples, have the utmost difficulty in taking him seriously when he says that we simply know nothing of the nature of God. And this, I think, is where the misunderstandings of the tradition begin.

If I may very briefly summarize what I have said so often elsewhere: Aquinas's Five Ways, as I read them, are sketches for five arguments to show that a certain kind of *question* about our world and ourselves is valid: 'Why the world, instead of nothing at all?' This is a question, in Aquinas's jargon, about the *esse* of things, their being over against nothing, not just their being over against some alternative or over against potentiality. Aquinas wishes to say two things: (1) that here we have a valid question and, (2) that we do not know how to answer it; or (1) God exists, and (2) God is an incomprehensible mystery.

Of course, there are plenty of philosophical reasons for thinking that the question is not a valid one, not one we could possibly ask – that we may say the words but, when we do, we are not asking a real question. It is by no means *obvious* that the question is valid, and it is precisely the point of the Five Ways to try to establish that it *is* a valid question, for it is one which, for one reason or another, we are impelled to ask. Whether any of these arguments, or any others, are convincing is not my present concern; I merely want to show what Aquinas thought he was doing. He thought he was validating a specifically Judaeo-Christian activity (which has since become a quite common general human activity) of asking in some form: 'What does it *all* mean?' or 'Why *anything* instead of nothing?' And he thought he was validating the questioning even though (or perhaps because) he provides no answer. We do not and cannot in this life know the answer, but we label it 'God' – *et hoc omnes dicunt Deum*.

To say that we have a valid question (one with an answer) is to say that God exists; for what we mean by 'God' is just whatever answers the question. Apart from knowing this, says Aquinas most insistently, all we can do is point, as systematically as we can, to several kinds or categories of things that the answer *could not be*. For one thing, whatever would answer our question could not itself be subject to the question – otherwise we are left as we were, with the same question still to answer. Whatever we mean by 'God' cannot be whatever it is that makes us ask the question in the first place. So, perishability, decline, dependence, alteration, the impersonality that characterizes material things, and so on, all these have to be excluded from God. This means that suffering is excluded.

Now, as I have said, it is extremely difficult for readers of Aquinas to take his agnosticism about the nature of God seriously. If he says 'Whatever God may be, he cannot be changing', readers leap to the conclusion that he means that what God is is static. If he says that, whatever God may be, he could not suffer together with (*sympathize* with) his creatures, he is taken to mean that God must by nature be unsympathetic, apathetic, indifferent, even callous. It is almost as though if Aquinas had said that God could not be a supporter of Glasgow Celtic, we supposed he was claiming God as a Rangers fan.

It is supposed that there must be lurking there *some* notion of what God is – frequently characterized as a 'Greek' notion. Not everyone misreads Aquinas quite so blatantly as Moltmann in the passage I quoted, but we do find it hard to admit that he really did mean what he said.

The people collectively known as 'Greeks' in this context did not, of course, have any notion of creation. That is to say they did not ask the typically Jewish (and thus Christian) question about the *esse* of things, the ultimately radical question that, for Aquinas, points us towards the unknown God. I should add at this point, perhaps, that the revelation of God in Jesus in no way, for Aquinas, changes this situation. By the revelation of grace, he says, we are joined to God as to an unknown, *ei quasi ignoto coniungamur* (*Summa Theologiae* 1a,12 and 1a,13,ad.1). God remains the mystery which could only be known by God himself, or by our being taken up to share in his own knowledge of himself, a sharing which for us in this world is not knowledge but the darkness of faith. For Aquinas, the distinction that Moltmann attributes to him would be senseless: we shall not, and could not, know the nature of the divine until we know *who* God is.

The Christian use for the word 'God', according to this tradition, depends on what I would call the 'creation question', and it seems to me that Edward Schillebeeckx has it exactly right when he says:

Enthusiasm for Jesus of Nazareth as an inspiring human being, I can appreciate – at the human level that is quite something in itself. But it entails no binding invitation, can bear no stamp of the universally human, unless it can be shown that the Creator, the monotheistic God of Jews, Muslims, Christians and so many others, is personally implicated in the Jesus event.[2]

In other words, the 'creation question' has to be prior to the fullest understanding we can have of Jesus. Our use for the word 'God' does *not* begin with christology. To put it at its simplest, we cannot ask the question 'In what sense is Jesus to be called Son of God?' without some prior use for the word 'God'. And, of course, the New Testament did have such a prior use. The NT is unintelligible except as the flowering of the Hebrew tradition and the asking of the creation question that became central to the Jewish Bible.

One of my first claims, then, is that the God of what I have called the 'tradition', the God of Augustine and Aquinas in the west, is precisely the God of the Bible, the God of Abraham, Isaac and Jacob, the God who is not a god, not a powerful inhabitant of the universe, but the creator, the answer to the question 'What does it all mean?', 'Why anything anyway?' This was essentially the question asked by the Jews, at least from Second Isaiah onwards, the question which, once asked, could not be unasked (except with great philosophical ingenuity), and this is the question which for mainstream Christian tradition gives us meaning for the word 'God'.

One of my worries is that by contrast with this biblical God, the God spoken of by those who insist on God's participation in the history of his people, sharing their experiences, their sufferings and triumphs, is perilously like one of the gods. This is particularly worrying when it is found amongst liberation theologians because it is the God of the Hebrews (who in the Jewish interpretation comes to be seen as creator) who is hailed in the decalogue as liberator; it is the gods (parts of history) and the whole religion of the gods that is seen to stand for alienation and dependency. 'I am Yahweh your God who brought you out of slavery; you shall have no gods.'

God the creator, who is not one of the participants in history but the mover of Cyrus and of all history, is the liberator fundamentally because he is not a god, because there are no gods or at least no gods to be worshipped. This leaves history in human hands under the judgement of God. Human misery can no longer be attributed to the gods and accepted with resignation or evaded with sacrifices. The long slow process can begin of identifying the human roots of oppression and exploitation, just as the way now lies open for the scientific understanding and control of the forces of nature. The doctrine of creation which begins as a Hebrew insight makes human science possible, including the scientific examination of human society and the forces that govern it and guide its history.

It seems to me a disastrous error to suppose that, just because Aquinas and the medieval schools took over with delight the instruments of Greek classical and post-classical thought and used and developed their logic and their language, they were therefore thinking in the way that, say, Plato or Aristotle thought. Aquinas, for example, takes words like 'substance' and 'accident' and uses them in his Eucharistic doctrine to say something that Aristotle would have thought unintelligible nonsense – about the change of a piece of bread not into another kind of thing, but into another individual. The technical word that Aristotle would have found so alien is Aquinas's word *esse* (it is the *esse* of the bread that becomes the *esse* of the body of Christ, as its accidents lose their accidental role altogether and become the symbols by which Christ is sacramentally present). Here is a change below the level of substantial change, as creation is deeper than substantial change, a change which is not a *mutatio* at all. *Esse* in Aquinas's jargon belongs to the doctrine of creation, of which Aristotle had no notion at all. He is content to deny, as does Aquinas, that the world could be *made*, generated. He does not, as Aquinas does, ask the Jewish question, the question of *esse*, of the existence of things not over against potentiality but over against nothing.

The notion that the adoption of Aristotelian categories, concepts and language, arguments and insights means that nothing will be said that

Aristotle would not approve is on exactly the same level as the notion that the adoption of Marxist categories, arguments and insights means that liberation theologians will or should say nothing but what is approved by Marx. Luther was, perhaps, the Ratzinger of his age.

Aquinas's Five Ways, then, which are, of course, a part of his theology, are an attempt to validate what I have called the Jewish question, the creation question, using the categories of Aristotelian and, to some extent, Platonic thought. Whether or not these attempts are much use to people who have moved to different ways of seeing the world, the *question* seems to remain, together with the challenge of validating it in the face of, for example, claims that such metaphysical talk cannot be thinking. But in any case this metaphysics of being arising from the notion of a creator God is a Jewish and not a Greek discovery.

To lose sight of the Jewish creation question is, it seems to me, to settle for worshipping an inhabitant of the world, to betray the biblical inheritance and to regress to a worship of the gods; it is a form of idolatry.

If, on the other hand, we accept the creator God, then he must be in no way passive with respect to the world, and this must mean that God does not learn from or experience the world and, in general, cannot be affected by it. It is this that worries people. If the creator is really incapable of experiencing suffering, what are we to make of God's compassion, or his wrath? Are we not in danger of making him indifferent? Even if we acknowledge that words like 'compassion' and 'wrath' are used metaphorically (because animal passions cannot be attributed to what is not material), still they seem to imply some kind of reaction to what is taking place. Must we deny this of God?

As with Celtic and Rangers, it does not follow that, if God is not affected by, say, human suffering, he is indifferent to it. In our case there are only two options open: we either feel with, sympathize with, have compassion for the sufferer, or else we cannot be present to the suffering, we must be callous, indifferent. We should notice, however, that even in our case it is not an actual 'suffering with' that is necessary for compassion, but only a *capacity* to suffer with. Sharing in actual pain is neither necessary nor sufficient for compassion, whose essential components are awareness, feelings of pity and concern. I can have all these three without myself suffering from the pain or tragedy that afflicts my companion, and conversely I may be smitten with exactly the same kind of pain without experiencing any compassion at all.

Compassion is clearly a feeling (and not simply an intellectual awareness of another's pain) but it is not the same feeling as the pain itself. But the creator God cannot even be said literally to experience this feeling of compassion.

Our only way of being present to another's suffering is by being affected by it, because we are outside the other person. We speak of '*sym*pathy' or '*compassion*', just because we want to say that it is *almost* as though we were not outside the other, but living her or his life, experiencing her or his suffering. A component of pity is frustration at having, in the end, to remain outside.

Now, the creator cannot in this way ever be outside his creature; a person's act of being as well as every action done has to be an act of the creator. If the creator is the reason for everything that is, there can be no actual being which does not have the creator as its centre holding it in being. In our compassion we, in our feeble way, are seeking to be what God is all the time: united with and within the life of our friend. We can say in the psalm 'The Lord is compassion' but a sign that this is metaphorical language is that we can also say that the Lord has no need of compassion; he has something more wonderful, he has his creative act in which he is 'closer to the sufferer than she is to herself'.

What is true of compassion has to be more generally true of all experience and learning. Unless we learn, we are ignorant, but it is not the case with God that he would be ignorant if he did not learn. And our learning and experience is a feeble shadow of God's understanding of the world which he makes both to be and to be intelligible.

Whatever the consciousness of the creator may be, it cannot be that of an experiencer confronted by what he experiences. I think that James Mackey does not choose his words carefully enough when he says of Aquinas:

He further distances from our world all discussion of real divine relation by stating quite baldly, 'there is no real relation in God to the creature'. Creatures, that is, may experience a real relationship of dependence on and need of God, but God experiences no such relationship to his creatures.[3]

For Aquinas, of course, the question is not one of experience. God simply does not have any relation of dependence on his creatures but he understands, with an understanding more intimate than any knowledge from experience, the truth about the dependence of creatures on his knowledge and love.

The point about the lack of real relation on God's part is simply that being creator adds nothing to God; all the difference it makes is *all* the difference to the creature. (Indeed, the gift of *esse* is too radical to be called a 'difference' since clearly the creature is not changed by coming into existence.) But it makes no difference to God not, of course, because God is indifferent or bored by it all, but because he gains nothing by creating. We could call it sheerly altruistic, except that the goodness God wills for his creatures is not a separate and distinct goodness from his own goodness. The essential point that Aquinas, surely rightly, wants to make is that creation fulfils no need of God's. God has no needs.

I am repeating at too great a length the familiar point that the God of Augustine and Aquinas, precisely by being wholly transcendent, *extra ordinem omnium entium existens* (*In Peri Hermenias* I, lect. 14, 197), is more intimately involved with each creature than any other creature could be. God could not be *other* to creatures in the way that they must be to each other. At the heart of every creature is the source of *esse*, making it to be and to act

(*Summa Theologiae* 1a,8,1). As is well known, Aquinas carries this through to its logical conclusion and insists that it must be just as true of my free acts as of anything else. To be free is to be independent of others. God is not, in the relevant sense, other.

So, I think it makes perfect sense to say both that it is not in the nature of God to suffer and also that it is not in the nature of God to lack the most intimate possible involvement with the sufferings of his creatures. To safeguard the compassion of God there is no need to resort to the idea that God as he surveys the history of mankind suffers with us in a literal sense – though in some spiritual way.

* * *

Here I come to my second argument. I think that the temptation to hold that it is in the nature of God to suffer arises because of a weakening hold on the traditional doctrine of the incarnation.

If, in accordance with the doctrine of Chalcedon, we say that the one person, Jesus, is truly human and truly divine, we can say quite literally that God suffered hunger and thirst and torture and death. We can say these things because the Son of God assumed a human nature in which it makes sense to predicate these things of him. In other words, the traditional doctrine, while rejecting the idea that it is in the nature of God to be capable of suffering, does affirm literally that God suffered in a perfectly ordinary sense, the sense in which you or I suffer.

If, with certain theologians, you regress from Chalcedon and affirm that Jesus is not literally divine, you at once block the way from saying that *Jesus* suffered and died to saying that *God* suffered and died. Nevertheless, since there is a profound Christian instinct that the gospel has to do with the suffering of God, these theologians are constrained to say that since God did not literally suffer in Jesus, God must suffer in some other way: as, for example, he surveys the suffering of Jesus and the rest of mankind. One consequence of this, of course, is that whereas a traditional Christian would say that God suffered a horrible pain in his hands when he was nailed to the cross, these theologians have to make do with a kind of mental anguish at the follies and sins of creatures.

May I be so impertinent as to remind this gathering of Aquinas's treatment of Chalcedon. I shall be brief. First a word or two about language.

Simple indicative sentences very commonly have two parts that we call subject and predicate. Words in the subject place are used to refer to what we want to talk about and words in the predicate place are used to say something about it. Which words are in which place is not to be decided by looking at the sentence but by wider considerations. (Thus, for example, Raymond Brown argues convincingly that in I Jn 2.22, 'he who denies that Jesus is the Christ', we should realize that 'the Christ' is the subject phrase of the clause.)

We can very often vary the subject phrase, using another of a different meaning, but so long as both refer to the same subject the truth of the statement made with the sentence will not be affected. Thus the phrases 'The Pope following Paul VI' and 'The Pope preceding John Paul II' have quite different meanings, but they can both be used to refer to the same person, so that, whichever one we attach to the predicate 'reigned for a very short time', we get an equivalent statement.

If, however, we put between the original subject and predicate phrases the additional words 'as is only to be expected' we get quite different statements: 'The Pope preceding John Paul II, as is only to be expected, reigned for a very short time' expresses a quite different innuendo from the other one. Similar changes will occur if we put the words 'as such' in the same position. As Aquinas puts it, the particular meaning of the subject phrase is thus drawn into the predicate and makes the whole thing a different sentence. Thus it is one thing to say 'God was nailed to the cross' but quite another to say 'God, as is only to be expected (or as such), was nailed to the cross'.

Thus, since both 'Son of God' and 'Son of Mary' can be used to refer to Jesus (for he was *ex hypothesi*, given Chalcedon, both divine and human), we make equivalent statements when we say 'The Son of God died on the cross' and when we say 'The son of Mary died on the cross'. But we do not make an equivalent statement if we put 'as such' in the sentence. Moreover, given Nicaea, if we can say 'The Son of God died on the cross' we can say 'God died on the cross'. Although 'God' here signifies the divine nature, it does not here, in the subject place, refer to that nature; it refers to what *has* this nature, in this case the man Jesus of Nazareth. The fact that Jesus was human means that there is a whole range of predicates such as 'was hungry' or 'was amused' or 'was tortured' which we can sensibly attach to the subject 'Jesus' to make ordinary literal propositions that may be true or false. I mean we can sensibly apply these predicates to Jesus in the way that we couldn't apply them to a piece of butterscotch or a star. Similarly, the fact that Jesus is divine entitles us to attach another range of predicates such as 'is creator', 'is eternal son of God', 'is omnipotent', and so on. The traditional doctrine of the incarnation is simply that both ranges of predicates apply to the same person referred to by the subject term 'Jesus'.

It is, of course, profoundly mysterious that this should be so, but it is not flatly contradictory, for the human and the divine, because they do not occupy the same universe (the divine does not occupy any universe), do not exclude each other in the way that two created natures would do. The divine omniscience of Jesus, for example, does not conflict with his human ignorance, for divine knowledge is not in the same universe of discourse as human knowledge. For Jesus to be omniscient is nothing other than for him to be divine; it is not a question of being better informed than a non-omniscient being.

Chalcedon, then, does allow us to say that God suffered, and suffered quite literally (and not even analogically) as we do. It is the doctrine that God is involved in the whole human condition not simply as creator but as having a created nature. It also means that there are certain things that we suffer that God did not suffer, like overhearing transistor radios or drinking Coke.

As I say, I think it is the loss of this doctrine by those who fear that to confess the divinity of Jesus would be to diminish his humanity that has led some of them to attribute suffering to God as such.

* * *

But there is more, much more, to be said than this and I am sorry that time will not allow me to say it as clearly and as fully as I would like. I shall just have to summarize it, perhaps enigmatically, perhaps unconvincingly. I want to argue that the doctrine of the incarnation is such that the story of Jesus is not just the story of God's involvement with his creatures but that it is actually the 'story' of God. There is one sense in which we must say that God has no life-story – and it is essential to my thesis to insist on this, as we shall see – but there is also a sense, the only sense, in which God has or is a life-story, and this is the story revealed in the incarnation and it is the story we also call the Trinity.

The story of Jesus is nothing other than the triune life of God projected onto our history, or enacted sacramentally in our history, so that it becomes story. I use the word 'projected' in the sense that we project a film onto a screen. If it is a smooth silver screen you see the film simply in itself. If the screen is twisted in some way, you get a systematically distorted image of the film. Now imagine a film projected not on a screen but on a rubbish dump. The story of Jesus – which in its full extent is the entire Bible – is the projection of the trinitarian life of God on the rubbish dump that we have made of the world. The historical mission of Jesus is nothing other than the eternal mission of the Son from the Father; the historical outpouring of the Spirit in virtue of the passion, death and ascension of Jesus is nothing but the eternal outpouring of the Spirit from the Father through the Son. Watching, so to say, the story of Jesus, we are watching the processions of the Trinity.

That the missions in time of Son and Spirit reflect the eternal relations is, of course, perfectly ordinary traditional teaching. What I am venturing to suggest is that they are not just reflection but sacrament – they contain the reality they signify. The mission of Jesus is *nothing other* than the eternal generation of the Son. That the Trinity looks like a story of (*is* a story of) rejection, torture and murder but also of reconciliation is because it is being projected on, lived out on, our rubbish tip; it is because of the sin of the world.

There is much to say both to try and justify this position and to bring out its implications, but just for the moment I want to look at its bearing on the question of the 'pre-existent Christ'. It is a part of my thesis that there is no such thing as the pre-existent Christ.

The pre-existent Christ was invented, to the best of my knowledge, in the nineteenth century, as a way of distinguishing the eternal procession of the Son from the incarnation of the Son. It was affirmed by those who wanted to say that Jesus did not become Son of God in virtue of the incarnation. He was already Son of God before that. The pre-existent Christ marks the development from the 'low' christology of the virgin birth that you get in Matthew and Luke to the 'high' christology of John, with the pre-existent Word in the beginning with God. Raymond Brown's brilliant discussion of this both in *The Community of the Beloved Disciple* (New York: Paulist Press, 1979) and in his Johannine commentaries (*The Anchor Bible*, vols 29, 29A, 30) is, I am afraid, conducted throughout in terms of the pre-existent Christ.

I wish to reject the notion from two points of view. In the first place, to speak of the pre-existent Christ is to imply that God has a life-story, a divine story, other than the story of the incarnation. It is to suppose that in some sense there was a Son of God existing from the eternal ages who at some point in his eternal career assumed a human nature and was made man. *First* the son of God pre-existed as just the Son of God and *then* later he was the Son of God made man. I think this only needs to be stated to be seen as incompatible at least with the traditional doctrine of God coming to us through Augustine and Aquinas. There can be no succession in the eternal God, no change. Eternity is not, of course, a very long time; it is not time at all. Eternity is not timeless in the sense that an instant is timeless – for an instant is timeless simply in being the limit of a stretch of time, just as a point has no length not because it is very very short but because it is the limit of a length. No: eternity is timeless because it totally transcends time. To be eternal is just to be God. God's life is neither past nor present, nor even simultaneous with any event, any clock, any history. The picture of the Son of God 'becoming' at a certain point in the divine duration the incarnate Son of God, 'coming down from heaven', makes a perfectly good metaphor but could not be literally true. There was, from the point of view of God's life, no such thing as a moment at which the eternal Son of God was not Jesus of Nazareth. There could not be any moments in God's life. The eternal life of Jesus as such could not precede, follow or be simultaneous with his human life. There is no story of God 'before' the story of Jesus. This point would not, of course, be grasped by those for whom God is an inhabitant of the universe, subject to experience and to history. I am not, need I say, suggesting that it can be grasped intelligibly by *anyone*, but in the traditional view it is the mystery that we affirm when we speak of God.

From the point of view of God, then, *sub specie eternitatis*, no sense can be given to the idea that at some point in God's life-story the Son became incarnate. But I also want to question the notion of the pre-existent Christ from another point of view.

From the point of view of time, of our history (which, of course, is the only point of view we can actually take), there was certainly a time when Jesus had not yet been born. Moses could have said with perfect truth 'Jesus of Nazareth is not yet' or 'Jesus does not exist' because, of course, the future does not exist; that is what makes it future. (There are people who imagine that the future somehow does exist, perhaps in the way that the past has a certain existence – in the sense that about the past there are fixed and settled true propositions.

But these people are, in my view, mistaken. They are especially mistaken when they say, as they sometimes do, 'the future already exists for God', for to say that is to attribute a mistake to God, and a philosophical mistake at that.) So, yes, Moses could have truly said 'Jesus does not exist', he could also have said with truth 'The Son of God does exist', and he could have made both these statements at the same time.

Now this fact *might* be called the 'pre-existence of Christ', meaning that at an earlier time in our history (and there isn't any time except in history) these propositions would both have been true – 'Jesus does not exist', 'The Son of God does exist' – thus apparently making a distinction between the existence of Jesus and the existence of the Son of God. But the phrase 'pre-existent Christ' seems to imply not just that in the time of Moses 'The Son of God exists' would be true, but also that the proposition 'The Son of God exists *now*' would be true. And this would be a mistake. Moses could certainly have said 'It is true now that the Son of God exists' but he could not have said truly 'The Son of God exists now'. *That* proposition, which attributes *temporal* existence ('now') to the Son of God, is the one that became true when Jesus was conceived in the womb of Mary. The simple truth is that apart from incarnation the Son of God exists at no time at all, at no 'now', but in eternity, in which he acts upon all time but is not himself 'measured by it', as Aquinas would say. 'Before Abraham was, I am.'

So, like those who speak in what I regard as a muddled way about the 'pre-existent Christ', I too wish to adopt John's high christology and say that it is not the incarnation that brings about the divine sonship of Jesus; but I suggest that the incarnation and the whole life of Jesus is the sacrament of divine sonship; it just is the divine sonship *as story*, as manifest in history.

I would be much happier in an odd way with the notion of a 'pre-existent Jesus' in the innocuous sense that, as I said, the entire Bible, spanning all history, is, all of it, the story of Jesus of Nazareth ('Moses wrote of me'). But that merely tells us how to read the Bible; it does not make any claims about the relationship of divine and human in Jesus.

So, in conclusion, I have been arguing three things: firstly, that the traditional notion of God, far from being some allegedly 'Greek' idea of a remote indifferent God, is a doctrine of the everpresent active involvement of the creator in his creatures; on this point I also claimed that the creator is a metaphysical notion of God and that we owe this metaphysics not to the Greeks but to the Jews and their Bible. Secondly, I suggested that the temptation to attribute suffering to God as God, to the divine nature, is connected with a failure to acknowledge that it is really God who suffers in Jesus of Nazareth. Thirdly, I suggested that the traditional doctrine of God, especially of the eternity of God and the incarnation, is at least capable of development to the idea that the whole set of stories narrated in the Bible is nothing other than the interior life of the triune God visible (to the eyes of faith) in our history.

I don't think you could have God more involved than that.

Notes

1   Jürgen Moltmann, *The Trinity and the Kingdom of God* (London: SCM Press, 1981), p. 12. Cf. Aquinas, *Summa Theologiae*, 1a,2,3.

2   Edward Schillebeeckx, *Jesus: An Experiment in Christology* (London: Collins, 1979), p. 12.

3   James Mackey, *The Christian Experience of God as Trinity* (London: SCM Press, 1983), p. 182.

4

Evil

At least in the western tradition nothing so affects our attitude to God as our recognition of evil and suffering. An important factor in the modern bourgeois indifference to God has been a cultivated exclusion of evil from our consciousness. It is not long since English moral philosophers searching for an example of moral evil could only come up with promise-breaking; the liberal imagination shied away from real sin, just as commercial advertising shies away from suffering. It is a commonplace that prisons and hospitals are not only institutions for dealing with crime and sickness but also for hiding them. If we break out of this cosy world and face the real state of affairs we are liable to two apparently contrasting reactions. We may reject God as infantile, as unable to comprehend or have compassion on those who suffer and are made to suffer in his world. On the other hand we may find, as Job did, that it was our own view of God that was infantile; we may in fact come to a deeper understanding of the mystery of God. The first 'atheist' reaction may indeed be a part of the second.

It is not my purpose here to offer positive suggestions about the transition from an inadequate view of God, through 'atheism', to a deeper understanding. I have set myself the minor task of removing one impediment on the way. We will not pass through this transition successfully if we let ourselves be trapped in the *philosopher's* problem of evil.

As it seems to me there is the problem or mystery of evil which is a dark entry into the mystery of God. Not to be aware of this, not to be confounded and overthrown by it, is not yet to have recognized God's love. But there is also a philosophical muddle about God and evil, and there is no reason at all to be confounded or overthrown by this.

This chapter is not, then, intended as some kind of anodyne for those who are facing the mystery of evil – whether they express their understanding in the form of 'atheism' or of a deeper awareness of mystery. It is a philosophical reply to philosophers who seek to show that the reality of evil proves that the ultimate source and meaning of the universe *cannot* be unconditional compassion and love.

* * *

I appear then as though in a lawcourt as counsel for the defence of God against his philosophical accusers. I seek to do no more than to answer *their* arguments.

The prisoner stands accused of wreaking all kinds of murder and mayhem, of running a world full of misery and malice. Evidence for the crimes lies all around us, and the question is whether God is really responsible, whether he should be judged guilty and perhaps whether he should get off on a plea of diminished responsibility due to unsound mind or natural ignorance.

May I say at once that I shall be falling back on that sound principle of English law that a God is innocent until he is proved guilty. It is not my job to prove that God is innocent; I am not going to explain how and why his activities have been good. I am simply going to refute the charges brought against him. I shall be dealing, in fact, with what his accusers have said about him.

At the end of this hearing I hope you will agree that God has not been proved guilty, but I expect you will be as puzzled as I am about his innocence. In other words, I hope it will remain a mystery to you why God has done what he has done; but you will at least agree that what he has done does not prove his guilt.

First of all what is the charge? The world is full of suffering and sin, and God committed this world; he openly admits to having done so. Nobody else interfered. There is no one else to take the blame from him. You might imagine a defence on the lines that the poor fellow couldn't help it, he's only a God after all. But this cannot be my defence for I hold that God is omnipotent and can do anything he likes that you could mention. (The only reason why you would have to say that he can't make square circles is that you can't mention them; the words cancel each other out so that you haven't named anything.)

But anything you *could* describe or think of God could do, and it is not difficult, surely, to think of a world with less suffering and sin than this one has in it. Indeed, it is hard *not* to think of such a world.

So, there stands the accused, perfectly capable of making a delightful, happy, painless world, but instead he has deliberately made this dreadful place. What possible defence can be put up for him?

Before I start my case for the defence, may I just say what I will *not* resort to. I have already said that I am not going to make a plea of diminished responsibility on the grounds of incapacity. I am not going to say that God is innocent because he is not omnipotent. Secondly I am not going to question the evidence: there are some people who would say that evil is not real, that it is only an illusion and if we look at it the right way it disappears like the ghost at the corner of the stairs. But I shall not be arguing that 'it's all in the mind', that nothing's good or bad, but thinking makes it so. I admit whole-heartedly that when someone says 'my toothache hurts like mad', or 'that cow is suffering from a disease', or 'Charlie is a wicked and depraved man', he is making quite literal true statements, just as literal and true as the statement that London is in England. So, I accept the evidence; evil is real. I shall not be using the 'unreality of evil' defence.

Thirdly, another defence is not open to me. This is the defence that at least some of the evil in the world is not caused by God but by the free actions of people. God, this defence goes, can hardly be held responsible for what people do freely, and a great deal of the awfulness of the world is due to the viciousness of men and women. Now, I hold that all my free acts are caused by God, that I do not act independently of God, and so I can hardly get my client off the hook by putting the blame on someone else.

So, I shall not defend God on the grounds that he is incompetent, or that the evidence is phoney, or on grounds of mistaken identity – that someone else did it. God is omnipotent, the world he made is full of evils and they were not put there by human beings independently of God.

1   I am going to argue that everything good in the world is brought about by my client.

2   I am going to argue that some kind of evil – suffering – what I shall call 'evil suffered', is a necessary concomitant of certain kinds of good, and God can only be said, therefore, to have brought it about in the sense that he brought about that good.

3   I am going to argue that another kind of evil – sin – what I shall call 'evil done', is not brought about by God at all. I shall grant that he could have prevented it, but I shall give reasons why this does not make my client guilty by neglect.

So, God brings about everything that is good and he does not directly bring about anything that is evil; if this can be shown it seems a sufficient defence, even if it leaves a great deal that we do not understand.

Let us now consider the evidence: and first of all let us ask what it is supposed to be evidence *of*. It is evidence of evil; but what do we mean when we say that something is evil or bad? I am using the words more or less synonymously, but I suppose that 'evil' has a rather more sinister ring in English than 'bad'. A bad man and an evil man are much the same, but a bad washing machine wouldn't ordinarily be called evil. Perhaps we usually keep 'evil' for moral evil, for the evil that belongs to human beings or to other creatures that are free and act deliberately, like human beings, devils and such like.

Let us look then, first of all, at badness. The charge is made that God made a bad world, when he could have made a better one. Let us see what this means.

First of all, I suppose you will agree that there is no such *thing* as badness, just as there is no such thing as redness. There are just bad things, as there are red things. You never get badness unless there is first of all something that exists that is bad, just as you never get redness unless there is first of all something to be red.

Badness is not like milk or chewing gum, something that a cow or a man or God might make; it is the *character* of something that has been made. The charge against God, then, is not that he made something called badness; there is no such thing. The charge is that some of the things he made are bad, just as some of them are red.

Now what exactly are we saying when we say that a thing is bad? Here we come immediately to a difference between badness and redness. For all red things share a *property* in common, the property of being red. If you know what it is like for an apple to be red then you more or less know what it is like for a pencil or a nose to be red.

But this won't work with badness; if you know what it is like for a deckchair to be a bad deckchair you do not for that reason know what it is like for a grape to be a bad grape. A bad deckchair collapses when you sit down on it, but the fact that a grape collapses when you sit on it is not what would show it to be a bad grape.

We call something a bad deckchair when it doesn't come up to our expectations for deckchairs, and we call something a bad grape when it doesn't come up to our expectations for grapes. But they are different expectations. And similarly when we say that a thing is a good grape or a good deckchair we mean that they do come up to our respective expectations for grapes and deckchairs. Goodness, like badness, is different from redness in that what it is like for one thing to be good isn't the same as what it is like for another. The fact that wine can be made from good grapes has no tendency at all to suggest that wine can be made from good deckchairs.

Now notice that whenever we say something is bad we are saying that it *doesn't* come up to expectations; we are saying, in fact, something negative about it. A bad washing machine is one that won't wash the clothes properly – notice that this makes badness a good deal less *specific* than goodness. If someone says he has a good washing machine, you know pretty well what it is like: it cleans the clothes quickly and efficiently and quietly and cheaply and so on. But if someone just says his washing machine is a bad one, you don't know yet whether it tears the clothes into strips, or soaks them in oily water, or just doesn't move at all when you switch on, or electrocutes the children when they go near it. It can be bad for an indefinite number of reasons so long as the one negative thing is true: that it doesn't come up to expectations for a washing machine.

So, badness is a negative thing. Please notice carefully that this does *not* mean that a bad washing machine always has to have a part missing: it is not negative in that sense. A washing machine may be bad not only because it has too little, as when there is no driving belt on the spin drier, but also because it has too much, as when someone has filled the interior with glue. Badness is negative just in the sense that a bad thing doesn't succeed in measuring up to our expectations. Badness, then, is always a defect, an absence, in this sense.

So, not only is there no such thing as badness in the sense that there is no such *thing* as redness (for redness, even if it is not a *thing*, is at least a positive quality of a thing); but badness isn't even that; it is the *lack* of some positive quality in a thing – the positive quality of being a clothes cleaner for example. And do remember that it is a lack of precisely that positive quality which we think is to be *expected* of a thing. We say 'That is a bad bottle' because it won't hold the liquid as we expect bottles to do; we don't say it is bad because it hasn't got a ten-foot neck, as we expect giraffes to have. So, badness is just a lack, but a particular lack.

Now does this mean that badness is unreal? Certainly not. Things really are bad sometimes and this is because the absence of what is to be expected is just as real as a presence. If I have a hole in my sock, the hole is not anything at all, it is just an absence of wool or cotton or whatever, but it is a perfectly real hole in my sock. It would be absurd to say that holes in socks are unreal and illusory just because the hole isn't made of anything and is purely an absence. *Nothing* in the wrong place can be just as real and just as important as *something* in the wrong place. If you inadvertently drive your car over a cliff you will have nothing to worry about; it is precisely the nothing that you will have to worry about.

So badness is quite real even though it isn't the name of a stuff like milk or even the name of a quality like redness.

Everything I have said about bad washing machines and bottles is just as true of bad men and women. We call a person bad (or in this case sometimes, evil or wicked) just because he or she doesn't measure up to what we think we can expect of human beings. Cruelty, injustice, selfishness, are just dispositions or activities that don't measure up to our idea of what a proper human being should be like; they are not fitting to a human being. We may find it a lot harder to be clear about what *is* fitting to a human being than we are about what is fitting to a washing machine, because all a washing machine has to do, so far as we are concerned, is wash the clothes properly; it is an instrument that we expect to function in a certain way. People, of course, aren't instruments in that way; they are not just good because they do some job well, and so the whole thing is more complicated. But it doesn't matter how we decide this matter and it doesn't matter whether we disagree about what makes a human being a proper human being; the thing is that if we call a man bad, we mean he doesn't measure up to whatever it is that we expect of a man.

Let us remember that with people, as with washing machines, to say that they are bad is not always to say that they lack some part or other. A washing machine may be bad and defective for very positive reasons, like being full of glue, and a man may be bad and defective for very positive reasons, like being full of hatred or lust. But what makes us call this bad is that just as the positive glue stops the washing machine washing, so the positive hatred or lust stops the man being human enough.

Now let us also notice that since badness is a defect it is always parasitic on good. I mean that you can't have badness unless there is at least some goodness, whereas you can have goodness without any badness. The two are not symmetrical, so to say. I mean that if a washing machine is to be a bad one, it must be at least good enough at being a washing machine for us to call it one. If I produce a cup and saucer and complain that it is a useless washing machine because it never gets the clothes clean, you will gently correct me and explain that what I have is not a washing machine at all. So, even the worst washing machine must be a little good, otherwise it is not even a washing machine and cannot therefore be a bad one. But it doesn't work the other way round. Goodness does not mean a defect in badness. You could, theoretically, have something that was just very good with no defects at all. You could probably have a perfectly good washing machine with nothing wrong with it at all, were it not for built-in obsolescence and the capitalist modes of production.

So now if we are fairly clear about what, if you want to be pompous, you can call the logic of the words 'bad' and 'good' and 'evil', we can take a look at some of the pieces of evidence against my client, God. There are I think two main exhibits.

There is the badness that *happens to* people and things: that is exhibit A. Then there is the evil that people *do*: that is exhibit B. I think this covers all the evil there is.

The first kind is evil that comes to something from outside, as when bacteria attack a healthy horse and it falls sick, or when a lion attacks a lamb and chews it up. The agent that brings about the unpleasantness is separate from the one that suffers.

The second kind of evil is evil that is not brought about by some outside agent but is self-inflicted, and this is moral evil or sin. I mean by this that if a man can show that what he did was not really due to him but was caused by something outside him – he was acting under the influence of drugs or hypnotism or something – then we stop blaming him, we say he hasn't really sinned, we sympathize with him as one who has *suffered* evil rather than as one who himself *inflicts* it.

Let us look first at the evil suffered in the world. Let us be clear that by no stretch of the imagination can this be attributed to the viciousness of men and women, or hardly any of it can. For millions upon millions of years before the human race even appeared, dinosaurs were setting upon each other or upon harmless plants and chewing them up, undoubtedly inflicting evil on them; a plant that has been chewed by a dinosaur is nothing like as good a plant as it was before. The lamb that is attacked by a lion speedily becomes a very defective lamb.

When however we look into the business of the lion eating the lamb we see that necessarily what is a defect suffered by the lamb is at the same time a fulfilment or achievement for the lion. The lion is being fulfilled, indeed he is being filled, precisely by what damages the lamb and renders it defective. In fact there can never be a defect inflicted on one thing except by another thing that is, in doing so, perfecting itself. When I suffer from a disease it is because the bacteria or whatever are fulfilling themselves and behaving exactly as good bacteria should behave. If we found a bacterium which was not engaged in inflicting disease on me we should have to judge that, like a washing machine that did not wash clothes, it was a defective or sick bacterium. The things that inflict evil on me, therefore, are not themselves evil; on the contrary, it is by being good in their way that they make me bad in my way.

Being eaten by a lion is undoubtedly bad for a lamb; it is not just that it *seems* bad from some point of view; it actually *is* bad from the lamb's point of view. On the other hand, it actually is good from the lion's point of view. Good and bad are relative, but they are not just subjective.

Thus if God is to make a lion, and a good lion, he cannot but allow for the defect of the lamb; that is the kind of things that lions and lambs are. It is no reflection on God's omnipotence that he cannot make good lions without allowing for damaged lambs. However omnipotent God may be, he cannot compose a string quartet for three instruments or five. It belongs to being a quartet that it is for four instruments; and in a somewhat similar way it belongs to being a lion that it wants to eat lambs. In general, it seems to me that you cannot make material things that develop in time without allowing for the fact that in perfecting themselves they will damage other material things. Life evolves in the course of the constant interaction of things which includes the damaging and destroying of things. But every occasion of destruction is, of itself, an occasion of good for the thing that is doing the destroying – always with the single exception of the free creature which may sometimes while destroying something else be simultaneously destroying itself, but of that more in a moment.

Ordinarily it is by being good little bacteria or good healthy lions that the agents of destruction work, and it is God who makes them to be good bacteria and good lions. He does not directly cause the defectiveness of the sick animals and chewed sheep that are the concomitant of this; for defectiveness as such does not exist, it is a mere absence. But in creating good lions we can certainly say that God brings it about indirectly that there shall be evil suffered. He brings it about because it is not possible to bring about this good without allowing for the concomitant defects. None of this, I submit, shows that God is guilty of deliberately proposing and bringing about evil.

You may be tempted to argue that it would be better not to have any lions at all. But if you think along those lines you have to end up thinking that it would be better not to have any material world at all – and indeed I think some Buddhist thinkers have reached this very conclusion. But then you do have to change the charge against my client. It is not that he has made a bad world but that he has made a material world at all. This does not sound a very damning charge. Most people are rather glad that he did so and even sometimes thank him for it.

Now it may be argued that God could have made a material world without *so much* sheer pain in it. But let us look at what is being said if we say this. Ordinarily, if I have a headache the doctor will explain what brought it about: it was, perhaps, that fifth whiskey last night. It was the whiskey behaving like good whiskey – as whiskey may be expected to behave – which brought about my headache. There is no mystery about my headache. Similarly with my cancer or my influenza. Always there is a natural explanation, and always the explanation is in terms of some things, cells or germs or whatever, doing what comes naturally, being good. Sometimes of course, and rather more often than he admits, the doctor is baffled. But he puts this down to his own ignorance. He says: 'Well, eventually we may hope to find out what is causing this, what things are bringing it about simply by being their good selves, but for the moment we don't know.' What he does *not* say is this: 'There is no explanation in nature for this; it is an anti-miracle worked by a malignant God.'

But that is what he would *have* to say if he thought there was more pain in the world than there need be. More suffering than there need be would be suffering that had no natural cause, that was not the obverse of some good, that was scientifically inexplicable. Now I do not think that anyone in a scientific tradition would believe in the existence of such suffering, except perhaps in one case: in the case of evil inflicted by a malignant free cause such as a wicked man or a demon. Given that his acts are free, then they are not caused and thus cannot be explained by the fulfilment of natural things like germs and viruses. But leaving that aside for the moment, the pain and agony of the world is just what you would expect to find in a material world – no more and no less. If we think otherwise we do not just give up belief in a good God, we give up belief in the rational scientific intelligibility of the world.

Of course, God could have made a kind of material world and then by a series of miraculous interventions prevented any suffering in it. He could have fed the lion miraculously without damaging any lambs, and so on throughout the order of nature. But such a world would have no reason or order within itself. Lions would not do things because they were lions, but simply because of the miraculous action of God. What we mean by the miraculous action of God is indeed simply the non-presence of natural causes and explanations. A miracle is not God intervening in the world. God is always acting in the world. A miracle is when *only* God is acting in the world.

A world without any defects suffered, then, would be a world without any natural order in it. No reasonable person objects to an occasional withdrawal of natural causes, a miracle from time to time; but a world without *any* natural causes, entirely consisting of miracles, would not be a natural material world at all. So, the people who would like my client to have made a material world without suffering and defect would have preferred him not to have made a world subject to its own laws, an autonomous, scientifically explicable world. But here again I would say most people are pleased that he made such a world which, so to say, runs by itself according to its own scientific laws. The accusation that God made it does not seem very damning.

Perhaps I should add a little note here about pain. You might find some people saying: yes, we can see how if lions are to be good lions then lambs will have to die, but why does it all have to be so agonizingly painful? Surely God could have stopped that. Not so; pain is, in fact, a good and necessary thing from one point of view. If the lamb were not hurt by the lion it would not be afraid of it – except maybe by a miracle, and then we are back with the previous discussion. I happen to know of a young girl who is highly intelligent but by some malfunctioning of the brain or nervous system is incapable of feeling pain. She once left her hand in a pan of boiling water and damaged it terribly because she was not warned by pain. She had a special frame strapped to her because of the damage she had done to her limbs by unnoticed collisions and accidents. Her case shows the value of pain, its evolutionary significance. If pain were unnecessary for our survival we would long ago have discarded it like our tails.

It is true of course that some pain seems to go above and beyond the call of duty. We can understand why it needs to hurt but not why it needs to hurt so much. Take dying of rabies for example. But I think if you investigated the matter, and taking into account that it is not just the human animal but all the other animals and even the rabies virus that has to be considered, you would find that none of this was without scientific explanation. The pain of rabies is not, like the warning pain of boiling water, useful to us, but it follows necessarily on what is good and useful for other things. I think, then, that Exhibit A, the pain and suffering of the world, has not sufficed to convict my client, God, of crime in creating this world. Let us then turn to Exhibit B, the wickedness of the world.

Here, I am bound to admit, my client faces his most dangerous threat. There are, as I have said, those who think otherwise. For them, wickedness, at least, is not due to God; it is an offence against God which he would rather not have happen. It is due to wicked human wills and the actions of these, being free, are not caused by God. God, they will argue, could have prevented evil, but only by making humans unfree; and just as it is a great glory to have a real material world with its own laws of action, even though this has to involve pain and suffering, so it is a great glory to have free creatures, even if this involves at least the risk of some sin and wickedness.

This cosy escape route is not, however, open to me. I hold that there is nothing existing in the world that God did not create. There is no being which does not depend on him. All my good acts are more due to him than they are to me, since it is due to him that they are due to me. He makes me to be *me*. So what about my bad deeds?

First I think we need to be clear that, unlike evil suffered, evil done, sin, is not an inevitable concomitant of good in the world. There could not be a material world, developing according to its own laws, without evil suffered. But there most certainly could be a material human world without evil done. A world without selfishness and greed and cruelty and domination would obviously be a happier, pleasanter, livelier, more sensuously enjoyable world than the one we have now. Evil suffered is the obverse of good achieved, but evil done has no connection with good at all, except accidentally. That is to say God may bring good even out of my evil acts, but in themselves they have no good aspect. This is because evil done, moral evil, is self-inflicted. In evil suffered there are two beings to be considered: the one inflicting the harm and the one suffering it (for one what is done is good; while for the other, it is evil). In evil done the harm is done to the agent which causes it.

In the case of the lion eating the lamb, what makes this bad for the lamb is that its lambness, so to say, is diminished. It becomes less like what we expect of a lamb; and what brings this about is the lion. But in the case of, say, Fred being unjust, what makes this bad for Fred is that his humanity is diminished. He becomes less like what we expect of a man, and what brings this about is Fred himself. In the lamb/lion encounter at least the perpetrator, the lion, is benefiting; but in Fred's act of injustice the perpetrator, Fred, is precisely the one who suffers.

Perhaps I should make that a little clearer because there may well be those who think that what makes an action morally wrong is the harm it does to others, and they may be a little surprised that I say that what makes an action morally wrong is the harm it does to the perpetrator. An action may be morally wrong *because* it does harm to others, but what we *mean* by saying that it is morally wrong is that it damages the perpetrator. I can after all do a great deal of harm to others without doing anything morally wrong at all. I may bring with me to a foreign country some deadly infectious disease that I don't know about, so that in a few weeks people are dying in agony because of my arrival. If so, I have certainly harmed them by my arrival, but I have not done anything morally wrong. If however I knew about it and went all the same, then you could well say that I was acting unjustly, that I was behaving in an irresponsible way in which no human being should behave, that I was defective in my humanity, that I was committing a moral evil. The moral evil would *consist* in the injustice and the way that I had diminished myself in acting like that.

When I am the cause of frightful things happening to others, the evil suffered is in them and is inflicted by me, but if in doing this I am acting unjustly (as would ordinarily be the case if I did it deliberately) the evil done is in me and consists in the diminishment of my humanity that injustice means. I do not mean by this that acting unjustly has a bad *effect* on me (making me a drearier person or whatever). I mean that acting unjustly *is* a bad effect on me, it *is* a diminishment of me, just as not being able to rinse the clothes is a diminishment of the washing machine. And the point is that this diminishment of me is brought about by me. So there is no separate agent to achieve something by diminishing me, as the lion achieves something by diminishing the lamb. Evil done is evil to the perpetrator himself. It is a dead loss with no good aspect to it.

Of course, morally evil actions may have good *effects*: my injustice may benefit my family, my adultery may give birth to a child. But what we mean when we say they are morally bad, if we think they *are* bad, is the defect that they are in me.

You will remember that when God was accused of damaging lambs, I was able to reply for him that what he was really doing was creating and sustaining lions. This was the good thing he was engaged in doing; the evil to the lamb was merely a necessary concomitant to this. But now in the case of moral evil, no such course is open to me. Moral evil is not the concomitant of some good. It is, as I said, sheer loss.

Of course God may bring good even out of my evil actions, and good may even be the ordinary consequence of my evil action; but that is not the point. The action itself has no good in it, and we cannot exonerate God simply on the grounds that it is for good ends that he uses evil means.

My defence is quite different. It is simply this: since there is no good at all, except incidentally, in a morally evil act, in evil done, there is nothing created there, hence no action of God. A morally evil act as such is an absence of something, a failure on my part to live as humanly, as intensely, as I might have done. Evidently, God does not bring about failure as such, for failure is not there; it is an absence. When, as in the case of the lamb, the failure is brought about by the fulfilment of something else, then indeed God can be said in a Pickwickian way to have brought about the failure, but only because he brought about the fulfilment of the lion. But here there is sheer failure on my part, not brought by the fulfilment of some outside agent, but simply allowed by me. So, God has no hand in it at all.

When I do evil I have a choice between what will fulfil me as a human being, as what I truly am, and some lesser good which conflicts with this fulfilment: say I have to choose between being just and being rich. There is no harm in being rich of course, unless, as it usually does, it conflicts with being just. If I then choose the riches unjustly I have failed in being human, and that is moral evil.

I could not, of course, act unjustly unless I existed and were sustained in being by God. I could not do it unless every positive action I took were sustained in being by God. My desire for riches is a positive thing, and a perfectly good positive thing, created by God. The only thing is that it is a *minor* thing. I should desire other things more than this. My failure to seek my true happiness and fulfilment, of course, since it is a failure, an absence, a non-being, is not created or sustained or brought about by God.

There are no such things as evil desires, there is only evil disproportion in our desires; human evil, moral evil lies in sacrificing great things for the sake of trivial things, it lies in the failure to want happiness enough. It is evident, then, that though it is due to God that any good and positive thing is due to me, it is not due to God that any moral failure is due to me. God does not make absences, non-beings, failures. On this count then my client is fully exonerated and his character has no visible stain on it.

But, and I think this will be the final argument from the prosecution, must we not admit that although God did not, of course, bring about my failure, he could, instead, have brought about my success? In fact it was the fact that God did not cause me freely to succeed that brought it about that I freely failed. There can be no doubt, then, that had he wished to do so God could always have prevented me from sinning – without, of course, in any way interfering with my freedom. For freedom does not mean independence of God. It means independence of other creatures. Thus although God does not cause me to fail to choose the good, he could easily have caused me to choose the good. In what way, asks the prosecutor, is my client's position any different from that of the careless helmsman who fails to steer the ship clear of the rocks? Is he not guilty of neglect in permitting me to sin?

Let me say just once more that there is no question of God *having* to permit me to sin in order to leave me with my freedom. *That* kind of argument belongs to a theory that freedom makes me independent of God. In fact God could have made a world in which nobody ever sinned at all and everyone was perfectly free. In such a world, if it were material and historical, there would certainly have to be suffering as the obverse of the good of material things, but there would be no need whatever for sin. Sin has no useful function in the world except by accident.

Is God, then, guilty by neglect? I think that he is not, for this reason. You can only be guilty by neglect if you have some kind of obligation to do something and you do not do it. It is the helmsman who is accused of neglect, and not the cabin-boy, because it is the helmsman's *job* to steer the ship. Now by no stretch of the imagination is it God's *job* to prevent me from sinning. In his mercy and kindness he frequently does so, and frequently he gives me the grace to repent of the sins I have committed, but this is not his job. There can be no sense in the idea that God has *any* job or is under any obligation; if he were, there would be something greater than God which constrained him. God is no more under an obligation to prevent me from sinning than he was under an obligation to create the world in the first place. He cannot therefore be said to be guilty by neglect.

* * *

I think I have shown that so far as evil suffered is concerned there is no more in God's world than is required by the existence of a natural material world subject to its own laws – indeed if you reckon in the miracles of healing there is slightly less suffering than would be expected. On the premiss, which I think you will accept, that the natural material world is a good thing to have (including, as it does, ourselves), we cannot then blame God for the necessary concomitant of some suffering. I think I have also shown that although there is no such case for the natural necessity of *moral* evil, the most we can say is not that God causes moral evil but that he does not prevent it – that he permits it; and I think I have shown that in not preventing it God is not failing in any duty and thus cannot be charged with neglect.

It remains, of course, that I have not the faintest idea *why* God permits moral evil. I know why there is suffering, because without it there would be no real animals, but I do not know why there is sin. This is an unfathomable mystery, but it is not a contradiction.

Suffering (of the lamb) is not, of course, a perspicuous sign of God's goodness, but the fulfilment (of the lion) which is its concomitant *is* a sign of God's goodness; in sin, however, there is no *manifestation* of God's goodness at all. But it is one thing to say that sin is *not a manifestation* of God's goodness and quite another to say that sin is a manifestation that God *is not good*. We do not know *why* the good God has made a world which does not at all times manifest his goodness, but the notion is not contradictory. Somehow the infinite goodness of God is compatible with his allowing sin. We do not know how, but it is good to recognize this for it reminds us that we know nothing of God and his purposes except that he loves us and wishes us to share his life of love.

5

Are Creeds Credible?

There is no doubt that faith is a bit of a nuisance. Wouldn't life be a lot simpler without it? Why can't we just accept what seems reasonable to us, reject what seems unreasonable and be mildly sceptical about the rest? This surely would be the civilized attitude, the attitude of the independent mind, a mind which is neither credulous nor arrogant, but coolly prepared to face the truth when it appears and to confront its own ignorance when that appears. But the faith business seems alien to all this.

We can't help feeling that what has happened is something like this: once upon a time, before we had perfected our modern critical techniques, when it was a lot easier to make mistakes about the world and human beings, there were a certain number of beliefs which it was quite reasonable to hold, and these were taught by men of authority and status. Gradually, however, there developed new ways of looking at the world and it began to be seen that the old views were inaccurate and out of date. But by this time there was a large vested interest in these views: there was a whole priestly class, for example, whose status and even livelihood depended on the acceptance of the old views. These people were only human, and naturally they felt it was a bad thing that the traditional opinions were being questioned, so they spread about the idea that it was a bad thing to question. Since it was no longer really possible to show that these old opinions were reasonable, the priestly class invented the idea of faith; we were to stick to the ancient beliefs but were now to hold them out of loyalty to a tradition, by faith instead of reasons. Of course this wasn't a deliberate plot to fool people. It was a more or less unconscious reaction on the part of a social class which needed to safeguard its position. You might ask how other people came to be taken in by this move. Well, part of the reason is that the modern world is rather frightening – not just our modern world but the modern world in any age. To keep up with the age we have to stretch ourselves to the utmost; we have to be adult and independent, and this is rather difficult. It is sometimes a lot easier to contract out, to live on nostalgia for the past. The religious beliefs which we are asked to take on faith come from an older time which seems to us more peaceful, less nerve-shattering than our own. These beliefs postulate a cosy intelligible world, rather like the world of the nursery when life was so much simpler, so a lot of people welcome the idea of faith because they are afraid to think for themselves, and all of us at one time or another have a hankering after this return to childhood.

This is, I think, a reasonably fair statement of a belief about beliefs which is pretty common these days. It was perhaps commoner in the last century than in this, but it is still widespread. It goes usually, in England at any rate, with a pleasant tolerance of religion. Some people hold that religion in fact is a good thing: this occasional indulgence in childishness is refreshing, it is good for mental health to relax in this way. No doubt this is why so many excellent philosophers and scientists and other highly intelligent people still maintain religious beliefs.

This is a belief which, as I say, goes with a great tolerance of religion and also an unfathomable ignorance of what exactly religious beliefs are, and of how religious people think.

I do not myself find it to be a very plausible account of the history of religious ideas. I think that one of the reasons why people cling to it in spite of its implausibility is that they find the idea of faith not only a nuisance but irrelevant. It is not so much the content of the creeds that bothers them as the fact that they are *creeds*. They feel they must give themselves some account of the idea of *faith* itself, to make if fit somehow into the human picture; and their explanation briefly is that the contents of the creed are so out of date and unlikely that they can only be held by faith: that was how faith was invented.

Because so many people honestly think this, I should like here to offer an alternative account of the relevance of faith. Why do we have faith at all? What is the theologian's account of faith? Let us come at it not first of all from the point of view of people who have not got it and for whom it is something strange and alien. Let us begin from the point of view of those who do have faith. What account do they give? Here we have to go back a long way. In fact we have literally to go back to the beginning.

God made creatures of all kinds, with all kinds of powers and capabilities. Human beings do certain things. They eat, laugh, get angry and do crossword puzzles; they explore the Antarctic or make Sputniks or string quartets, and we are delighted but not surprised. We say, 'Naturally, that is the kind of thing that people do'. Similarly tigers eat and get angry, and again we are not surprised. We say it is natural enough, it is just what we should expect of a tiger. Different kinds of behaviour are natural to different kinds of things. When a horse behaves like a horse we think it quite natural, but if a man behaves like a horse we are surprised and ask for an explanation. So if X behaves like a horse, and we think it natural for X to behave like a horse, then this is because we think X is a horse. If we don't think it natural for X to be horsing around, it is because X is not a horse. A horse is just a thing which *by nature* behaves like a horse.

Can we give an account of what is natural to human beings? This is notoriously difficult. Remember that we mean 'what is natural to humans as humans'. Some people think of 'natural' behaviour as simply the kind of behaviour that we have in common with other animals, but here we mean any behaviour at which we have no need to be surprised. In this sense it is just as natural for people to build a nuclear power station as it is for them to eat and sleep. We are not astonished at any of these things in the way that we would be completely astonished if, for example, a horse were to write a sonnet. We are lost in admiration for scientists, but we do not think they have superhuman powers; if a horse wrote a poem we would certainly think it had super-equine powers.

As people get better and better at controlling their environment it becomes increasingly difficult to set limits and say, 'Well, anyway it could never be natural for a human being to do *that*,' as we can fairly easily predict that it will never be natural for a tiger to do *that*. Five hundred years ago if you suggested that someone might launch his or her own private moon, people might have believed you, but they would have said 'Yes, someone might do that by magic, or by being in league with the devil, or by a miracle'. What they wouldn't have believed is that someone could do such a thing quite naturally, in perfectly natural ways. Yet this we now know is the case. But whatever we may be able to do now or in the future, whatever may come naturally to us, there is one thing which could never be natural to us. We could not be naturally divine.

Remember, I pointed out that if something behaves like a horse naturally, then it is a horse; and similarly if man behaved like God by nature, it would be because he is God. If it were ever 'perfectly natural' for a man to have a divine nature as it is perfectly natural for him to elaborate quantum mechanics, then he would be God. God is the only being which is by nature divine. Not even the omnipotent God could make a creature which was by nature divine. It is not that God cannot make lesser creatures easily enough, but he finds greater creatures a bit more difficult, and finally finds it impossible to make a creature with the same nature as himself. It is not a question of difficulty. When we say that God could make a creature with the same nature as himself, we are saying the same sort of thing as when we say he couldn't make a square circle. God couldn't make a square circle, not because he is not powerful enough, but because a square circle is a contradiction, something that couldn't be made; the phrase 'square-circle' is a self-cancelling one, it could not be the name of anything. In the same way, a creature which is by nature divine is a contradiction; it is a creature which is uncreated, and the phrase 'uncreated creature' could not be the name of anything.

But the astonishing teaching of Christianity is that God has, so to speak, done the next best thing. He could not make man by nature divine, but he has given him divinity as a gift. This is what we call grace. We do share in the divine nature, we do behave like God, but not by nature. We can do what God does, but in God it is natural, in us it is not – we call it super-natural. Just as it would be super-natural to a horse to write a poem, so it is super-natural to a human being to behave like God. This means that our divinity must always come as a surprise, something eternally astonishing. We could never get used to it and say: 'Well, naturally enough'.

Now one of the things that sharing in God's life involves is sharing in his knowledge of himself. This share in God's self-knowledge is called faith; it is a kind of knowledge we have not by nature (we never could have it by nature) but as a gift. It is because faith is part of our divinity, and because our divinity can never be *natural* to us (it can only be natural to God), that faith cannot be quite assimilated into ordinary reasonable human life.

What does it mean to share in somebody else's knowledge? Especially somebody else's self-knowledge? Before answering this, I must further explain that faith is only the beginning of our share in God's self-knowledge. It is a very imperfect kind of sharing. Our sharing will not be complete and perfect until we see God in heaven. As a way of knowing, faith is the lowest kind of knowledge, much inferior to human science; it is only superior to this, and more important, because of the things that we know by faith, and the fact that finally it will develop into the vision of God.

Again, what does it mean to share in somebody else's knowledge? Well we can best understand this by comparison with the ordinary way in which one of us can share in another's knowledge – the business of teaching. Take a boy at school. He learns from his teacher. He comes to believe certain things because his teacher has told him. He is beginning to share in the teacher's knowledge, but for the moment he only shares in it in a very imperfect way. For the moment he simply believes it on authority – because the teacher has said so. He has not thought it out for himself. He merely has faith. When he grows up he sheds this faith and begins to have opinions which are really his own. This, I take it, is the essential difference between adult education and a school. A school is a place for training. A university is a place for discussion. In a school we try to get a child to believe the fundamental things that society recognizes as true and important. In a university we try to carry on a continuous critical discussion. (That incidentally is the reason why there are good arguments for having Catholic schools in a non-Catholic state, but none whatsoever for having a Catholic university.)

The point is that coming to share the knowledge of another means beginning with faith in the other person. There has to be a basis of faith on which to build. There are, as you know, children who are handicapped and unable to learn and grow up, simply because they lack this fundamental sense of security and trust in the adult world, the faith in the teacher which is a prime necessity. But of course, the purpose of this faith is to bring the child to maturity when it will cease to have faith, when it will lose its dependence on the teacher and be able to think things out for itself.

Notice that to shed your faith in your teachers does not necessarily mean to disagree with them – though, in fact, normal people go through a period of reaction against the actual beliefs they have been brought up in; it is the simplest way of manifesting the change over from belief to independent knowledge. But such coming to maturity does not necessarily mean disagreeing with the teacher. You may go on holding the same opinions, but now hold them as a matter of your own judgement and no longer as a matter of faith.

These two stages, first faith, and then seeing things for yourself, take place also in the matter of sharing in God's knowledge. But here it is not a matter of growing up in our human life, but of growing up in our divine life. The point of maturity, when we lose our faith and see for ourselves, is the point at which we begin to see God in heaven.

Now somebody might want to object that this confirms all their worst suspicions. They always thought that religion was a matter of childishness, of a sort of arrested development which keeps us in the schoolroom throughout our lives, unable to think for ourselves. And here we are admitting it.

In answer to this I should say that there is such a thing as arrested development in human things (and a very bad thing it is) when people refuse to think for themselves and look round for some human authority to tell them what to think. Such people are afraid of the responsibilities of growing up. They want to remain children forever – like the loathsome Peter Pan. What is wrong with such people is that when they have an opportunity of thinking for themselves they refuse it and cling to their faith. They are offered a higher and more mature way of knowing, but they won't have it.

In divine things, however, this is not the situation. These are things that we *cannot know any other way* except by having faith in the teacher, God, who tells us about them. They are not things we could find out for ourselves. They are not the kind of things we could naturally know. Our knowledge of them is super-natural. We are not refusing an offered opportunity, we are not avoiding a higher, more grown-up approach, because there is in this life no higher way available. The boy who refuses to have faith in the teacher *may* be acquiring a grown-up critical sense and beginning to think for himself, or he *may* be simply refusing to learn. I imagine it must be one of a teacher's most difficult jobs to decide which of these is happening. But, in the case of divine things, those who refuse to have faith are always in the latter class. They are not starting to think independently because about these things it is impossible to think independently. They are merely not thinking at all. They are not displaying their maturity. They are merely playing truant. Of course genuine arrested development, the refusal to grow up, to be mature, is possible in the divine life as in human life. People may deliberately refuse the maturity which is offered to them in the vision of God. They then remain in that state of perpetual arrested development that we call hell.

The divine life does indeed grow in us even on earth; but we never reach full maturity; we never dispense with faith until we actually see God face to face. Now the question is: what is the relation between this divine life (and divine knowledge that we call faith) and human life (and human knowledge)? Some people have held that they are actually opposed to each other. You know that kind of person who thinks that you can't be a saint unless you're very slightly ill; this sort of person tends also to think that you can't have faith unless what you believe is humanly incredible. They think of faith not as a matter of knowing or of learning, but rather as a matter of courage, a leap into the unknown, a quixotic championing of the absurd. Now faith is certainly a leap into the unknown in the sense that what you believe is something that cannot be known by ordinary human power. But it is a leap which precisely tries to make this *known*. It is not a rejection of knowledge, it is an effort to know more. To get to know more by trusting in a teacher.

There are two sets of people who think of faith as the acceptance of the absurd. People in the first set go on to say what a splendid thing faith is: it means a reaching out beyond all human criticism; the man of faith does not care about the carping objections of mere logicians, etc. People who belong to the second set go on to say what a dangerous and foolish thing faith is, and for the same reason. It seems to me, however, that both these sets of people are wrong. I would claim that our divinity (one manifestation of which is our faith) transcends our humanity, but is certainly not opposed to it. The Spirit of Christ by which we live is not destructive but creative. It does not reject anything human.

What does it mean to say that the divine life transcends the human? Simply this: that because we are divine we have a destiny, a purpose which is beyond any purpose we could have as merely human. However we envisage human fulfilment, human perfection or human happiness, our divine purpose is far beyond this, and because we have this greater end in view we organize our human life with a view to something greater than it.

Let me return to my comparison with the child and its parents or teacher. Left to themselves, children will organize their world in certain terms – this or that is important, this or that is unimportant, and so on. On the whole the world of children will be organized in terms of their desires and pleasures and pains, though there will, of course, be hints of a larger world, a dim recognition that there is a lot more in life than all that. Now when the parent or teacher comes on the scene this enclosed world is broken into. Because of what they learn from their teachers, children will reorganize their world. They will believe that certain apparently unimportant things are really very important – like washing and learning to write. They cannot see why these are immensely important, but normally, and if they have the right sort of relationship with their teachers, they will believe that they are, and be prepared to sacrifice their own scale of values for their sake. Their purpose as potential adults transcends their child's purpose, but again, because they really are children and really are potential adults, there is no fundamental opposition between the two. Education does not *have* to make children miserable. There have been educationalists who thought that you were not really educating children unless they are doing something they actively dislike. These are like the people who think that faith has to be absurd. On the other hand, of course, there have been people who thought just the opposite: that you are not really educating children unless they do what they like. These are like the people who say that there can be no belief which transcends any human reason. This is a refusal to believe that the adult world transcends the child world.

The divine life, therefore, because it transcends human life, will involve some re-organization of human life towards a larger world, the world of eternity. But here we meet an additional complication. It is not just a matter of re-orienting human life because a certain amount of repair work is needed first. Briefly, according to Christian belief man was created with divine life as well as his human life, but he lost his divinity by the fall and this also damaged his humanity. The result of this is that we need to make certain efforts of re-organization even to lead a properly human life, never mind a divine one. In fact without the grace of divine life we are so enfeebled that we cannot even manage the job of living a human life. We have so much tendency to wishful thinking, to taking what we would like to be true, that if we try to run our lives simply on the basis of what seems good to us, we are liable to act in a less than human way. Even in order to live a human life, therefore, we need to make certain sacrifices, to give up things that seem at first sight desirable, to do a certain amount of violence to what look like ordinary human tendencies.

It is merely by extension of this that our divine super-natural life demands certain sacrifices, but what it does not and cannot demand is a sacrifice of the fundamentally human things. It cannot make demands which are really contrary to human dignity, for it is a *super*-natural, not a *sub*-natural life that is in question. It may make demands which look at first sight contrary to human dignity, but this will be merely because we do not know all the facts. Thus a man may suffer all kinds of indignities rather than deny his faith, and this may seem absurd to those who do not know all the facts (i.e. do not themselves believe). But the supernatural life can never make demands which are genuinely contrary to human dignity. Above all, it cannot demand that we do what is wicked or believe what is false. The divine teacher does not tell us things which are self-contradictory or false. It is always possible to show even to someone who does not believe in any article of faith that these do not involve an absurdity. Christians must, it seems to me, believe that it is always possible to dissolve any argument brought *against* their beliefs; this itself is a matter of their faith. That creeds are not *incredible* is itself a part of the *creed*. In this minimal sense of reasonable, in which we mean 'not unreasonable', faith is certainly reasonable. Nobody can produce an absolute knock-down argument to show that the believer is talking nonsense. Of course, someone may produce an argument which seems to me knock-down. It is no part of the faith that all believers will be able to answer all possible objections against the creed. But it is part of the faith that any objection is answerable in principle.

I think that nowadays quite a lot of people would be prepared to accept this. They would grant that Christianity does somehow always manage to elude the critic (just when he thinks it caught in a nice contradiction, theology somehow slips through the logical net). They are prepared to grant that, in this sense, Christianity is not unreasonable – it is not sheer nonsense. But the Christian often goes further, and certainly I would want to go further. I would claim not only that Christianity is logically coherent, but that also it is reasonable, in the sense that if people consider it coolly and calmly and objectively, there is a very good chance of them coming to believe in it. Of course most people these days don't have much of a chance of considering anything at all, even a detergent, coolly and calmly and reasonably. But there are some circumstances where this ought to be possible. I do not say that any investigator will find knock-down arguments to prove that Christianity is true; indeed I am sure that this cannot happen – just as sure as I am that there are no knock-down arguments against it, for we are dealing with the super-natural, which cannot be arrived at by merely logical means. The kind of argument one has in this sort of matter is not a simple linear argument from these premises through these means to that conclusion. What you have, as Newton pointed out, is a convergence of arguments each pointing towards the conclusion but none of them absolutely settling it. This is the case in all human studies – history, for example. The sort of argument by which someone may come near to Christianity is much more like an historical argument than a mathematical one.

Now there are some people who will admit even this. They will admit that Christianity is reasonable even in this sense, that it is not merely logically coherent, but also a pretty reasonable hypothesis. They will admit that there is a lot of evidence of one kind and another to suggest that Christian beliefs are true, just as there is a lot of evidence of one kind and another to suggest that telepathy is quite common or that Queen Elisabeth I was in love with Essex. What they find so unreasonable in Christians is that, instead of saying that Christianity is highly probable, they claim to be completely certain. When you do establish something by this kind of probable and convergent argument, you have every right to hold it as your opinion, but you have no right to claim absolute certainty and to be sure that you will never meet a genuine refutation of it. This is what finally seems unreasonable about faith to the open-minded liberal sceptic. And here I can agree with him. In this sense I am prepared to admit that you might call faith unreasonable.

It is not unreasonable in the sense that it is absurd or incoherent. Nor is it unreasonable in the sense that there are not good reasons for it. But it is, if you like, unreasonable in that it demands a *certainty* which is not warranted by the reasons. I am completely certain that I am in Oxford at the moment. I have all the evidence I need for certainty on this point. It is true that I admit the logical possibility that I may be drugged or dreaming or involved in some extraordinarily elaborate deception. But this doesn't really affect my certainty. Yet the evidence which makes it reasonable to hold, for example, that Christ rose from the dead comes nowhere near this kind of evidence. One might say that the evidence in spite of all probability does really seem to point to this fantastic conclusion, but it is certainly not the kind of evidence which makes me quite sure and certain. And yet I am more certain that Christ rose from the dead than I am that I am in Oxford. When it comes to my being there, I am prepared to accept the remote possibility that I am the victim of an enormous practical joke. But I am not prepared to envisage any possibility of deception about the Resurrection. Of course I can easily envisage my argument for the Resurrection being disposed of. I can envisage myself being confronted by what seems to me to be unanswerable arguments against it. But this is not the same thing. I am prepared to envisage myself ceasing to believe in it, but I am not prepared to envisage either that there really are unanswerable arguments against it or that I would be justified in ceasing to believe it. All this is because, although reasons may lead me to belief, they are not the basis of my belief. I believe certain things because God has told them to me, and I am able to believe them with certainty and complete assurance only because of the divine life within me. It is a gift of God that I believe, not something I can achieve by human means.

It is important to see that faith is not an additional reason. It is not that you can get so far with reasons and then you have to stop until faith comes along and carries you the extra bit to the end. You cannot arrive at belief *by* human reason but you can get the whole way there *with* human reason. You may come to see that it is reasonable and come to believe it with absolute certainty at one and the same moment. Or, as most of us do, you may come to believe it with certainty and afterwards find that it is quite reasonable. Or you may come to see that it is reasonable but never believe it with divine faith. A great deal of nonsense is talked about the psychology of belief on the assumption that reason and faith are always temporally distinct, that faith cannot come until one has finished with reason and waits poised on the brink to make a leap into the unknowable. This can happen, but it is only one of many possibilities and not the most common, at any rate in my experience.

Since faith means believing something because God has revealed it, the only things we can believe are things that God has revealed. Now these are of two kinds. God has first of all revealed things about himself and his plan for human salvation which we could never have known about if he had not revealed them and given us faith in his word. But God, says the Christian, has also revealed some things that we could perhaps have discovered for ourselves without his revelation. I mentioned that as a result of humanity's first rejection of divine life even our humanity itself is damaged. One of the most important results of this is the chronic disease of wishful thinking, which makes it extremely difficult to arrive at the truth even by ordinary human means, especially in anything which directly affects man himself (only consider the amount of rubbish which is talked about politics). This means that, although it is possible, it is extremely unlikely that people shall by themselves arrive at the truth in certain matters which are of the first importance for human happiness, such as the existence of God himself, and certain basic moral principles which we need to maintain our human dignity. For this reason God has revealed some of these things even though we could theoretically arrive at them by human reason. Of course, if he is to reveal anything, he must reveal his existence. You could hardly believe something because he said it if you did not also believe he existed. But, besides this, God has also revealed certain truths in ethics (e.g. the prohibition of murder) which people could have arrived at by themselves. It is important to see that if it happens that someone does arrive at these things purely by use of reason then he or she cannot be believing them. Belief means accepting truths because they have been revealed by God. If you have succeeded in proving something then you don't believe it because it is revealed; you believe for the good reasons which you have found. Thus the same proposition may be accepted by some because they have proved it, and by others because God has revealed it. What is impossible is that one and the same person at one and the same moment should both believe and know, both accept on God's word and accept for his or her own reasons. I speak here, of course, of proof. Faith is not incompatible with seeing that something is reasonable, but it is incompatible with proof. Often, of course, one cannot easily answer the question 'Do you believe this by faith or can you prove it?' I am sometimes convinced intellectually by arguments for the existence of God, and, at the moment of conviction, I suppose I do not have faith in God's existence; I have something better: knowledge. But afterwards I can say 'Well, maybe I was being misled, perhaps there are important flaws in that argument'. But I do not for this reason doubt the existence of God. This shows that habitually I believe it rather than know it.

Finally, it is most important to see that the function of reason does not cease with the coming of faith. Faith, as I have said, is a part of our divine life. It is a share in God's self-knowledge, and it is a part of our knowledge. Although it remains something learned, although it is never something we can think out for ourselves, it is something we can think about for ourselves. This thinking about what God has told us is called theology, and this is by far the most important function of human reason in relation to faith. The apologetic function by which we seek to show up fallacies in arguments directed against our beliefs, and the preliminary function in which we try to show that it is reasonable to hold these beliefs, are both only minor jobs of the theologians. Their real business is to think about what is revealed, to see how one part fits in with another, to see the whole thing as a coherent human thing, not arbitrary slabs of information given us to 'test our faith', but all as knowledge given to us 'for us and for our salvation', as we say in the creed.

6

Doubt is not Unbelief

I do not here wish to give some kind of psychological account of the state of belief in general and doubt in general – if there are such things. My focus is on Christian belief. So I think we should begin by looking at what belief means in the sense that we use it, say, at baptism, when the answer to the question 'What do you seek from the Church?' is 'Belief'.

'I believe in God.' I don't think the best way to begin understanding this is to compare it with 'I believe there are nine planets (though I've never counted them)' or 'I believe Australia is there (though I've never seen it)'. I think, as I'll be saying presently, that 'I believe in God' does have to do with believing that some propositions are true. But I don't think you can start there.

One way to start is with the model of a child and her parents. One thing that is necessary for the health and growth of children is that they should believe that their parents love them. This is almost as necessary as food and drink, and, indeed, without it the children may die because of refusing food and drink. This belief is necessary for their health. When you hear someone say that faith is necessary for salvation, remember that this is just the same thing in bigger words, words that reach down to a deeper level of belief and health. The whole of our faith is the belief that God loves us; I mean there isn't anything else. Anything else we say we believe is just a way of saying that God loves us. Any proposition, any article of faith, is only an expression of faith if it is a way of saying that God loves us.

Have you ever thought of the extraordinary unconscious arrogance of western Christians who think that they are being broad-minded and ecumenical when they talk about the 'Great World Faiths': Hinduism, Buddhism, and so on? This is wrongly to try to squeeze these religions into a Christian mould. Buddhists don't think they have a great world faith. They are not in the least interested in faith. Nor are Hindus. Jews are, of course, and so are Muslims, but they really belong to the same family as Christians, and it is Christians who make a great fuss about faith. And this is just because they see the relation of people to God on the model of the relation of children to their parents, or to adult society in general.

Think some more about the very young child. First of all, her faith that she is loved is not something that she works out by assessing her world and coming to a conclusion. It is something *given*, taken for *granted* (in the literal sense). Indeed if it is not granted, if she is deprived of the belief that she is loved, she will not even be *able* to assess her world at all. She will go more or less crazy.

The child doesn't arrive at or achieve her belief that she is loved. It is a precious gift which is just there, like the gift of life itself. But it can, of course, be destroyed. It is notoriously possible for adults, and especially parents, to erode a child's faith, to leave the child insecure and uncertain that she is loved, uncertain therefore of her own value, uncertain that she matters. The love of parents and later of other friends may fail; they may betray us. Indeed, I think we have a whole society (known as the Free World) which is so structured as to destroy belief in love, to eat away at the confidence people have in each other, to replace friendship by competitiveness, generosity by domination and submission, community by national security, love by fear.

The Christian notion of God is based on a belief in a love which simply can never fail. God, for the Christian, is the lover who accepts us absolutely and unconditionally, quite regardless of whether we are nice or nasty. We put this simply by saying that God loves sinners. This is what the cross says, and that is why it is the centre of Christian faith. God cannot fail to love us, whatever we do. But we can fail to believe this.

Children, of course, quite quickly come to realize the importance of their parents' love. And, quite soon, they need to be reassured about it. It is not enough for them to be told, to be kissed and cuddled and so on. They need to test it out. Lots of the misbehaviour of children is experimental – making sure that the love will still be there under all circumstances. I think that some of the things we class as doubt are often quite like this. Testing out not so much God's love for us as our belief in it – discovering how far our faith can go. This seems to me not so much a good thing or a bad thing as an *inevitable* thing – as inevitable and necessary as the infuriating behaviour of children.

So Christianity sets great store by faith precisely because it sees our relationship to God, to the ultimate mystery behind and beyond the universe, our relationship to the creator, the source of all being and meaning, as a personal one – not just the relationship of a work of art to the artist, of the poem to the poet, of the thing made to the maker, but of the child made to the parent. We are not just what God has made, though that is tremendous enough. We are whom God loves. This is the gospel. This is what we believe. We believe in belief, belief in God's love, as the ultimate thing about us. This is as essential to the divine life we have been called to as is a child's confidence in her parents to the human life into which she has been born.

Faith is a kind of knowing that God loves us. It is not just a feeling or a mood, but a kind of understanding or knowing. And knowledge, for us, is the answering of asked questions. That is why our knowledge is expressed in language and in the form of statements or propositions. People who say that faith is not 'propositional' because it is a personal relationship are, I think, very muddled. Faith is not just a feeling of happiness because of the beloved. It is what that feeling of happiness is based on. The happiness and joy are sensible, human, and awake (not like the happiness of being high or drunk), just because there is a reason for it. It is based on a belief, a belief that can be and has to be expressed in language – whether the language of words or of other symbols such as sacramental rites or the crucifix.

Faith can be, and has to be, expressed in propositions. But it isn't about these propositions; the propositions themselves have continually to be tested to make sure that they are expressions of faith and not of something else, expressions, that is, of belief in God's love for us. The trouble arises because faith, like the human persons who have it, is a communal, social thing. You cannot have faith without the community of believers and its tradition any more than you can have a human being without human society and human history. So any expression of our faith is also invariably an expression of our loyalty to, our belonging to, this tradition and community. This is not a bad thing. Indeed, it is an absolutely necessary and good thing, for faith belongs to human animals. The difficulties begin to arise (it is part of the dangerous process of eroding our faith) when we pay less attention to the doctrine as expressing our faith in the love of God for us, and concentrate simply on the doctrine as expressing our loyalty to our fellow Christians, to the church. That is why we have to test and criticize our doctrines to question both what we are making of them and what use the church itself is making of them. Are they degenerating simply into an expression of loyalty? Are they really still about God's love?

This is a kind of doubting because it is a kind of questioning, and it is an integral part of faith itself. It is the kind of questioning that is called theology. The object of theology is to see the traditional teachings of the church as a unified whole, unified around the gospel that God loves us. Only when we see what the church teaches about sin or grace or the Eucharist or the Trinity as all part of a revelation of the love of God – *only* when we see this – do we begin to understand these doctrines. And the only way to see this is to question them and to question our understanding of them.

Quite often we simply cannot see the relevance of some doctrine, or we suspect that its origins lie in some power struggle in the church rather than in the preaching of the gospel. Quite often the thing seems simply unintelligible or daft. It seems to me that the sensible reaction in such cases is neither to accept the doctrine blindly simply because you were told it at school, nor to reject it uncritically for the same reason. The sensible reaction is one of questioning and doubt. It is a reaction that demands a certain amount of work and thought. It is doing theology.

Occasionally, if you do this, you will find that what you always thought was a 'teaching of the church' turns out not to be that at all but simply what a lot of past theologians have thought – the so-called doctrine of Limbo, for example. Sometimes you find that what you always took to be the meaning of the doctrine is not what it actually means, that, for example, in the eucharist the body of Christ is physically located disguised as bread – that Christ can be 'the prisoner in the tabernacle'. It is especially true of moral matters that what is called the teaching of the church often turns out to be just the prejudices of the last generation but one preserved because the church is inevitably a rather conservative and conserving institution.

Sometimes the thing will be baffling; sometimes the job of making sense of some teaching will still be quite intractable – well, you must not expect to solve all problems quickly, and here it seems to me that your acceptance of this doctrine remains dark, your faith still co-exists with doubt in this area. The doctrine in question cannot be any kind of nourishment to your Christian life. It remains dormant for you. But this is not disbelief. I think a startlingly large number of Christians are this way about such absolutely central doctrines as that of the Trinity. It is a pity, though, if you simply say: 'Well that is all very difficult, so let's just ignore it and get back to Our Lady of Fatima or the fellowship of the eucharist.' It is a pity because if you just do that the chances are that you have an inadequate and infantile view of Our Lady and of the eucharist.

None of this, though, is disbelief. Disbelief is quite other. To understand this we need to get back to our model of the child and her parents. What happens to the child who has lost faith in her parents' love? The first thing is fear – a fear that she does not matter, that she has no value or importance. This is the fear that St John says is cast out by love, by being loved, by knowing you are loved.[1] The child who is deprived of love is characteristically defensive. She is terrified of admitting any inadequacy or guilt – I mean terrified of admitting it even to herself. She becomes gradually self-righteous, convinced of her rightness, with a conviction that conceals, and is meant to conceal, a deep anxiety. She is not able simply to accept herself, warts and all, as valuable because someone loves her. So she has to create a self-image for herself, a self-flattering image. She will have to protect her importance by having power over others. She will be terrified of being at the mercy of others, vulnerable to them. She will guard her self-image with possessions which make her independent of others. She will at all costs protect what she calls her 'freedom', meaning her isolation from others and the demands they might make on her. She will see the world as a place fundamentally of competition and struggle in which she has to win, rather than of friendship and co-operation.

All that is an image of disbelief. If you fail to believe that the most important and fundamental thing about you is that you are loved, if you fail to believe in God, then you have no recourse except to believe in yourself. All sin arises from the deep fear that is involved here. You only have to ask yourself why in the end you have sinned on any particular occasion. If you think hard enough and honestly enough, you will trace it back to fear, fear that you will not matter, that someone is threatening the importance or status or wealth you have carefully built up for yourself, fear that you are missing out on some experience that makes you you. Tracing sins back to their single root in such anxieties is as important as tracing all Christian doctrines back to their root in the faith that we are loved. In fact it is part of the same process. All sin is a symptom of faithlessness or uncertainty about being loved, as all belief is an affirmation of that love.

The societal and political manifestation of disbelief (of belief that we make ourselves and are only what we make ourselves) is, of course, the world of liberal individualism – the world of isolated individuals asserting their freedom against each other. And, of course, if this is what society is like, you need a state whose job it is to control and limit the freedom of its citizens. The world that believes in the autonomous free individual also has to believe in the bureaucratic state. Society is seen as a perpetual struggle between these two – sometimes emphasizing the individual, sometimes the collective. But all this is the world of disbelief, the world without God.

This is the world from which Jesus came to redeem us, to give us faith in his Father's love so that we do not need to assert ourselves and our innocence and our rightness, so that we can relax and confess the truth about ourselves, so that we stop judging ourselves and others because we know that it doesn't matter: God loves us anyway, so that we are liberated enough to risk being vulnerable to others – liberated enough to risk loving and being loved by others, liberated enough to know that we belong to each other because we belong to God. In that world we will not cling fanatically to particular formulas and doctrines simply because they are our security, any more than we cling to our own righteousness. We can be relaxed either way. In such a world a belief that we are called to share in divine life, and do already share in it, can go with a clear awareness of our own weakness and inadequacy and sin. And in such a world believing in God's love can go with a critical awareness of the weakness and inadequacy of our ways of expressing it. Our belief can and, indeed, must go with a certain kind of searching and questioning, a certain kind of doubt. Faith will exclude doubt altogether only when it ceases to be faith and becomes the *vision* of the eternal love which is God.

Note

1   1 John 4.18.

7

'He was Crucified, Suffered Death, and was Buried'

I don't know whether you've noticed how completely different this article of the Nicene Creed is from all the other articles in the creed. All other articles talk religious language or speak of marvels that only a believer could take completely seriously: 'born of the virgin Mary, on the third day he rose from the dead, the Holy Spirit the Lord and giver of life …' and so on. But this just flatly says that Jesus was crucified, died and was buried, rather horrible facts but perfectly ordinary facts that would have been known to any spectator in Jerusalem that day and in fact are quite well known to us. Nobody but a crank has the slightest doubt that Jesus was crucified and died and was buried; it is a piece of historical information on a par with the fact that Prince Charlie lost the battle of Culloden. There is no need to be a Christian to know about this; you just have to be ordinarily well-informed.

So already there is a tiny problem here – what is it doing in the creed? The creed is supposed to be full of things that make demands on our faith, on the commitment of the whole man, and the Lord knows what. What is this simple piece of ordinary history doing there? It's as though you had a creed saying: 'And I believe that the Holy Spirit is poured forth in our hearts because of the resurrection of Christ, and that Huddersfield is in Yorkshire.' It's not as though the creed put a religious interpretation on the matter, as though it had said

Jesus died as a sacrifice, or he died to make atonement for our sins, or he shed his blood of the new covenant. It just quite starkly states the empirical facts. Indeed, some creeds go out of their way to emphasize the sheer vulgar historicality of the thing by dating it: 'He was put to death under Pontius Pilate.' One word used, 'crucified', does suggest an interpretation of the affair as we shall see. Yet it is precisely not a religious interpretation but a political one. If only Jesus had been stoned to death that would at least have put the thing in a religious context – this was the kind of thing you did to prophets. But nobody was ever crucified for anything to do with religion. Moreover the reference to Pontius Pilate doesn't only date the business but also makes it clear that it was the Roman occupying forces that killed Jesus – and they obviously were not interested in religious matters as such. All they cared about was preserving law and order and protecting the exploiters of the Jewish people.

It all goes to show that if we have some theological theory that only certain kinds of proposition can follow the words 'I believe that ...' we should be very careful. We can believe that the Holy Spirit proceeds from the Father and the Son, which really isn't an empirically testable statement, and also that Jesus was killed, which is. But this article isn't just an oddity in the creed. This oddity is the very centre of the creed. It is the insertion of this bald empirical historical fact that makes the creed a Christian creed, that gives it the proper Christian flavour. It is because of this vulgar fact stuck in the centre of our faith that however ecumenical we may feel towards the Buddhists, say, and however fascinating the latest Guru may be, Christianity is something quite different. It isn't rooted in religious experiences or transcendental meditation or the existential commitment of the self. It is rooted in a murder committed by security forces in occupied Jerusalem around the year 30 AD.

Most of the creed is expressed in language that could fairly be called mythological (I suppose it is no longer necessary to insist that mythological language is just as good as any other and at least as likely to tell the truth as any other), which makes it relatively easy to relate it to other mythological forms. There are creation and resurrection myths all over the place and Christianity can be related to them. And a good thing too. What *anchors* the creed is the totally non-theological cross. And I think it is highly significant that in popular tradition (which is where you would expect to find the Holy Spirit at work) the cross is the central image representing our belief. From time to time there are mythological or at least interpretative crosses – crucifixes that show Christ the King in glory, or that show Christ in an attitude of prayer, or with his arms outstretched to welcome all people. But all these, excellent though they are in their own way, are a minority thing. The image that stands at the centre of popular Christianity just shows a dying man nailed to a piece of wood. And this is just a picture of an historical event. I hasten to add that this is not *just* a popular tradition. It is a tradition that very early got itself into Scripture. One of the very earliest Christian writings (earlier than any of the Gospels), St Paul's first letter to the Corinthians, says 'we preach Christ crucified' and 'I decided to know nothing amongst you except Jesus Christ and him crucified'.

There is then a certain stark and literal simplicity about this article of the creed and I would like to look at it with the same simplicity. There are of course endless interpretations of Jesus of Nazareth, and most of them help to shed some light on him. You can, for example, take the titles used of him in the New Testament; you can tease out what would be meant by calling him Messiah or the Servant or Son of Man or Son of God, or you can unravel what is meant by saying he is light of the world or bread of life. You can examine what is meant by saying that he came to save the world or that he came as our redeemer. And all these are useful things to do. But if you have not started with very simple things these others are likely to lead you into strange pathways. Take the last for example. It is agreed that Jesus is in some way our redeemer – the word is used in connection with him around a dozen times in the New Testament, where it is furthermore agreed that it was by his cross that he redeemed the world. But then the questions begin. To redeem means to buy back, as when you give money to the pawnbroker and get back the thing you hocked, or when you pay money to a kidnapper to redeem someone who is captive. And I suppose you would redeem someone from jail or from a debtor's prison by paying the money he owed. People have asked questions like *what* did Jesus pay *to whom* in order to get back *whom*. Most people have thought Jesus was paying a debt due to God that was owed by man, but some have thought he was paying a ransom due to Satan who had captured man. And so people got around to saying that what Jesus was doing on the cross was paying back something owed by man; and pretty soon they were saying that this was why he allowed himself to be crucified.

You get a similar process with the notion that Jesus is our High Priest, as it says in the Letter to the Hebrews. If he was a priest then he offered sacrifice. What did he sacrifice? Himself on the cross, of course. To whom did he offer himself? To the Father, of course. Excellent; and pretty soon people are saying that Jesus went to calvary in order to offer this sacrifice of our redemption. Then again there were people saying that Jesus, like the Servant in Isaiah, took on himself the burden and punishment of our sins: 'by his punishment we are healed'. Although he had no sin himself he took on himself the penalty of our sins. And pretty soon they are saying that he submitted to the cross in order to take the penalty of sin off our shoulders and onto his own. Sometimes people have said that Jesus paid the debt or offered the sacrifice or took the punishment of sin *instead* of us – the so-called 'vicarious' theory. And sometimes people say that he did this in *the name of* the whole human race – the so-called 'representative' theory.

Now all these views (and a great many more) can help to shed light on Jesus and are therefore not a waste of time. But they all have one interesting feature in common. They all end up as answers to the question 'Why did Jesus decide to be crucified? What was the reason for the Cross? Why something so strange as the crucifixion for the Son of God?' Now my belief is that the ordinary Christians who have kept the crucifix or the sign of the cross as their creed – a visual one that is just as good as a verbal one – never had this problem at all.

The ordinary people deep down in their understanding, have never had the slightest puzzle about the cross. They have taken it for granted. Why naturally the man was crucified. Aren't we all? Whether they would put it into words or not, they felt deep down that crucifixion really does express what life is about. This is not easily acknowledged; to begin with it is something we are afraid to face – that the deep things in life are suffering and death. Not the only things in life of course; and life that is really humanly lived consists in making value out of suffering and death amongst other things. But the deeply significant things are always tied up with suffering. You can tell this by simply listening to the music and poetry of the people. For the most part the really great songs are about love and sorrow and death. I do not believe that this is a morbid aberration. I think that if you can articulate the deep meaning of life in terms of death by means of songs or sacraments, you are free for the wildest celebrations of sheer joy and love of living – these celebrations are freed from the task of carrying the final significance of life and for that reason can be as exuberant as you like. There is a magnificent Irish tune called *Rosin Dubh*, the dark rose (meaning Ireland), which expresses indescribably all the sorrows and suffering of Irish history and I have hardly ever heard it played without it being immediately followed by the liveliest and fastest air available. This is partly, I suppose, a psychological effect. You simply cannot bear to be left with the ending of *Rosin Dubh*, or the player doesn't want to sound portentous, but partly I think the exploration of tragedy releases us for simple happiness.

Anyway I think ordinary people have taken the crucifixion for granted in one way; what has made the cross the symbol of hope and consolation is that it is a symbol of God. It says the divine reaches down even to those depths of the human reality, the depths we scarcely dare to explore.

So what I am saying is that the question 'Why did Jesus opt for crucifixion' is a misplaced one. Of course he was crucified; he was human wasn't he? This is the central thing I want to say: that Jesus died of being human. More than that, all humans die, but he was so human he had to be killed.

He was and is a man like us in all things but sin. 'Like us in all things but sin' doesn't on the face of it sound very like us. We all I think have a suspicion that if you took away our sins and vices, especially our minor vices, we would first of all be very different people, but also we would be less human and less likable people. There is something repellently inhuman about the man or woman with no weaknesses who is always rather chillingly perfect. I hardly need to say, I am sure, that this feeling is based on a hopelessly negative idea of virtue. Virtue, whatever else it means, at least means being more human; it would not be virtuous if it did not. Sin, whatever else it means, means being less human, more stiff, cold, proud, selfish, mean, cruel and all the rest of it. It is not in fact our sins that make us attractive. Weakness, of course, is frequently attractive, but just because it is human weakness, that is virtuous weakness. There is a perfectly definite virtue involved in letting yourself be helped by others, and a perfectly definite vice in declining to be helped. What makes us more human is, of course, being more loving. And sin is a defect in this love. To say that Jesus was without sin just means that he was wholly loving, that he did not put up barriers against people, that he was not afraid of being at the disposal of others, that he was warm and free and spontaneous. That is what really lies behind that portentous sentence 'He spoke as one with authority'. It makes him sound so magisterial and solemn. In fact it just means that what he said came straight from him, warmly and immediately. He was never looking over his shoulder at the textbooks and traditions.

There is, of course, a lot more to be said about the relationship between love and humanity and sin and inhumanity. In fact, when we talk of sin and of love we are operating at a depth in man at which his humanity transcends itself. We are concerned with our divine life. All I want to insist on at the moment is that the fact that Jesus was without sin doesn't mean that he was cold and inhuman, but rather just the opposite. It means that he was liberated, free and spontaneous, really able to love and, as I say, not afraid of others, not afraid of being with others at their mercy.

Any man like this is, of course, at risk. He is going to be first exploited and then destroyed. This is the fact of life recognized by all those ordinary people I was talking about who take crucifixion for granted. This is no world for love. There is a twist or a contradiction in our human life that means we build a world unfit for humans. The only way to get by in it is to restrict your humanity rather carefully, otherwise you will get hurt. The world is not totally unfit for human habitation, but it can take just so much of it. You have to ration your love, keep a wary eye out for enemies, if you want to survive. Now Jesus did not ration his love, so naturally he didn't last.

To believe in the cross, as distinct from knowing it happened or expecting it in the circumstances, is to believe that this challenge to the world at the cost of destruction is not only right but the key to what human life is about, that in this act we have the revelation of the divine.

We live in a world that cannot afford too much humanity, too much love. Love is permissible on the surface down to a certain relatively shallow level, but beneath that, what keeps chaos at bay, what keeps our world fairly stable, is not love but domination and fear (Hobbes gives a perfectly accurate account of all this). Any clear, cool, unsentimental look at our world shows us that in the end the last resort of society is to violence, to the appeal to fear, whether it be the threat of punishment or the threat of social collapse. It is not that people go around all the time anxiously living in fear of the police. There is no need for this. But the police and other men of violence are there waiting in the wings in case they are needed. As a matter of fact people do go around in anxious fear, but it is not directed at the police. Sometimes it is just a formless anxiety, a general fear of the world and of other people. This is not just a picture of our own society. It is true in varying degrees of every human society we have yet built – notably it was true of colonial Palestine under the Roman empire. In a subject country massively occupied by Roman troops it was quite obvious that society was based on fear. Roman order was preserved by harassment, torture and killing.

It was equally true that the religion of the people was based in a more subtle way on fear. Not officially on fear of hell. Hell is not mentioned in the Old Testament as a place of eternal punishment. Nor for that matter is it mentioned in the writings of St Paul. It was Jesus who popularized this idea. Nonetheless the religion of the Jews at the time of Jesus seems to have been based on the domination of God. It was certainly better to be dominated by God than by any human emperor or king. The law of Yahweh was a great deal more humane than the laws of most of the countries round about. But it remains that the covenant relationship between man and God was seen in terms of domination and subjection.

The thing is that both the social order and the religious order depended on the imposition of law. The only alternative that could be envisaged was chaos. And Jesus posed a threat to both the political and the religious establishment because he proposed what he claimed was a third possibility: neither domination nor chaos but love. Now this, to the unsentimental eye, is evidently rubbish – unless you have a very special kind of love available. To attempt to sustain an even slightly human society on the kind of thing that we ordinarily know as love is ridiculous and also almost certainly dishonest. People who want to get rid of laws and substitute love are quite often people who find illegal domination easier than using law. What was special about Jesus was not that he produced the theory that people might live by love – that was a tired old theory that had been discredited many times in most people's experience – but that he produced the love. The kind of relationship that he had with his friends, and the kind of relationship he enabled them to have with each other, was something quite new. Here was something that *could* be the basis of a third possibility, neither law nor chaos.

Or was it? Was there here something really new, or was Jesus just another unconscious charlatan setting up a personality cult of himself instead of the law? I must stress again that abominable as the Roman law was, particularly in the colonies, it was better than some others, and certainly better than the horrors of paganism. It is understood that if someone proposes to dissolve these structures, ramshackle as they are, you want to be pretty sure he has something better to offer than a personality cult.

There can be no doubt that Jesus sounded as if this is what he was offering. His alternative was not a philosophy or a theology or a social theory or a political programme. It was simply himself. Believe in *me*, he says.

The whole question of Jesus turned on whether he really was or was not offering a quite new kind of relationship with people – or as people were subsequently to put it, pouring forth the Holy Spirit. And of course the only way to tell this was to respond to Jesus, to accept him or reject him, to have faith in him or not.

The thing is that your response to Jesus was not just your judgement of him. It was also a judgement of you. Since what Jesus in fact offered was a truly free, liberating relationship, the question really was whether you were prepared to accept this, whether you were frightened by such freedom or whether you were prepared to take the risk. If you did not take the risk then you did not recognize what Jesus was offering; you immediately explained it away.

I say all this so that you will be more able to understand the reactions of the police and the priests, the guardians of the law. It was, as Jesus himself kept saying, so much easier for the poor and the despised and the social outcasts than for those with heavy social responsibilities. The poor could accept him for what he was. The establishment had always to be calculating just where he stood and what his role was in their scheme of things. It was easier for Galilean peasants than for sophisticated city dwellers in Jerusalem. It was easier for the weak than for the strong.

Anyway the religious leaders in general failed to see what Jesus was offering them. They could not open their hearts to him, so hearing they did not hear and seeing they did not see. In consequence they viewed him simply as a blasphemer setting himself up against the law of Yahweh, against all the religious traditions of the people of God. It was necessary to be rid of him. This would not be too difficult because the colonial powers were naturally suspicious of any popular leader and Jesus had begun to have a mass following particularly amongst the peasants and working class. Generally speaking, as might be expected, the collaborationists who worked in the colonial power were the upper class Sadduceans together with the Herodian party grouped around the Herod family, who had been set up as puppet kings in the territory outside Judea. Judea itself, including Jerusalem, was under the direct rule of Pontius Pilate.) Things were made rather worse by the fact that some members of the zealots, the underground revolutionary movement, were associated with Jesus, although Jesus clearly disagreed both with their aims and their tactics (they were traditionalists looking for a theocratic Jewish state, and their ideology was pretty similar to that of the Pharisees), the Romans would not pay attention to such subtle distinctions. As a popular leader he would be lumped together with the zealots.

The fact that Jesus aroused the suspicions of the Romans by the sheer fact of having a mass following not only made it relatively easy to dispose of him; it also gave an added motive for doing so. Caiphas, himself appointed by the Roman authorities, put it quite simply. If we let him go on he will provoke a Roman backlash. We will have an Operation Motorman and our people will be beaten up and killed and have their homes wrecked by the soldiers. Caiphas, in fact, feared that Jesus would provoke what the zealots finally did provoke in AD 70 on a much bigger scale when Jerusalem was ravaged in a hideously bloody act of repression. Of course the author of John's Gospel, who quotes Caiphas, was writing after these events and in the light of them. But there is no need to suppose that he misinterpreted the reaction of the religious establishment.

This I think broadly explains how Jesus came to be crucified, to die and be buried. Things had come to head after the Palm Sunday demonstration when it was obvious that Jesus had very widespread and enthusiastic support.

It was first necessary to discredit him in Jewish eyes, to get a conviction of blasphemy against him. One Jewish writer on this theme maintains that what was really happening here was that, in order to protect him from the Romans, the Jewish leaders were trying to persuade Jesus not to make dangerous messianic claims. But this theory has not been generally accepted. I think it more plausible to hold that they wanted first to excommunicate him and deprive him of popular Jewish support, and then to see that the Romans did the actual execution job by suggesting that he was a kind of zealot. To present him as an enemy of both the Jewish people and of the Romans was the neatest way of getting rid of him, and they succeeded. There was never much difficulty about getting the Romans to crucify someone. It was the normal punishment for political opposition. In the state in which Palestine was at this time there were probably several crucifixions a week (Josephus records seeing 2,000 people crucified at once on one occasion). We naturally see the crucifixion of Jesus as an outstanding and awe-inspiring event, but for the Romans it was just one amongst others. The gospels record that two men were executed on the same day as Jesus and there may well have been a number of others.

That is the death of Jesus as seen from the public point of view, as it might have been reported in the contemporary left-wing press. What about it from Jesus' own point of view? It is clear that very early on Jesus recognized that the love he offered presented such a threat to the establishment that he was sooner or later going to be destroyed. Of course, the evangelists writing with hindsight attribute to him various quite specific prophecies about his death on the cross, and there is no good reason to think these are pure invention; on the contrary Jesus would have had to be very imperceptive and very foolish to think that he could get away with it. It is only very foolish and inexperienced people who imagine that love is welcomed. Real love is a dangerous disturbing and subversive force. If you offer it to the world then, as John has Jesus say, 'The world will hate you.' Jesus knew that his attempt would fail, knew that he would be defeated; but he remained faithful to his mission from the Father.

To conclude, it is clear that if the kind of love that Jesus offers inevitably results in his being crucified, the same kind of thing is going to be true of those who receive his love and are liberated in their turn and able to pass it on to others. Crucifixion in some way is the destiny of every Christian. It does not have to be public execution. That only occurs when the love of Christ takes forms that are recognized as immediately dangerous by the ruling class. But for every Christian his or her death is to be a death that expresses the love of Christ, the Holy Spirit. There are just two kinds of death, the death that, like Christ's death, is the operation of the Spirit, or the death that simply means the organism has ceased to function. To die as Christ did filled with the Holy Spirit is to conquer death; death then becomes simply the presupposition for the transformation of humanity in the resurrection. But that is another matter.

8

'Nobody Comes to the Father but by Me'

In the fourteenth chapter of St John's Gospel we find Jesus saying 'Nobody comes to the Father but by me'. Can we really take that literally? Can we even take it seriously? 'Nobody' (he is talking about the whole human race) 'comes to the Father' (he means God) 'but by me' (he means himself). There are, I think, around four or five thousand million people alive today and countless millions have lived in the past; and most of them (apart from a few eccentrics) have thought about God one way or another, communally or individually. I mean they have thought about the mystery that things are, the mysterious purpose of human life or however they have put it; and they have sought to come to God. There have been great religions devoted to meditating on these things, whole civilizations sustained by some kind of worship of God; there has been endless striving to come to the Father. And now, amongst all these teeming millions, it is being asserted that, after all, nobody comes to God except through this individual carpenter in Palestine.

The egoism is breathtaking. Surely there must be some mistake.

Let us then think about this for a minute or two.

First of all, St John is not saying that nobody sees or understands God except by getting to know Jesus of Nazareth. People can seek to understand God, they can wrestle with this problem or explore this mystery quite apart from faith in Jesus Christ. John does not think they will get very far, for he says 'No one has ever seen God'; but having faith in Jesus Christ will not get them any further. People can seek *a way of life* in which to be united with God; they can try to come to the Father quite apart from faith in Christ. They will not get very far; but they will not get any further by having faith in Christ.

Christians are not people who think that because they have faith they have an advantage, that they are better informed about God than other people or have reached a position closer to God than other people, that they have discovered the secret of coming to the Father. Christians do not claim to have any secret and private knowledge about God or to have discovered any new secret way to the Father.

We come to the Father in Jesus Christ not because he has revealed to us the way by which we may go. (In John 14 Thomas wants to know about this and Jesus tells him that is not the point; that is not what he offers.) We come to the Father in Christ simply because Jesus is the way in which the Father comes to us: not first our way but the way the Father comes, the Father's truth, the life of the Father. And when the Father comes to us in the human life of Jesus it is not to show us how to know, how to be successful at coming to him or successful at anything else. He comes to us, after all, in a complete failure, in one who suffers and is defeated. He comes to us as a condemned and despised and executed criminal.

The *Word* of God is made flesh not to tell us something, not to make us better informed; he does not show us how to teach the world new secrets; what he shows us is our ignorance, our failure to understand. Christians *claim* that they know nothing of God. Christians think that anyone who claims to know God has set up some kind of idol in place of God. Christians say they are in the dark; it is the special darkness they call faith. Christians are not *proud* of being in the dark; they just know that they *are*. Christians are not proud of failing and being defeated by the powers of this world; they just know they constantly will be, if they love as Christ loves. They would much rather not be in the dark and not be defeated, but they don't think it matters all that much because their faith is not in themselves, in *their* success and *their* understanding. Their faith is in the power of God, which appears as weakness, and in the wisdom and understanding of God, which appears as folly. And they know it is by accepting this darkness and accepting this defeat that they will be given victory in light.

The thing that does make Christianity unique, really different from any of the other wisdoms and religions that I know, is not that it has a special secret but that it has no secret at all; it has nothing special to it. It has no way of its own, no truth or wisdom of its own, no life of its own. It has nothing of its own to offer: it just asks us to accept, to submit to, whatever God has to offer. It asks us to accept *the way and the wisdom and the life* which is God's. And if you ask 'What is that?', Christianity will not take you to a book, a recital, a code of laws; it will only take you to a defeated human being hanging from a cross. For the secular world looks for wisdom but we preach Christ crucified … the power of *God* and the wisdom of *God*.

I am sure you all know the nasty story of the ecumenical gathering when one Divided Christian says to another: 'After all, aren't we all going to the same God, you in your way, and I in his.' But that really is what the Gospel says. It makes no claim to know the way, except to refuse to believe in any such claims. There is no Christian way of perfection that is better or worse than anybody else's: the actual Gospel is that we do not need it since God is taking humankind, the human race, to himself. There are, indeed, ways we can learn to be more human, to grow in human virtues; and from the Ten Commandments onwards, Jews and Christians have played a large part in this search for human decency. There are no ways we can learn to become divine, to come to the Father: making us divine is God's business.

It was always an illusion to suppose that by wisdom or ascetic practices, by meditation or by building the Tower of Babel, we could come to the Father. The good news is that the Father comes to us. In one way, a negative way,

Christians do perhaps understand God better; because they won't have any substitutes, any idols, any gods. They have the sort of clearer, uncluttered, understanding that atheists have – except that most atheists cultivate some little idol of their own on the quiet. But apart from that, Christians don't expect or want *their* understanding of God to improve; they want to be taken over by God's understanding of God – and they don't mind much if, at the moment, this seems like nothing but greater ignorance for them.

This is what John is talking about at the beginning of his Gospel when he calls Jesus the Word of *God* made flesh. Jesus is God's Word, God's idea of God, how God understands himself. He is how-God-understands-himself become a part of our human history, become human, become the *first* really thoroughly human part of our history – and therefore, of course, the one hated, despised and destroyed by the rest of us, who wouldn't mind being divine but are very frightened of being human.

In Jesus, says the Christian, we do not understand God but we can watch God understanding himself. God's understanding of God is that he throws himself away in love, that he keeps nothing back for himself. God's understanding of God is that he is a love that unconditionally accepts, that always lets others be, even if what they want to be is his murderers. God's understanding of God is that he is not a special person with a special kind of message, with a special way of living he wants people to conform to. God's understanding of God could not appear to us as someone who wants to found a new and better religion, or recommend a special new discipline or way of life – a religious code laid upon us for all time because it is from God. God's understanding of God is that he just says: 'Yes, *be*; be human, but be really human; be human if it kills you – and it will.' The Law of God is a non-law; it has no special regulations. The Word just says: 'I accept you as human beings; what a pity you have such difficulty in doing this yourselves. What a pity you can only like yourselves if you pretend to be super-humans or gods.' God could never understand himself as one of the gods, only as one of the human race.

Let us be absurd for a minute and try to imagine what it means for God to understand himself. I don't mean try to think or understand it (of course we cannot do that). But let us try to *imagine* understanding that limitless abyss of life and liveliness, that permanent explosion of vivacity and awareness and sparkling intelligence and, of course, humour. And remember that in understanding himself God will thereby be understanding all that he has done and is doing, all that he holds in being, every blade of grass and every passing thought in your mind. The concept he has of himself in all this is his Word. This is what is made flesh and dwells amongst us in the human suffering and dying Christ.

And in contemplating his life in this Word, in this concept, in contemplating all he is and all he does, God has surely a huge unfathomable joy, and immense excitement and enjoyment in all the life that is his and all the life he has brought into being. God takes immensely more joy in one little beetle walking across a leaf than you can take in everything good and delightful and beautiful in your whole life put together. If he gets that pleasure from one beetle he has made, think then what joy he takes in being God. This limitless joy is what we call the Holy Spirit.

To be able, through faith, to share in Christ, in God's understanding of himself, to be in Christ, is to be filled ourselves also with this joy, this Holy Spirit. It is a joy so vast that we can only faintly sometimes experience it as our elation and joy, just as our sharing in God's self-understanding hardly at all seems to us an understanding, a being enlightened. We have a life in us, an understanding and a joy in us, that is too great for us to comprehend. Quite often it has to show itself as what seems its opposite, as darkness and suffering. The Word of God is Christ crucified. But it is God's way and the truth of God and the life and joy of God. And this is in us because we have faith. We have been prepared to go into the dark with Christ, to die with Christ. And we know that this means that we live in Christ. And that life, the divine understanding and joy that is in us, will one day soon show itself in us for what it truly is. And we shall live to the Father, through the understanding which is the Word made flesh, in the joy which is the Holy Spirit for eternity.

9

Prayer

I want to talk about the theological problems associated with the idea of prayer, that is to say I am going to talk about prayer at, at least, one remove and this will inevitably be unsatisfactory. I am wholly in agreement in the end with the view that prayer (like loving) is something you only begin to understand, something you only see as justified, if you do it. So in one way the answer to someone who asks: 'What is the point of prayer?' is 'Pray and you'll see'. But it isn't a satisfactory answer because there are a whole lot of people who do pray and do not see clearly: I, for one, and probably a whole lot of you. Praying may be a necessary condition for seeing the point of praying but it certainly is not sufficient. 'Pray and you'll see the point of praying' is not anything like as simple as 'Taste lychees and you'll see why people eat them' because the whole point of eating lychees is that they taste nice, whereas the whole point of praying is not in the satisfactory experience of praying – at least I cannot believe that it is. I usually do not find praying a deeply satisfying experience.

Though you have to be careful here: there are satisfying experiences that are immediately satisfying, like drinking good Irish whiskey, but there are other satisfactions that occur only over long periods of time, like having a decently furnished room. A well-furnished room is not breathtakingly beautiful (like the Irish whiskey), but it is very satisfying to live with, and if you get rid of it simply because it doesn't give you an immediate kick, you will notice the lack of it only maybe a long time later. So I have to be careful about saying that

I usually don't find praying a deeply satisfying experience. It is true I hardly ever get a kick out of it, it almost never takes my breath away, but if you are deprived of, say, a decent liturgy for a fairly long period of time, you discover an important gap in your emotional life. I might as well say at this point that I think there is a mistaken tendency, more especially in the United States but to some extent in the United Kingdom, to design the liturgy for too immediate a satisfaction. I have been with the 'underground' groups in the American Church who do not really feel they have celebrated a Eucharist unless they get some kind of immediate experience of personal warmth and enhanced sensitivity. I think the liturgies designed by these people are very frequently in bad taste. I agree with those critics who find the *Missa Normativa* a little dull, except that I do not think it is altogether a criticism. A room furnished in good taste is a little dull compared to one covered in psychedelic posters saying 'Love is Love' and 'Mary, the ripest tomato of them all'.

The Mass a Prayer?

But I must not let myself be carried away by passionate conservatism. In one way the reforms of the liturgy have made us at least more urgently and explicitly aware of the problem of prayer. So long as the liturgy was in the nature of an abstract painting it could be regarded as more or less callow to ask what it represents, what it means. Our fathers just told us: 'Go to Mass every week and you will find it somehow a meaningful and supporting experience.' For children this was sometimes rationalized in terms of meeting and having little chats with Jesus, but the basic teaching was: here is a mystery, something like a great work of art that has significance that can be expressed in no other way; never mind what it 'means', just enter into it. And lots of Catholics of a past generation who had almost no aesthetic sophistication, who had a crudely rationalist and utilitarian approach to any painting or literature, were in fact able to appreciate the Mass precisely in this abstract way. These Catholics had in fact the usual problems about prayer but they were not very worried about them because prayer was not central to their lives. What was central was the mystery of the Eucharist.

And now we have these people coming along and saying that Mass is itself a prayer. This is explosive because of course the Mass is immediately devalued. The enormously complex mystery of the Mass has become a mere prayer. It is like saying that Chartres Cathedral is really just an advertisement for the Roman Catholic Church.

I am quite sure that what I am saying here must be quite unintelligible to many of you who were brought up in other Christian traditions, traditions in which prayer is quite central; for you, to say that the Mass is a prayer is to make it meaningfully religious for the first time. But I am speaking from the English Catholic or perhaps the Irish English Catholic standpoint. If to people like me you say that the Mass is a prayer then you really do have to restate what you mean by prayer – that is if you want me to take you seriously. The Mass is the terrible mystery of our union with Christ – compared with this, 'saying your prayers' is almost a triviality. That is one reason why the problem of saying what we mean by prayer has become urgent for Catholics.

Prayer of Petition

There is a special problem too now about prayers of petition. These have for a long time been less than respectable. For many years now people have been a bit furtive about actually praying that they will pass an exam or that their wives recover from a dangerous illness. They did it, of course, but they were rather embarrassed to have to mention it in public. It was rather a disreputable weakness, not exactly a secret vice, but certainly not something to talk about.

And now, for heaven's sake, we have these 'Prayers of the Faithful', all out in the public church. We have people openly acknowledging that they want something and apparently expect God to get it for them. We get over this a bit by asking for large-scale things like world peace – indeed with any luck the whole episode can be turned into a political credo to follow the theological one, but you cannot altogether get away from the fact that here are these adults asking God for the things they want.

Since all true progressives are expected to favour this liturgical reform and at the same time all true progressives think the prayer of petition is probably a lot of silly superstition, they have a problem here. Haven't they?

Well what I think I want to say about all this – and I don't know whether I can say it convincingly – is that if you are going to make serious sense of the idea that the Mass is a prayer you have to interpret prayer in terms of the Mass. All prayer is going to have to take its meaning and point from the sacrifice of Christ; we shall simply have to scrap all the metaphors about the all-powerful kindly father up there whom we can sometimes get through to and draw his attention to what we happen to need; we shall really have to get back to the traditional view that all providence is in Christ, that predestination is the predestination of Christ – that no one comes to the Father except through Christ.

As to petitionary prayer I can only contribute what I find to be the immensely illuminating insight of Thomas Aquinas, which as is so often the way with insights (especially St Thomas') turns the whole problem upside down very neatly.

Prayer, God, Christ

But first of all, is the problem of prayer not the problem of God? People feel that if only they could be a bit clearer about who or what God is they would see more sense in praying to him. Now I am afraid it is going to have to be the other way round. The problem of God is the problem of prayer. I am *not* saying this in a pietistic tone of voice: all these intellectual problems would just go away if you all got down on your knees and prayed a bit more. I am saying that maybe the way we understand God is as 'whatever makes sense of prayer'. I would say: we understand God as the other end of the personal relationship which is prayer, except that this might take us back into seeing prayer as a 'personal relationship' with a god, which would bypass the passion of Christ. In the end I suppose I want to say that God is what makes sense of prayer because God is what makes sense of Christ.

Love and Be Killed

What do I mean by saying that God is what makes sense of Christ? The Gospels insist upon two antithetical truths which express the tragedy of the human condition: the first is that if you do not love you will not be alive; the second is that if you *do* love you will be killed. If you cannot love you remain self-enclosed and sterile, unable to create a future for yourself or others, unable to live. If, however, you do effectively love you will be a threat to the structures of domination upon which our human society rests, and you will be killed.

This point is well put by Rosemary Haughton in her book *Love* that I have just been reading. She is casting doubt on the idea that correct instruction and orthodox teaching are the proper way of inculcating or evoking loving behaviour. She says:

If effective teaching on the importance of compassion and brotherly concern were sufficient to bring it into existence, the continuous, imaginative adver- tising campaign on behalf of famine and war relief organizations would have resulted in the virtual overturning of the world economic system, in favor of the 'developing' countries. In fact no such outbreak of love has occurred or is likely to occur, otherwise such advertising would probably be forbidden by law, since the economic stability of the Western world depends on the non-development of the 'developing' countries. A serious outbreak of love in the world would bring the markets crashing down. This may sound shockingly cynical, but an examination of the figures for world trade confirms it.[1]

If you do not love you will not be alive: if you love effectively you will be killed.

The life and death of Jesus dramatizes this state of affairs. His attempt to set up a community of love in Galilee was a threat to the colonialist and clericalist establishment and so he was killed. It was a death, as we say in Canon II, that he freely accepted; he was prepared to totally identify with the condition of his fellow men. He refused to defend his life's work at the cost of compromising what he saw as his mission. He was prepared to see all that he had apparently achieved come down in ruins, to see his fellows deserting him, scattered and demoralized. He accepted all this because he did not wish to be the founder of anything, the man of power who would compel the coming of the kingdom. He wished only to do what he called 'the will of his Father', which was simply to accept the condition of humanity, to seek the fullness of humanity in love and to accept the failure that characterizes loving humanity. This is what the crucifixion says. *Ecce homo.* This is what happens when you are really human. But the primary Gospel message is that Jesus was raised from the dead – that is to say that God exists. For the only God we Christians know is He who raised Jesus from the dead. God is what makes sense of the senseless waste of the crucifixion. The existence of God means that the failure, the total failure, which is the act of love is a new kind of triumph.

In the crucifixion Jesus casts everything upon God. The crucifixion says that the coming of the kingdom is not to be an achievement of Jesus but a gratuitous act of the Father's love. The kingdom is to come as a gift.

A gift means an expression of love. When we thank someone for a gift we are thinking through the gift to the giver ('thank' and 'think' come from the same root). To say 'Thank you' for a gift (or as the Greeks would say, to make a eucharist of it) is to recognize it, to think of it, as a communication of love. Gift is an expression of an exchange of love. To believe in the resurrection, to believe in God, is to believe that the resolution of the tragedy of the human condition comes as a gift, as an act of love encompassing mankind. The crucifixion–resurrection is the archetypal exchange of prayer and answer to prayer. On the cross Jesus casts himself upon God, not because he has not come of age, not because he lived before the age of technology and therefore lacked the means for constructing the kingdom, not because he needed a 'god in the gaps' to do what science and technology might have done had he lived 2,000 years later, but because he was wholly human, wholly free, wholly loving and *therefore* helpless to achieve what he sought. If he had wanted something less than the kingdom, if he had been a lesser man, a man not obsessed by love, he might have settled for less and achieved it by his own personality, intelligence and skill. But he wanted that all men should be as possessed by love as he was, he wanted that they should be divine, and this could only come as a gift. Crucifixion and resurrection, the prayer of Christ and the response of the Father, are the archetype and source of all our prayer. It is this we share in sacramentally in the Eucharist; it is this we share in all our prayer. But the crucifixion, the total self-abandonment of Jesus to the Father, is not just a prayer that Jesus offered, a thing he happened to do. What the Church came to realize is that it was the revelation of *who* Jesus is. When Jesus is 'lifted up' – and for John this means the whole loving exchange of the lifting up on the cross and the lifting up which is the resurrection – he appears for what he is. It is revealed that the deepest reality of Jesus is simply to be *of* the Father.

This is the news about ... Jesus Christ our Lord who, in the order of the Spirit, the Spirit of holiness that was in him, was proclaimed Son of God in all his power through his resurrection from the dead. (Rom. 1.3-4)

We are preaching a crucified Christ ... who is the power and wisdom of God. (1 Cor. 1.23)

Prayer and Sonship

Jesus is not first of all an individual person who then prays to the Father. His prayer to the Father is what constitutes him as who he is. He is not just one who prays, not even one who prays best. He is sheer prayer. In other words, the crucifixion/resurrection of Jesus is simply the showing forth, the visibility in human terms, in human history, of the relationship to the Father which constitutes the person who is Jesus. The prayer of Jesus which is his crucifixion, his absolute renunciation of himself in love to the Father, is the eternal relationship of Father and Son made available as part of our history, part of the web of mankind of which we are fragments, a part of the web that gives it a new centre, a new pattern.

All our prayer, whether the Mass itself or those reflections from the Mass that we call our prayers, is a sharing into the sacrifice of Christ and therefore a sharing into the life of the Trinity, a sharing that is the Spirit. All our prayer is, in a very precise sense, in Spirit and in truth. For us to pray is for us to be taken over, possessed by the Holy Spirit, which is the life of love between Father and Son. When our prayer is the prayer of the people of God *as such*, when it is the prayer of *the Church as a whole*, it is a sacramental expression of this life of the Spirit. That is what we mean by the sacraments, and this is what we primarily mean by our prayer; but the people of God pray individually too, or in small groups which do not claim to represent the whole Church. And here too their prayer is a living by the Spirit.

So our stance in prayer is not simply, or even primarily, that of the creature before the creator but that of the Son before the Father. At the most fundamental level, the level which defines prayer as prayer, we receive from the Father not as creatures receiving what they need to make up their deficiencies, but as the Son eternally receives his being from the Father. Our praying is an expression in history of our eternal trinitarian life. Those who feel that to express our eternal divine life in the form of asking for what we need is a little undignified and unworthy of man come of age, need to be reminded that the Son when he expressed his divine life in history emptied himself taking the form of a slave, and being found in human form humbled himself.

The Spirit Prays in Us

I remember a 'progressive' theologian providing an unintentionally hilarious account of being tempted to pray as his airplane took off down the runway, and how he sternly rebuked himself for this temptation and was able to preserve his dignity as an adult human being. This kind of crass and vulgar criticism of prayer can only arise because the author's notion of prayer is essentially pre-Christian. Behind it lurks the image of the great power 'up there' whom we can shout at and who, if we are lucky, will hear us and provide us with magical help. You remember all those prayers – particularly extempore prayers – that supply God with the necessary information: 'Almighty Father, as you doubtless saw in *The Times* this morning ...' or 'Almighty Father, paradoxical as it must seem to you ...' No, for traditional theology, prayer is not our attempt to gain the Father's attention; prayer is not in fact primarily a human activity, it is something we do in virtue of being divine. It is, to use the traditional language, the work of grace in us, the expression of our trinitarian life. 'Whatever you ask in my name ...' All prayer that really is prayer is in Christ's name; it is offered in virtue of our identification with Christ, our sharing in the sonship of God. The notion of the needy creature simply appealing to his creator is not merely an inadequate account of prayer; it is not prayer at all. It involves an initiative on the part of the creature, building a city and a tower that will reach up into the heavens. All true prayer is the work of grace, that is to say the initiative is from the Father drawing us into communion with his Son. 'In this is love, not that we loved God but that he loved us … We love because he first loved us.' What makes the theologian's story of himself primly deciding not to pray from the highest possible motives so comic is that the man clearly regarded *his* decision as the ultimate truth of the matter. He seems unaware of the depth within the free human decision: the depth of grace. I don't, by the way, at the moment want to go into the whole mystery of freedom and grace – of how a decision can be wholly mine, wholly free and simultaneously wholly the work of God's grace. If you feel hung up on this perhaps you could just make do with St Augustine's remark that God is closer to me than I am to myself. Grace is not something that comes at me from outside to constrain my freedom; it is a depth within me more central to me than what I call my self.

We must keep this firmly in mind: it is *God* who prays. Not just God who answers prayer but God who prays in us in the first place. In prayer we become the locus of the divine dialogue between Father and Son; we are in Spirit and truth. It is when we forget this that we get tangled up about petitionary prayer. There are some people who think that prayer of thanksgiving is OK, but that prayer of petition is somehow superstitious. It is hard to see the logic of this. If we are thanking God for what he has done, then surely we are seeing it as having been his free gift, an expression of his love, as something that would not have happened but for his personal love for us. If we are allowed to see what has already happened as God's free gift, and to thank him, what is wrong with seeing what has not yet happened as his free gift also, and asking for it?

Not Manipulation of God

Of course the real objection people make to petitionary prayer is that it looks like manipulation of God. Here is God just about to make it rain for the sake of the farmers and their crops in the fields around Clyst Honiton. Then he overhears the urgent prayer of the vicar who is running his garden party that afternoon, and he changes his mind. Then there is always the question whether the louder and lustier prayers of the farmers may make God hesitate again. The critics ask rather smugly: 'How is it possible for God to satisfy everybody, to hear all prayers, since good people frequently want incompatible things?'

But all this is to forget that it is God who prays, that my prayer is the action of God's grace in me. My prayer is not me putting pressure on God, doing something to God; it is God doing something for me, raising me into the divine life or intensifying the divine life in me. As Thomas Aquinas puts it, we should not say: 'In accordance with my prayer: God wills that it should be a fine day'; we should say: 'God wills: that it should be a fine day in accordance with my prayer.' God brings about my prayer just as much as he brings about the fine day, and what he wills, what he has willed from eternity, is that this fine day should not be, so to say, just an *ordinary* fine day. It should be for me a *significant* fine day, a sign, a communication from God. It should be a fine day that comes about through my prayer. Now what does that mean? It means that I can truly describe the fine day not just as a fine day but as an answer to my prayer, as a revelation to me of God's love, a sudden privileged glimpse of the generosity of God. The fine day becomes for me a sacrament of the love of God. Not a sacrament in the full sense precisely because it is just *for me* and not a revelation for the whole Church. It is *my* faith that has made me whole.

In the last analysis there is no *essential* difference between an apparently ordinary fine day becoming in my faith, for me personally, a medium of communication with the Father, a revelation in Christ, and the mystery of apparently ordinary bread and wine becoming in the faith of the whole Church the body of Christ himself. Of course there are differences: for instance the answers to my prayers are exuberant scintillations of God's revelation, God just does it for fun now and then, whereas the prayer of the whole Church as such, the sacramental prayer in the strict sense, is always answered. We can be *sure* that the apparently ordinary bread and wine have become the body of Christ; we cannot in the same way be sure of an answer to our personal prayer. Or perhaps we should put it more precisely: the answer to the prayer of the whole Church in the Eucharist is at one level *specified*; the bread and wine become the body of Christ (at another level, though, it is not specified, I mean at the level of what this will mean for those taking part). The answer to my private prayer on the other hand is not specified; it may be answered in ways I do not expect. More about this in a moment for I must hasten to add, lest there be heresy hunters around, that an ordinary, fine day does not change by being an answer to prayer whereas bread and wine *are* transformed into the body of Christ – but I don't at the moment want to go into eucharistic theology. I only want to point to the thing that the two have in common: when God makes it that the fine day shall really be an answer to my prayer, and when God makes it that bread and wine should really be the body and blood of Christ by involving it in the prayer of the whole Church, in both cases he is revealing himself, making us see (in faith of course) the meaning of his love. 'In faith of course' because the bystander will not see the bread and wine as the body of Christ. These revelations like all revelations are a matter of the divine life in us, part of our sharing into the life of the Trinity that we call faith.

Praying for the Right Things

Another final word about prayer of petition. It is something that I learned from Victor White OP and seems to me well worth passing on. Victor maintained that one important reason why people found it difficult to pray was that they prayed for the wrong things. By this he did *not* mean that they prayed for merely material things instead of for spiritual things; on the contrary he meant practically the exact opposite. He meant that people pray for things they don't really want but have been told that they ought to want. You feel you *ought* to want the grace to be nice to your next-door neighbour or you *ought* to want your mother-in-law to recover from her painful gumboil or you *ought* to want passionately to see a cure for AIDS, but as a matter of cold fact what you *really* want most of all is a short holiday in North Wales. But it would be 'selfish' to pray for that, so you resolutely turn your mind to more high-minded things. Victor maintained that what people call distractions in prayer are just their real wants and concerns breaking in on the bogus wants and concerns that we think are the only suitable ones for prayer. If you get 'distractions', he said, take a good look at them and see what wants and needs they spring from and pray about those – whatever they are. When you are really praying for what you really want you won't be distracted – the prayers of people on sinking ships are rarely troubled by distractions; they know exactly what they want. The prayer of petition is a matter of bringing ourselves, in the form of our wants and needs, into the presence of the Father. If we come before the Father not in our true selves but in a disguised and respectable form, pretending to be high-minded and altruistic saints, then we will not make any contact at all.

Prayer of petition is a form of self-exploration and at the same time self-realization. If we are honest enough to admit to our shabby infantile desires, then the grace of God will grow in us; it will slowly be revealed to us, precisely in the course of our prayer, that there are more important things that we truly do want. But this will not be some abstract recognition that we ought to want these things; we will really discover a desire for them in ourselves. But we must start where we are. Children will never mature if they are treated as adults from the age of two, with no concessions to their infantile emotional needs. Children must begin from where they actually are. Similarly we will never grow in the life of prayer if we begin by imagining that we are St John of the Cross. We have to begin in our own infantile imperfect grasping state. All that the Father requires of us is that we recognize ourselves for what we are. He will attend to the growing. He will grant the increase.

I think the process is expressed pretty well in a poem by the Hindu Rabindranath Tagore – which Rosemary Haughton quotes:

> Time after time I came to your gate
> with raised hands, asking for more and yet more.
> You gave and gave, now in slow
> measure, now in sudden excess.
> I took some, and some things I let
> drop; some lay heavy on my hands;
> Some I made into playthings and broke
> them when tired; till all the wrecks and
> the hoards of your gifts grew immense,
> hiding you, and the ceaseless expectation
> wore my heart out.
> Take, oh take – has now become my cry.
> Shatter all from this beggar's bowl:
> put out this lamp of the importunate
> watcher, hold my hands, raise me from
> the still gathering heap of your gifts
> into the bare infinity of your uncrowded presence.

Prayer, then, whatever stage we are at, is an entry into the mystery of the crucifixion of Christ, a sharing into the eternal exchange between Father and Son. That is why prayer is really a waste of time. The incarnate form of our prayer may be concerned with getting something done, forwarding our plans, and the generosity of God is such that he will let himself be incarnate even in these ways. But the very heart of prayer is not getting anything done.

It is a waste of time, an even greater waste of time than play. Play is after all something that can be justified in terms of getting something done, some human achievement. I do not mean that play can be reduced to a relaxation that fits someone to return to work – though our own production-obsessed society is in danger of thinking this. But play, even valued for its own sake, is not a total waste of time; it has to do with a certain kind of human achievement.

For a real absolute waste of time you have to go to prayer. I reckon that more than 80 per cent of our reluctance to pray consists precisely in our dim recognition of this and our neurotic fear of wasting time, of spending part of our life in something that in the end gets you nowhere, something that is not merely non-productive, non-money-making, but is even non-creative. It doesn't even have the justification of art and poetry. It is an absolute waste of time; it is a sharing into the waste of time which is the interior life of the Godhead. God is not in himself productive or creative. Sure he takes time to throw off creation, to make something, to achieve something. But the real interior life of the Godhead is not in creation, it is in the life of love which is the Trinity, the procession of Son from Father and of the Spirit from this exchange. God is not first of all our creator or any kind of maker. He is love, and his life is not like the life of the worker or artist but of lovers wasting time with each other uselessly. It is into this worthless activity that we enter in prayer. This, in the end, is what makes sense of it.

Note

1   London: C. A. Watts, 1970, p. 135.

PART TWO

ETHICS AND MORAL THEOLOGY

10

The Good Life

Is there something to be *discovered* which is, in fact, the good life? Could I be *mistaken* about the character of the good life and describe it in mistaken ways? Are moral judgements really statements which may be true or false, or are they merely expressions of a speaker's desires and feelings? And is there really such a thing as *the* good life? Or is there merely the kind of life that I or someone else would *like* people to live?

I think that the view that moral judgements are not true or false but merely expressions of feelings or desire is one of those philosophical positions that nobody would hold unless she thought she had to, unless she thought that any alternative position must be untenable. It is held in the way that John Locke (1632–1704) held that secondary qualities, like colours, do not belong to physical objects, or the way that Aquinas held that God brings about my free actions.[1] Both these very implausible-sounding views were held because the apparently common-sense alternative was thought to be impossible. (The fact that in my view, whereas Locke's implausible view was wrong, Aquinas's was right, is neither here nor there for present purposes.)

The common-sense view, held by most people, and even most off-duty philosophers, is that we are saying something *true* if we say that imprisoning innocent people is wrong or that rape is wicked. People who deny these propositions, we think, are not just bad (and perhaps not even bad), but mistaken. People only come round to thinking of such apparent propositions as expressions of will (of, for example, a sheer desire to bring about a society without such activities as rape) because they have become convinced that badness or wrongness *could not* be a property or characteristic, part of the description, of human activity; it could not be something we *observe* or *discover* in the world. They have become convinced that to say that some action is bad is to compare it with what it ought to be, and that what something ought to be is not an object of our experience. They have become convinced that we only see what is there and that when we look at the world we can only see what *is* the case, not what *ought* to be but is not the case. And they think that there is no way of deducing what ought to be from what is. What is the case, the facts, can be stated truly, or else we can be mistaken about them; but whether something ought or ought not to be, its value, can only be something we aspire to or want, or can only be something that we know others want.

You might think that we can save the objective, factual, status of values by claiming that *God* wants us to do certain things and not others. If values were simply a matter of *your* will or *mine*, they would be subjective and not a descriptive feature of things in the world. But, so someone might reason, since they are a matter of God's will, which is unchanging, we can make objective statements about values if we happen to know what it is that God wills. We would then mean by 'a bad action' 'something that God, as a matter of fact, wants us not to do, something that transgresses his commandment'. This would be an objective matter. It *is the case* that God does not want this done.

It would be an objective truth, however, at what I have called the second level. When we record that God does not want (has forbidden) some activity, we are speaking like the anthropologist who records that the Greeks did not want people to eat their dead parents. And nothing seems to follow from this about the nature of human activities in themselves, just as human activities. A view which would seek to make rational sense of ethical judgements simply in terms of the will or law of *God* is no less voluntarist than one which seeks to make sense of them in terms of *my* will. In neither case is any rightness or wrongness, goodness or badness, attributed to the human action because of what it is in itself.

So we seem left with, and thus compelled to, the view that it is one thing to give an account, a description, of what is the case, which, because it is 'value-free', will contain nothing but verifiable truths; and quite another human activity to speak of the moral value of this or that piece of behaviour: this latter does not tell us descriptive truths; it simply expresses the attitudes or options or feelings of the speaker, or, perhaps, of God. *Ought* (prescription) can never be derived from *is* (description). The classical statement of this conclusion comes from David Hume (1711–76). In his *A Treatise of Human Nature* he famously writes:

> In every system of morality, which I have hitherto met with, I have always remark'd, that the author proceeds for some time in the ordinary way of reasoning, and establishes the being of God, or makes observations concerning human affairs; when of a sudden I am surpriz'd to find, that instead of the usual copulations of propositions, *is*, and *is not*, I meet with no proposition that is not connected with an *ought*, or an *ought not*. This change is imperceptible; but is, however, of the last consequence. For as this *ought*, or *ought not*, expresses some new relation or affirmation, 'tis necessary that it shou'd be observ'd and explain'd; and at the same time that a reason should be given, for what seems altogether inconceivable, how this new relation can be a deduction from others, which are entirely different from it.[2]

'You cannot derive an *ought* from an *is*.' After Hume, this doctrine attained almost the status of a dogma in western European thinking.[3] It has, however, been questioned in recent times. And it is, indeed, highly questionable. The thing looks, in the first place, not quite so obvious if instead of talking about what *ought* to be, we talk about what is *good* or *bad*. For the kind of ethical thinking that I shall be trying to expound, doing what you *ought* is just one particular kind of morally good behaviour. It is behaviour that is sanctioned by just law, and obedience to such law is good because it is necessary for living in society, and living in society is part of the good life. So for this way of thinking *ought* is a secondary and derivative idea.

Let us, then, formulate the problem thus: Can we say that something is *good* because of what we know that it *is*?

People who follow Hume think that while you can, in principle, give a complete account of what a piece of human behaviour *is* in objective terms, upon which all observers can agree, you cannot derive from this the proposition that the behaviour is morally good or bad, that this is a subjective matter for each observer.

But this doctrine looks, in fact, pretty strange. For in every ordinary use of 'good' and 'bad', saying that something is *good* because of what it *is*, is *exactly* what we do. According to Humean thinkers, there is one tone of voice in which we say exactly what is being done, what a piece of human activity is, and quite another in which we praise it or say it is good or bad. But the truth seems to be that this separation of values from facts is ordinarily thought of as the mark of someone who is not very good at making value judgements, someone who is not a reliable guide to what is good or bad.

I once switched on the television and recognized, with a shudder, that it was showing yet another programme devoted to ice-skating. I was just about to change channels when I saw two people doing the most amazingly beautiful things. I was an instant convert to ice-skating, or, at least, to watching it, and I subsequently discovered they were people that everyone else had known about for months. I watched them avidly and incessantly. One day I was watching them and saying things like 'Beautiful', 'Lovely', 'Marvellous' – all expressions of value. With me was a friend who was equally enthusiastic but also knew something about ice-skating. He expressed his enthusiasm by saying things like 'Say, look at the way she did that …', and there followed a stream of arcane jargon. The air became thick with talk about double salchows, the toeless lutz, reverse walley jumps and the double cherry flip – all of which expressions were describing scientifically, and I suppose accurately, what my skaters had just done, or, in some cases, not done. It was I, the ignorant amateur, who used what are supposed to be pure value expressions, whereas the person whose opinions and value judgements were worthy of respect (the one whom my skaters would have been pleased to hear) expressed his view that something was *good* precisely by describing what it *was*. In this case, the account of what it was, *was* an account, and the best account, of it being good.

But, of course, an objector may say: 'That is all very well for ice-skating, but we are talking about morals. It is one thing to say that X is a good ice-skater and quite another to say she is a good person.' And this, of course, is true. But it would surely be very strange if the word 'good' in 'good skater' were used in some *totally* different way from its use in 'good person' – as though we were just making a pun with the word (a pun which, if it is such, is strangely made in many different languages). It would be very odd if 'good skater' could be spelt out in factual descriptions of what skaters do or can do (complex and open-ended descriptions, no doubt), whereas 'good person' were merely an expression of my feelings or desires.

I think people are forced into this very odd assertion because of a certain prejudice about persons. They are willing to agree that ice-skating is a particular definite art and activity – even though it is what I would call an open-ended activity. By calling it open-ended I mean that it is not just a technique which you either learn or do not learn. It is itself developing. What ice-skating henceforth involves will differ as new experts at it arise. Still, it is a definite human activity. These people I speak of, however, are unable to admit that human living, being a person, could be a definite human activity even in that open-ended sense. There may be many arts and skills within being human, but being human itself is not an art or skill. You may practice these arts well or badly, but you cannot practice being human itself well or badly. Now while I think, as I shall be saying, that there are important differences between those dispositions we call skills, such as are constitutive of being a good skater, and those dispositions we call virtues, which are constitutive of a good person, nevertheless I think that being humanly good involves something very like skills.

The bone of contention here is this: To call people ice-skaters is to speak of them in terms of a role or function or a job they perform which they can therefore perform well or badly. But when we call people human beings, are we in any sense ascribing some role or function to them which they could perform well or badly?

The answer which I shall label 'individualist' says that we are certainly not. The human subject simply exists and that is that. The philosophers called 'existentialists' were, I think, asserting this with especial emphasis. Saying that 'existence is prior to essence', they seem to have meant that people first of all just *are*, and what categories they may fit into, what kind of being they are, what relationships they have with others, is a subsequent and secondary matter determined, in the case of 'authentic' people, by their own choices. Human beings may, for their own purposes, ascribe functions to things. I may make a spoon in order to eat my porridge, and it will be a good one if it fulfils the purpose I have given it, and a bad one if it doesn't. In a similar way, a group of people may invent the art and institution of ice-skating and similarly decide what makes for good skating and what for bad; all these purposes are ascribed by the decisions human beings make. We cannot, says the individualist, in the same way speak of human beings themselves as having been ascribed a purpose or role. Of course, human beings can be *given* roles, as when we appoint them as teachers or carpenters, and then they may be judged on objective grounds as good or bad teachers or carpenters. But we do not appoint people to be human beings, and so we cannot on any objective grounds say that they are good or bad human beings. For this individualist way of thinking, *purposes and roles are always human artifacts*: there are no purposes prior to human decisions; there are no purposes for human beings in themselves.

For this way of thinking, human societies are themselves simply human artifacts. There is no difference in principle between the *polis* and a club which a few congenial friends might decide to set up. I have called this way of thinking 'individualist' because it starts from the position that to be human is simply to be an individual; we are not equipped at birth with any role or function; we ascribe roles or adopt them by our own decisions. It is because people believe this to be self-evidently true that they are compelled to say that the phrase 'good man' must be used in a totally different way from 'good skater' or 'good spoon'. In the latter cases, 'good' can be spelled out objectively in terms of what is the case about the skater or spoon because their goodness is functional; in the case of 'good man' it cannot, because to be human is not to have a function.

Now, one way of replying to the individualist is to say: 'Ah, but it is not only human beings that ascribe purposes. God, too, can do this, and he has given human beings a purpose: we are thus objectively good or bad insofar as we fulfil these divine purposes in our lives.' Now this could mean one or other of two quite distinct things. It might mean that God has *happened to* give human beings a purpose as, if I have lost one of my chessmen, I might happen to use a button as a pawn. In that case God might easily not have had any purposes for human beings to be good or bad at, but he has in fact given them these roles to play, these jobs to do, these commands to obey. But if this is what is meant, my role as a piece in God's game is not in principle different from my role as a skater or teacher. I might not have had, but in fact do have, this role as, say, a teacher, and in virtue of that I can be a good or bad teacher. But just as the role given me by the Education Committee concerns my being a good *teacher* and not, as such, a good *person*, so the role given me by God would not concern my being a good person. God happens to have given me the job of, say, honouring my father and mother, and because of this I can be judged as a good or bad honourer of my father and mother, just as I might be judged a good or bad teacher. But in neither case would I be judged a good or bad human being. The penalties for being a bad honourer of my father and mother may be stiffer than the penalties for being a bad teacher, but that does not make any difference in principle. This kind of appeal to God as a role-ascriber does not, therefore, help us to find an actual role or purpose for the human being as such.

The other thing that might be meant by the appeal to God is not that God simply *happened* to equip human beings with a job or role but that in creating them as human beings God created things that intrinsically and necessarily, and of their nature, have roles or functions. God could no more have created a human being without function than he could have created a triangle without three sides.

Well that is fine: but in that case there is no need to bring God in at all (just as you do not have to bring in God to explain why triangles have three sides). If what you are claiming is that God just had to provide human beings with a role to be good or bad in, if what he created were to be human beings because *that is the kind of thing that a human being is,* then you need to show that that *is* the kind of thing that a human being is. And if you can do *that,* you already have a sufficient answer to the individualist without mentioning God at all.

So the appeal to God is either inadequate or unnecessary. If the individualist is to be answered, it can only be by trying to show that just to be human is, in fact, to have certain roles or functions – so that we can speak of people being good or bad at being human just as we can speak of them being good or bad at ice-skating. And this, I think, *can* be shown starting from the fact that to be human is to be political, to be part of a *polis.*

Let me retrace the thread of the argument: I want to show that just being human (not being human *plus* being, for example, a teacher or a mineworker, but just being human) involves having a role or job, such that we can not only say of people that they are good or bad teachers or mineworkers, but just good or bad *tout court,* good or bad people, in a way that can be spelled out by describing how they behave. Certain kinds of objectively describable behaviour would count as a reason for saying that someone is good or bad *tout court*, just as certain kinds of behaviour would count as a reason for saying that someone is a good or bad teacher or ice-skater. To say 'He can give an accurate though simplified account of the notion of surplus value, intelligible to an audience of non-economists, in twenty minutes' just *is* to say that, in this respect, he is a good teacher. I want to argue that to say 'He would give you the shirt off his back' just *is* to say that, in this respect, he is a good man. In other words, 'good man' is a descriptive expression just as 'good teacher' is. And I argue this because I argue that everybody is ineluctably political. The reason why being human entails having certain functions to fulfil and roles to play (which may be done well or badly) is that to be human is to be part of a society of other human beings. To say 'This is a human being' is not like saying 'This is a red blob'. It is more like saying 'This is a gear-lever'. It would be hard to know what to make of the question 'Is this a good red blob?' But it is not at all hard to make sense of 'Is this a good gear-lever?'

Central to this argument is the claim that society is not the product of individual people. On the contrary, individual people are the product of society. There has to be at least some form of family society for people to be born at all and to survive and be brought up in a human way. And if you think of the family in the absolutely minimal terms of two parents producing a child, this structure itself depends on larger structures which ensure its survival and stability. The simplest social contract theory which supposes that individuals could come together initially for mutual support and protection to form a society is incoherent because it supposes these individuals to be already in possession of what only society could provide – institutions such as language, contract, agreement, and so on. The emergence of *homo sapiens* cannot have been (except maybe by a miracle) the evolution of strangely talented individuals. It must have been the evolution of new forms of animal grouping. We have to imagine the emergence of animal groups whose coherence is more and more a matter of conventional signs, language, rather than of innate signals. With this emergence of language, we begin to have rationality. Rationality is a special way of being in a group. It is because there is some form of linguistic community that there are rational individuals or 'persons'.

A linguistic community is a special sort of grouping in a very radical sense, for it changes the meaning of the word 'grouping'. The notions of whole and part are transformed. An individual person is, indeed, part of a society, but not simply in the sense that a gear-lever is part of a car. Individualism owes its popularity (despite its implausibility) to the sense people have that it must be wrong to treat persons as mere fragments or segments of a larger whole, as cogs or gear-levers. And this is understandable. There are, of course, totalitarian ways of thinking which are nothing but the obverse of individualism, which owe their popularity (despite their implausibility) to a craving people have to be treated as mere fragments of a larger whole, the craving to be rid of responsibility, to hand over decisions to the party, or the church, or the company, or the state. Both individualism and totalitarianism depend on the same mistake about the relationship of member and community in a symbol-using society. They see it as just like the relationship of part and whole in a pre-linguistic, non-rational group.

In the new kind of grouping, however, the linguistic community, what the part receives from the whole – language and rationality, the symbols in which she can represent herself to herself – are precisely what makes possible her specially human kind of individuality.

Let us contrast human individuals with cats. All cats are individuals; but this is because they are all born different and have had different things happening to them. But human beings are distinct from each other not just because of that. What they are like is the product not just of birth and what has happened to them but of their own rational decisions. Because we represent our *world* to ourselves symbolically, and because we can represent *ourselves* to ourselves symbolically, we can make free choices which determine our individuality. Our individual characters are importantly the product of our own decisions – though not, of course, only of our free decisions. It is just because of our insertion in the symbolic institutions of the linguistic society that we can, to a greater or lesser extent, make ourselves, possess ourselves and be free.

Moreover, we are free just to the extent that we are inserted in this human way into human community. It is the child who has been welcomed into the society of her family and friends, and encouraged to play a full part in it, who is able to be herself and be free. She has acquired the self-confidence and self-acceptance that comes of being accepted by others. And so it is at every level: it is by being parts that we are wholes. Community and individuality are not rivals. The individual who can stand over against the community, who can make a critical contribution to the tradition of the community, who can make a genuine contribution to revolution, is the product of that community and tradition. The individual, you might say, is the way in which a linguistic community develops itself historically. Other animal groupings do not have individuals in this sense. They do not have a *history*. They only evolve.

So it is through belonging to the community that you can make yourself the kind of person you are – so that you are not just passively made but actually make yourself, determine your life and character. In this way you make yourself the kind of person who can yet more make herself, whose life is more and more her own. This is, to speak generally, the role or task or function that belongs to being human. It is the task of entering more into the life of the community so that you can enter yet more; or, what is the same thing, it is forming your personality by your own decisions so that you have the personality which is more and more capable of making its own decisions. And this, still speaking generally, is what virtue is about. Virtues are dispositions to make choices which will make you better able to make choices. The aim of virtue is to be virtuous. Or, to go back to the other way of putting it, virtues are dispositions to enter into community, not to be absorbed in some lifeless way by a collective, but to develop those specifically symbolic, linguistic, rational relationships with others which we can sum up in the word 'friendship' and which are characteristic of the groupings of human animals.

This is, of course, to speak generally. There are many virtues and, while they all have as their long-term aim the community life of persons, they are each concerned with particular human activities. And a study of the virtues must be a study of the manifold ways in which people interact in the community of friendship.

If this is true (and I have only sketched it in the crudest way), there are many objections to be answered and qualifications to be made. But if it is true, then since to be a human being is to have the task of making yourself, the task of entering into the life of the community so that your life is more and more your own, then we have a basis for saying that, just as a good teacher is one who teaches well, so a good human being is one who enters into community well. The good human being is the one who is, in this sense, politically good. Aristotle's *Ethics* is simply the first part of his treatise on politics, on the life of the *polis*. If this is so, we ought to be able to describe what a good human being is in much the same way as we can describe what a good teacher is.

I am far from suggesting that you can easily describe what a good teacher is, or lay down simple rules for good teaching. It is fairly clear what a good typist is: he types accurately, neatly and quickly, and that is it. Typing is simply a technique. It is not so easy to say what a good secretary is, for acting as a secretary involves many techniques. Being a teacher is more open-ended still, and being a human being immensely more so. There are clear rules for what counts as good typing. We cannot be anything like so clear about what counts as a good human being. Still we can say quite a lot. And that is what ethics is about.

What I have been saying has all been exceedingly abstract – far more abstract than, for example, Aristotle allows himself to be in his *Ethics*. There does not exist such a thing as a community in general any more than there is such a thing as a horse in general. There is, perhaps, not yet even a community in general in the sense of a single community of mankind of which particular communities are parts. There is certainly a single biological community, a 'family of man', a species in which we are all interfertile. But there is not yet a single political community. There are only particular geographical and historical communities, and to be a human being is to be born and brought up in one (or sometimes more) of these, with its own culture and tradition. A human being does not become herself by entering into community in general or into humankind, but by being educated into and responding creatively and critically to the tradition of her place and time.

The process of being educated in virtue is not one just of acquiring ideas. It is a matter of day-to-day living amongst particular structures and customs, as distinct from other structures and customs. It is in this sense a material business, a matter of this human body amongst others, even though the *way* of being amongst is not simply bodily in the sense that, say, a chip is amongst others in a computer, or even in the way that a wolf is amongst others in a pack. It is, as I have said, a matter of being amongst others through symbols and conventional signs. But these are still particular material symbols. Every language is a particular material language. The symbols of a society involve myths, manners, stories and language that belong especially to this people and not to others.

So even if we can show how we might make the phrase 'a good person' a descriptive expression in one culture, we have not yet shown how it might be universalized, how we might have a meaning for it which could be universalized, how it could be valid just for anybody of any culture who belonged to the human species. We face here the relationship of the biological and the historical/political, the two senses of human unity. And this is not just a theoretical but a practical problem. I suspect that we can speak of 'natural law' just to the extent that we have solved the practical political problem of bringing the biological and historical together, insofar as we have achieved 'one world', and not just one species.

Once we have taken account of the linguistic, the political, the historical (in order to make our case for seeing human beings as functional, role-playing beings), we have departed from the universality of the sheer biological species. Of course, membership of the biological species itself involves certain roles, especially sexual ones. But the natural life of a human being is immensely more complex than her sexual and species life alone. So although I can share my sexual *productivity* universally, being in principle interfertile with any member of the species of the opposite sex, when we come to cultural and moral creativity (and, thus, a transformed sexual creativity) – the activity by which I can create, not just the next generation, but myself and my own generation – we are in the realm of the local.

Notes

1   For Locke, see *An Essay Concerning Human Understanding* (1689), Book II, Chapter VIII. For Aquinas, see *De Potentia*, 3, 1.

2   *A Treatise of Human Nature*, Book III, Part I, Section 1. I quote from p. 469 of David Hume, *A Treatise of Human Nature*, ed. L. A. Selby-Bigge, 2nd edn, revised by P. H. Nidditch (Oxford: Clarendon Press, 1978).

3   In a famous paper, 'Hume on "Is" and "Ought"' (*The Philosophical Review* LXVIII [1959]), Alasdair MacIntyre argues that, in the text I have just quoted, Hume is not, in fact, propagating an is/ought dichotomy but merely attacking one particular way (by an appeal to belief in God) of deriving what ought to be from what is. Hume does this, says MacIntyre, in order to prepare the way for his own more 'Aristotelian' appeal to human passions and desires. It seems to me, however, that, on the face of it, there is a difference between Hume's appeal to our empirically 'observed' passions and the Aristotelian appeal to human needs, interests, desires and happiness. MacIntyre himself stresses this in later writings. Cf. *After Virtue* (London: Duckworth, 1981), esp. Ch. 16.

11

Politics and Virtue

To be a human being is to be a part of a larger whole. It is not just that human beings *join* groupings, as people join tennis clubs or political parties. There is a community to which we belong simply in virtue of being human. It is not one that we join, one that *we* constitute. It is a community that constitutes *us*. But what does this mean? In turning to this question I first want to compare and contrast our belonging to a community with the way in which other animals belong to a greater whole.

To be a dog is to be part of the species of dog. This is not merely a logical matter; it is not like saying that the dog belongs to the class of animals whose names in English begin with 'd' or to the class of four-footed beasts. When we say a dog belongs to a certain species we are referring to a distinct material entity, the race of dogs which has existed for a certain amount of time, has a certain evolutionary development and so on, and of which the dog is a physical part. There is no way of being a dog except by being born of members of this species. A very great deal of the important facts about a dog have to do with its derivation from this species – for example, a great deal of its behaviour can only be explained on this basis. An individual dog is the way the species is carried on (the way in which certain genes persist).

Now the same, of course, is true of the animal species *homo sapiens*. But in our case the thing becomes much more complex because what we belong to is not just a biological species. It is also some kind of linguistic community.

And, while political or social communities constitute us rather in the way the biological species does, we also creatively respond to and modify them. Indeed, the linguistic community just *is* a community of such responsive and creative animals. In order to preserve itself in being, to be what it is, the linguistic community has to maximize the creativity of its members. If its members were determined by the community in the absolute way in which the individuals of a species are determined by their genetic structure, there would not *be* any linguistic community.

So there is a complexity or tension intrinsic to a linguistic community – at least by contrast with any mechanistic model of it. One cannot understand such a community successfully on the model of the parts going together to make a machine, or even on the model of the organs together forming an animal body (though that is a good deal nearer to the truth). It is characteristic of an animal that its parts are *organs* (tools, instruments). Their parts each have a life of their own which is simultaneously the life of the whole animal. The eye and brain of the dog have an operation quite distinct from the operation of the nose and brain. But both are the seeing and smelling of the animal as a whole. That is why what they do *counts* as seeing and smelling. Eyes cannot see, only the animal with eyes. This fact about an animal *is* the fact that it is alive; this is what Aquinas would refer to as its being animate, having an *anima* (soul).[1]

Now this supplies us with a quite useful, even if inadequate, model for the linguistic community in which each member has an operation which is simultaneously the operation of the totality. This operation is the creation of *meanings*, which is the use of material things, like movements and sounds and marks, as *signs*. When I indulge in such creation I cease to be acting just as me, just as *this* individual. I enter into the language. That is why my statements, for example, are not just bits of *my* biography but have an objectivity, which transcends me. This is connected with the interesting fact that in the sentence 'I think that p' (where p stands for any proposition you like) the clause 'I think that ...' can always be dropped without loss (except in the special usage in which 'I think' means 'I'm not sure', or in the usage according to which you are supposed to take note, not of what I think, but of the fact that *I* think it). 'I think that p' is not, in general, a statement about *me* at all. Its role is just to assert that p is the case.

This means that in creating meanings, in using language, I behave in a way that is not simply individual. Aquinas makes the same point when he says that the act of understanding is not a corporeal act, that when understanding I transcend my materiality, which for him is my individuality.[2] Matter for him is the principle of individuation, of privacy. Averroes (Ibn Rushd, 1126–98) took this point very seriously. He maintained that there is no such thing as an individual mind. There is but one mind (as we might say, the language, the *discourse*) and we individually latch onto that. For Averroes, what is particular to each of us is not strictly our understanding, which is universal, but the images we form when we think, which are material. Aquinas wrote one of the great western philosophical classics, a little book called *De Unitate Intellectus contra Averroistas*, to argue that Averroes and his fans were going too far. In my thoughts, Aquinas agrees, I do indeed transcend my individuality. But, he says (and surely correctly), my thoughts are still *my* thoughts and no one else's. In some ways, Averroes resembled certain modern structuralists for whom: (a) thoughts are in a language which speaks *through* the individual; and (b) literature is the product not of the private genius of the individual but of the culture or language itself. If Aquinas were writing today, I think he would, amongst other things, be engaged in literary theory, trying to steer a way between the older notion of the individual genius (with the 'author's intention') and the disappearance of the individual altogether in structuralism. For Aquinas, the spiritual is the *communal*. It is the immaterial, while materiality is individuality, privacy, subjectivity, isolation. So Aquinas speaks of even the animal senses as 'spiritual' because their operation is also an operation of the 'community', the whole animal to which they belong.

This, of course, places Aquinas at the opposite pole from the Cartesian way of thinking according to which it is the spiritual that is private (a matter of my subjective consciousness) while it is the material, the body, that is public. For Descartes, we reach our real spiritual selves by withdrawing from the public material outside world into our own centres of consciousness. Not so for Aquinas.

It is true that Aquinas very frequently uses the metaphor of 'interior' versus 'exterior' when speaking of our spiritual or immaterial activities. It was a metaphor he inherited from Augustine. But he never speaks of subjectivity or *privacy*. My thoughts really are *my* thoughts, he insisted against Averroes. But they are not, and could not be, my *private* thoughts, except in the trivial sense that I do not always have to read or talk aloud. For Aquinas, I can use the common public language in which my thoughts are formulated to speak silently to myself as well as to speak to others. And, so Aquinas thinks, nobody need know what I think since I can keep a secret and tell lies. For him, however, that is not to say that thoughts are *essentially* private.

This very brief, and perhaps not very intelligible, excursus into Aquinas's theory of mind is intended to show how we are constituted as who we are not just biologically, by the species, but also culturally, spiritually, by the linguistic community, the *polis* in which we live. A *polis*, says Aristotle,

> is something more than a pact of mutual protection or an agreement to exchange goods and services; for in that case [separate states like the] Etruscans and Carthaginians, and all others with contractual obligations to each other, would be taken as citizens of a single *polis*. Certainly, they have trade-agreements, no aggression pacts, and written documents governing their alliance. But this is very different from being one polis with one citizenship … neither is concerned with the *quality* of the citizens of the other, or even with their behavior, whether it be honest or dishonest, except in dealings with members of the other *polis*. But all who are concerned with

lawful behavior must make it their business to have an eye on the goodness or badness of the citizens. It thus becomes evident that that which is genuinely and not just nominally a *polis* must concern itself with virtue. Otherwise, the community (*koinonia*) is a mere alliance .... The *polis* is intended to enable all, in their households and their kinships, to live *well*, meaning by that a perfected and independent life.[3]

Aristotle is not, I think, suggesting that there might simply be an alliance or a non-aggression agreement *instead* of there being a *polis*. On the contrary, what he means by an alliance can only subsist between what are already constituted as states. What he is arguing against is an attempt to construe the *polis* itself as a very minimal kind of relationship, like an international agreement or a trade-post – the attempt, in fact, of modern neo-conservatism. He goes on: 'There arise in the *polis* the family connections, brotherhood, common sacrifices, games which draw men together. But these are created by friendship, for the will to live together is friendship. The end of the *polis* is the good life and these are the means towards it.'[4]

So to summarize: the *polis* is that because of which there are linguistic animals at all, and the purpose of the *polis* is that these animals should flourish, should live the life becoming to them, which is simply to live fully in the *polis*. In this sense, by existing so that its members may lead the good life, the *polis* exists *for its own sake*. For Aristotle, politics is the study of how to maintain the *polis* and the first part of that study is ethics. This is the background to Aquinas's treatment of virtues. He says: 'Since man by his nature is a political animal, moral virtues, insofar as they are natural to him, are called political virtues, for on them depends his behaving well in social life.'[5] This interesting text is not, indeed, central to Aquinas's treatment of virtues. In it he is simply explaining the term 'political virtues' (an expression in use in his time). But it illustrates very well the Aristotelean assumptions in his thinking.

The *polis*, then, needs that people should be virtuous. It is also the means by which people become virtuous and grow in virtue. This is what the *polis* is for, so we are here speaking of the healthy *polis*, the one that fulfils its function, one that really grows as a *polis*. This, of course, provides us with a critical standard by which we may judge any particular historical society. To what extent does it foster the virtues of its citizens? Aristotle laments the state of Athens 'nowadays' by comparison with 'the old days': 'Formerly, as is natural, every one would take his turn of service [sc. in political office]; and then again, somebody else would look after his interest, just as he, while in office, had looked after theirs. But nowadays, for the sake of the advantage which is to be gained from the public revenues and from office, men want to be always in office.'[6]

Well, of course, we are all a bit like that. So any actual society is not only the source of virtue for its citizens but also corrupt and the target of the virtuous person's criticism and challenge. But even the most corrupt society with a ruling class bent almost exclusively on its own private material advantage needs that its citizens should be inclined to act justly. It is not simply that it needs that people should do the things that justice demands, like telling the truth and not defrauding each other (for people might do these things out of fear of punishment or for some other reason); it is necessary that people should themselves be *inclined* to act in this way, be disposed to act in this way, and this is for them to have acquired the virtue of justice. People who are disposed in this way, people who love justice, are, of course, very liable to become a threat to the ruling class of a corrupt society. But this is just one of the contradictions inherent in the unjust society – it cannot afford to guard against the threat by getting rid of justice altogether. That would be to descend from free enterprise and competition into sheer chaos.

One who has the virtue of justice, then, is one who has learnt to want the things that are just. It is not that he acts justly because he wants to *have* something else, like honour, or to *avoid* something, like prison. Honesty may well be, in the end, the best policy, and that, perhaps, is why it is a virtue at all. But, as Archbishop Whateley of Dublin (1787–1863) says in the *Oxford Dictionary of Quotations*: 'Honesty is the best policy; but he who is governed by that maxim is not an honest man.' A child learns to read initially because she wants to please her parents or teachers, so the reading is seen as good because it has good ulterior consequences. This shows itself in the fact that if those same consequences can be achieved in some other, and perhaps easier, way (say by pretending to read a passage that is known off by heart) the child may well prefer to do this. Similarly, the man who does the just thing for the sake of praise and honour might do an unjust thing if the same reward were available for it. But in consequence of continued reading at her parents' behest, the child in most cases discovers that books are delightful in themselves and that reading is a good and pleasant way of spending time. She enters whole new worlds of imagination and so on. She is now reading for its own sake and there is no longer any point in ever pretending to read. It is the good *intrinsic* to reading that she seeks, no longer an ulterior consequence. Now education involves a similar process with regard to acting justly. We begin by acting well because we want to please our parents or others. We end by wanting to be the kind of person who is just and not cowardly and so on, just as the child wants to be a reading person: in both cases, it is a matter no longer of pleasing the grown-ups, but wanting to *be* grown-up.

The just person is one to whom the just thing appeals. We may contrast that with the law-abiding person. True, the just person will in many (perhaps most) cases be law abiding, but there is a difference. By 'the law-abiding person' I mean one who acts in a certain way precisely because the law commands it. Her formal object, you might say, is the law itself. It is the keeping of the law that matters to her, not precisely the nature of the action done. Such a person, then, will do *whatever* the law commands; and what counts as a command of the law is to be determined by discovering who is the legitimate authority and what this authority has in fact decreed. In this sense, the law-abiding person applies an *external* criterion to the action. I mean that when you have described the action in human terms, it is an *additional*, external fact that it is commanded or prescribed by some authority. The just person, however, who acts because she loves justice, or out of justice, is not applying an *external* criterion. For to be just is to want, to be disposed, to do things that are just. And whether something is just, unlike whether it is commanded, depends simply on the nature of the action itself. A disposition is internally related to its object. The disposition of justice is simply the disposition to do just things and to refrain from unjust things. So the virtue has to be defined by beginning with the nature of the things that are just, and this we will be looking into in a moment.

First, though, there are two questions I should like to open for discussion. The first is this: I mentioned earlier that in the statement 'I think that p' the first three words are in some way both misleading and redundant. They make it look as though the statement were a proposition about me, as though 'I' were the name of the subject being talked about. In fact, this is not so, as is shown by the redundancy of the apparent reference to me. This, I suggested, is connected with the speaker's capacity to transcend her individuality and materiality. Now it seems to me that 'I want to do X' is a rather similar case. It looks on the face of it like a piece of autobiography just as 'I think that p' looks like a piece of autobiography. But in neither case are we dealing with a statement about a subject (me) that is named by the first word of the sentence, 'I'. In 'I want to do X', the first two words are almost as redundant as the first three words in 'I think that p'. If you shave them off, you get simply 'to do X'. Now that, of course, unlike 'p', is not a sentence, at least not an ordinary one, but a clause, and so the cases are not exactly the same. Nevertheless, there are even English usages in which 'to do X' would be a sentence. Hamlet says: 'To sleep: perchance to dream: ay, there's the rub ...' Now, here 'To sleep' is not just the name of an action or whatever. It expresses a wanting to sleep (the sleep of death) which is then checked by the thought of the dreams. There is in any case no difficulty at all in imagining a language in which desires would always be expressed simply by sentences like 'O, to be in England', or 'O, to get my hands round his throat'. This would have the advantage that such expressions would not be likely to be confused with autobiographical remarks about the speaker. The speaker both in 'I want to do X' and in 'O, to do X' is saying the same thing. She is indicating that doing X is concretely (not just in a general way) *desirable*. She is not talking about herself. Just as the speaker in 'I think that p' is indicating that p is *true*, she is not talking about herself.

I mean to suggest that 'I want to do X' differs in an important way from 'I would get a kick out of doing X', which *does* seem to talk about me, to add a piece of autobiography. Of course, '*I* think that p' differs a great deal from '*She* thinks that p', which is a piece of biography and in which the first three words are by no means redundant. Similarly, '*She* wants to do X' is a piece of biography. But 'I want to do X' does not itself say anything about me; it expresses a desire to do X, or, what is the same thing, expresses the concrete desirability of doing X. 'I want to do X' no more announces the discovery of the fact that I have a desire in me than 'I think that p' announces the discovery that I have a thought in me.

The second thing I want to notice before going on to asking what just actions are is that the virtue of justice raises what we might call the 'Thrasymachus question' in its purest form.[7] Let me explain.

Suppose we establish that people need society; and suppose we establish that society needs people to be just. Does it follow that people need to be just?

Thrasymachus – but, for the sake of brevity, let us henceforth call him Fred instead – certainly needs society. He needed it in order to be born, to learn to speak and to receive all the education, all the skills, that he has. And this society could not have existed without there being a preponderance of people who acted justly most of the time. And this could not have been achieved unless most of them possessed to some degree the virtue of justice. You could not have a literate society unless most people got beyond the stage of reading to please others and arrived at the state of reading for their own enjoyment.

Similarly, you could not, I think, have a society in which people acted justly unless most of them had got beyond the state of simply doing it out of desire for rewards or fear of punishments.

Fine: but is there any reason that Fred could have as to why *he* should be just? Fred, we may suppose, is perfectly prepared to act justly when it is rewarded, but equally prepared to act unjustly when that brings *its* rewards. This means, by our account of the matter, that he is not a just man. Now why should he be (so long as other people are)?

I do not think that it is a valid answer to say that, as a mater of fact, in the long run justice always will be rewarded and injustice punished by the all-seeing God. This is not because Fred may doubt the existence of such a celestial police force and tribunal, but because to do just acts simply from calculation of celestial rewards and punishments is not to act justly. Christians, for example, hold that to do just acts simply and solely to avoid going to hell will not prevent you from going to hell. What will prevent you from going to hell is charity, and that is quite different.

I would try to answer this question (Why should Fred be just?) by first noting that I address my answer to Fred. I am trying to give *him* a reason for being just. A great deal now hangs on what *for him* would count as a reason for doing anything. Now being just is *itself* having certain kinds of reasons for doing things or not doing them. A just man will see it as a good reason for not making a confession under threat of torture that it would be cowardly. To have a virtue *is* to count certain considerations as reasons for acting.

Perhaps it is the case, then, that Fred who asks 'Why should I be just?' is simply an unjust man asking *his* typical questions: What's in this for me? What is the external reward or punishment involved in doing this or being like this? Now these are just the questions I might imagine a child asking before she can read. (Of course, being a child, she would be unlikely to ask the question, but she would behave as one who had asked and answered the question by saying: 'In order to please these grown-ups, or at least not to offend them'.)

This fact about the child does not throw us into philosophical perplexity. We simply set about teaching her. She will find out for herself reasons for thinking it intrinsically good to be able to read (to acquire and develop the disposition or skill of reading). And what is true of the literate child is also true of the non-just child. She too discovers in doing just acts that their desirability does not lie simply in, as she first supposed, pleasing the grown-ups. She finds them intrinsically desirable. Now perhaps the difference between Fred and the child lies in nothing more than that he asks the question explicitly in a way that the child would be unlikely to. If so, the proper response is not to seek to answer this question in his terms, but to do for Fred what we do for the child – persuade him to do what is in fact just in the hope that he will begin to find justice desirable for its own sake.[8]

Now, there is a fairly obvious objection to all this. When the child or Fred grows up to value justice 'for its own sake', and not for love of rewards or fear of punishments, is he not simply *internalizing* these rewards and punishments? Have we not simply succeeded in creating in him a super-ego so that he is pleased with himself when he has pleased his internal monitor and feels guilt when he has displeased it. Whether the monitor is external or internal to Fred makes no difference to the real question, which is whether the good Fred sees in doing the just act is external or internal to that act. Someone who does just acts in order to be praised by his conscience is no more just than someone who does them to be praised by other people – that is, if you mean by 'conscience' a 'still small voice' or super-ego.

This objection is powerful because it does seem to describe accurately what often happens. We do often induce just such a super-ego or 'still small voice of conscience' which is no more than an internalizing of the pleasing-the-grown-up phase. But I would argue that in that case the educational process has failed. Supposing a child did indeed get beyond the phase of reading to please her teacher, but then merely passed into a phase in which she read because she felt guilty not to. (This is not an altogether imaginary case. Lots of people read Dostoievsky or Proust because they would feel guilty if they did not.) In such a case, the external teacher has simply been internalized, but the educational process has failed. It has failed because the child has not come to recognize the goods internal to reading. Can we not similarly say that the person with the super-ego or conscience has simply failed to see the goods internal to acting justly?

I think that if we are to make this comparison (between the skill of reading and the virtue of justice) stick, I need to say a little more about what happens when the child discovers the goods inherent to reading. It is not just that she experiences a new sensation which she happens to like. Someone who has hitherto only really liked sweet sherry might come to discover the pleasure of a light dry claret; someone whose chief indulgence has been in eating Turkish Delight might be startled to find how delicious curry can be. In such cases, there is undoubtedly a progress because a new pleasant sensation has been found. But so far as that goes the progress might have been the other way round, from claret to sweet sherry, from curry to Turkish Delight. In either case, it would have been a simple addition to the catalogue of nice tastes.

Now discovering the goods inherent to reading is *not* like that. It involves something we might call an enlargement of the capacity for experience. The child finds a new way of being in the world. The world is no longer restricted to what she and her immediate circle experience. She can share the experience and imagination of vast numbers of others. She has, most importantly, discovered a new activity, a new way of being *active*, which is very different from discovering a new sensation, a new way of being *passive*. In fact, learning to enjoy story-books and other books is part of growing up. It is the kind of thing that (except for special accidental circumstances) *no one could ever regret*. To have discovered the goods inherent to reading is to have become in one respect a more fulfilled, a more excellent person with many more possibilities and opportunities open to one.

Now when I want Fred to become just, it is this sort of thing I want for him. The problem is merely to get *him* to want it for himself. I think that the only way to do this is to discover the complex things that he does want (which will turn out to be by no means simply pleasing sensations), and to indicate how the practice of just acts is involved in these activities and how the disposition to act fairly is needed for them, so that he begins to recognize his own desirable activity as involving justice together with other virtues and thus begins, perhaps slowly, to see that justice is desirable. It is not just an argument or just a way of acting, a regime that we are prescribing for Fred, but an 'argumentative regime', a matter of reasoned practice or of the practical reason. I will convince Fred that he has reason to be just, not merely by talking (theoretical or 'speculative' reason) nor by brainwashing, simply bullying him into doing just actions for so long that he begins to bully himself (the development of a super-ego or conscience), but by persuading him to engage in reasoned activity, activity in which he is analysing what he is doing and why: exercising him in the question, given the facts, 'What is it reasonable to do?' In fact, Fred and I would be engaged in what Aristotle or Aquinas would recognize as ethics – a study which is not simply about how to *talk* about being good but is intended to *make* people good as well. For Aristotle, ethics was part of politics. In our own day, very little that he would see as ethics is taught in the philosophy departments of universities (or at least not until very recently). The people he would recognize as doing ethics today would be people engaged in a certain kind of political thinking. Aristotle would most certainly have deep disagreements with Marxist thinkers, but when he heard them say 'Philosophers have sought to explain the world, the point is to change it', he would recognize them as at least on his wavelength. However wrong they may be, what they are wrong about *is* ethics.

So part of our task with Thrasymachus or Fred is to show him that acting justly is involved in things he wants to do and engage in. A preliminary to this is getting rid of his illusion that what he wants is not to engage in activities and do things, but simply passively to receive experiences. It is, or at least it used to be, quite a common belief amongst philosophers that a man might hold that the only reason for doing anything is to get an experience (a pleasant, satisfying experience) as a result. The logic of this view is that if you could get the experience some other more convenient way you would not bother with the activity. Aquinas in discussing what he calls *beatitudo*, blessedness, the end of human activity, begins by asking if it could be constituted by what amounts to various kinds of experience. He ends by arguing that it has to be itself an activity. Fundamentally, his reason for thinking this is that it is in its proper activity that a thing reaches its perfection. It exists, so to say, at full stretch; it is itself most fully.[9]

One convenient modern device for making the same point is Robert Nozick's 'Experience Machine'.[10] You have to imagine some kind of tank in which you can float and in which you can be plugged into electronic devices which stimulate your brain to receive any experience you choose, in any variety you choose. The only stipulation is that you will have to be in the machine for the rest of your life.

The first part of the 'thought experiment' is to ask whether you yourself would choose to be plugged into any series of pleasurable bodily sensations as you lay in the tank. To answer 'No' to this is to see the point of Aquinas's rejection of such pleasure as equivalent to blessedness.

But the machine is more versatile than that: it can go through the successive articles of *Summa Theologiae* 1a2ae,2, giving you experiences of being rich, honoured and famous. And, finally, it can give you the sensation and pleasure of activity. It can simulate for you all the experience you would have in winning the London and New York Marathons, or discovering the cure for cancer, or writing a play as great as *King Lear*. Now how about that? Would you choose a lifetime in which you have these experiences while as a matter of fact you are doing none of these things but simply floating in a tank in a laboratory? The question is: Would you now choose to be so plugged in, not would you enjoy yourself once plugged in. Once plugged in you would in fact be unable to want your situation changed. So this too depends on your decision now.

To discover that you would not want this illusion, however satisfying, is to discover that it is not the *satisfying* but the *satisfactory* life that we really want. By 'satisfactory', I mean (etymologically) the sufficiently (*satis*) made (*factum*) life, the life which in actual *fact* is fulfilled. It is, as John Finnis points out in his discussion of the Experience Machine, to see the point of Aristotle's remark that 'no-one would choose to live with the intellect of a child throughout his life, however much he were pleased at the things that please children'.[11] As Finnis puts it, 'The experience machine could give you the experience of writing a great novel or overcoming danger in company with a friend; but in fact you would have done nothing, achieved nothing. When in the end your brain rotted in the tank, it could be said of you that from the time you plugged in until you died "you never lived"'.

Now, if Fred will come along with us thus far – if he recognizes that his happiness lies not in experiences themselves but in certain kinds of activities – then it may be possible to show him the worth of justice and other virtues by showing how they are implied in such activities.

There is a very large (perhaps indefinite) number of complex fairly large-scale activities which people find worthwhile and wish to engage in. Plainly, I am not going to even try to deal with them all or to find any general principles upon which we could deal with them in bulk. What we need to do is to look at each such activity as it occurs to us and see how in fact it is carried on.

I am going to instance making and maintaining a family. I am concerned here with what Peter Geach calls 'large-scale worthy enterprises' and Alasdair MacIntyre calls 'practices'. These are all parts of what Aquinas calls political or social life. Aquinas sets this within the context of what he calls *the* end of man, blessedness (*beatitudo*), and he seeks to show that the political virtues, the cardinal virtues, take their place in the deepest meaning of human life, which is our vocation to the heavenly *polis*, the divine life. Philosophers of the kind that we might call neo-Aristoteleans often agree in rejecting Aquinas's argument to show that there is one last end for mankind. They accuse him of the familiar logical slip of moving from 'every human activity has some end' to 'there is some end that every human activity has' (i.e. some one end). I am inclined to think they are right about this – though of course the fact that Aquinas produces a bad argument for some doctrine does not make that doctrine false. I would like to argue that the place for considering the unit of mankind's purpose, the single last end common to all people of all cultures, is at the *end* of the study of ethics rather than the beginning. I agree with Geach that there are sufficient grounds for seeing the virtues as goods and for under-standing, at least in part, their significance if we simply look at the 'large-scale worthwhile activities' in which people do in fact want to engage.[12] When we have done that, if we discover a necessity for the virtues, then we can widen our sights to the whole political community (politics as the greatest large-scale worthwhile activity), and from there to what we might call the politics of mankind. And it is here that we will see coming towards us the politics of the Bible, meeting us from, so to say, the other direction.

But for the moment let us just consider the various large-scale activities: I mean large-scale by contrast with, say, knitting or bricklaying. Here is MacIntyre's attempt to give an account of what he calls a 'practice' in one large-scale complex worthwhile sentence. Remember when reading it that he has in mind some such activity as 'the making and sustaining of family life'.

By 'practice' I am going to mean any coherent and complex form of socially established cooperative human activity through which goods internal to that activity are realized in the course of trying to achieve those standards of excellence which are appropriate to and partially definitive of that form of activity, with the result that human powers to achieve excellence, and human conceptions of the ends and goods involved are systematically extended.[13]

Let us look at that as an account of making and maintaining a family life, which is quite likely to be one of the activities that Fred may want to engage in.

Having and maintaining a family as an activity of parents is complex, coherent (in the sense that it is a distinguishable form of activity with its own pattern to it) and, of course, co-operative – and here the cooperation is a matter not only of relations between the two parents and their children but also many other agents and agencies essential to family life, like grocers, schools and so on.

In maintaining a family we are concerned with goods internal to activity. That is: we do not maintain a family in order to realize some good which might have been attained some other way. In this sense, running a family is 'for its own sake'. These goods are achieved in the course of trying to achieve certain standards of excellence that belong to running families (making sure that the children are healthy, adequately fed and clothed, educated and so on, that the family forms a coherent unity in friendship, that it plays its part as a family in appropriate social activities, hospitality and all the rest) with the result that human powers to achieve these excellences are systematically extended, so that not only do these parents get better at the job but throughout a section of history the activity of maintaining a family becomes better understood and practiced. And finally throughout such a personal life and such a history the idea of what a family *is*, and what the goods are that belong to it, are gradually revised and extended. To put it simply, by trying in practice to be good parents we deepen our notion of what it is to be a parent.

You may well feel that in these last respects the family is not a particularly good example to take. It is highly debatable whether the modern family is a great improvement on families of the past – though hardly debatable that it is an improvement on some, especially in the more recent past. But this is where it matters that all our practices are interlocking and the family is radically affected by changes in the economy and in society in general. MacIntyre's own preferred examples of practices are such things as the practice of physics or portrait-painting or architecture.

Now if you think of what is involved in engaging in such a practice as running a family it becomes clear fairly soon that it cannot be done unless it is possible to rely on the justice of others and unless others can rely on your inclination to act justly. Without this there could not be the stability over time and over varying circumstances that is essential to rearing a family. Faithfulness to vows, regard for the rights of husbands and children and wives is plainly required – and it is not simply that people will act in accordance with just demands but that they should cultivate the disposition to act in this way, which comes from continually so acting: in other words, from the virtue of justice.

Again, a family will tend to fall apart if the people involved are simply at the mercy of their passions. If they let their anger rip or else repress it only with an effort of will so that it goes underground, if they act upon every passing sexual attraction, or again merely repress this with an effort of will, if, in fact, they lack the virtue of temperance, the project of a family is doomed. And such virtues are acquired precisely in this kind of context. Courage is required in adversity, and the patience that goes with courage. And, of course, above all there is required the moral/intellectual virtue of good sense, knowing what to do in order to realize the goods of family life in these particular circumstances. These human qualities or dispositions are distinguishable from the skills that are also associated with maintaining a family, like being able to cook; and one important distinguishing feature is that these qualities or virtues turn out to be required in other important fields of activity. Maintaining a university department, for example, does not, except very marginally, involve being able to cook, but it does demand just those human qualities that are needed in the first case. We are dealing here, then, with dispositions which are necessary for a particular worthwhile venture or practice but are not confined to or defined by that practice. There are skills required for a good ice-skater which simply constitutes her as a good skater; but she will also require certain virtues in order to become and remain a good skater which go beyond skating and it becomes possible to speak of the dispositions proper to a human being as such, or at least the dispositions belonging to any human being in this culture, in this historical epoch. I am not of course suggesting that because so-and-so is a great skater, she is for that reason a great and outstandingly good human being; I am suggesting that without some of the human qualities that we would praise in any human being we come across, it would not be possible to be a great skater. She may well counterbalance this with terrible human failings. But some of the virtues need to be there.

But this raises the question of the unity of the virtues. Can you have a genuine virtue while being otherwise quite vicious? Aquinas held that you could not. A thoroughly unjust man could not be truly courageous. He could only have a semblance of courage.[14] In the end, Aquinas held that no virtue is authentic unless it is, as he puts it, informed or enlivened by charity.[15] Others have disagreed with this. For the moment we might at least say that you can have some virtues more intensely, and others quite feebly.

This, then, is how I would deal with Fred (Thrasymachus). I would try to show that there are human virtues which are necessary to practices in which he wishes to engage, in which he will find some part of his happiness. The deliberate cultivation of these virtues is thus seen to be necessary to a happy adult active life. Certain of these virtues, such as courage and justice, will dispose him to act in ways that may bring disaster to him: he may be crucified. This is a risk that he needs to face if he is to engage in such adult life and, of course, courage is itself the virtue that will enable him to take such a risk. The alternative, however, is to live the half-life of the man floating in the tank, to opt for not growing up because growing up may involve unpleasantness. To someone who says that he does opt for such a passive life of immaturity there is, I think, nothing to be said.

I do not, by the way, think that it can be shown to anyone that being virtuous is always going to be in his interests, always going to ward off disaster. I do not think it will do to say that human beings need virtues even if it kills them; to say, as Geach puts it, that 'Bees need stings even though an individual bee may perish by stinging'.[16] This response is not good enough because it is not an argument directed at an individual bee who is asking precisely whether to use its sting or not. The analogy does not work because it is always fatal to the bee to use its sting. Justice and courage, however, are not always fatal and perhaps will never be in a particular life. Whether they will be fatal is a matter of chance. What is certain is that they are necessary to adult happiness.

Notes

1   *De Spiritualibus Creaturis*, II and *De Anima*, 13.

2   *Summa Theologiae*, 1a,79.

3   Aristotle, *Politics* III, 9.

4   Ibid.

5   *Summa Theologiae*, 1a2ae,61,5. My translation.

6   Aristotle, *Politics*, III, 6.

7   Thrasymachus of Chalcedon was a Greek sophist active during the last three decades of the fifth century BC. He appears as a character in Plato's *Republic* where he raises the question 'Does it pay to be just?'

8   Aristotle says of very eccentric views ('opinions … held by children and by the diseased and the mentally unbalanced'), 'The holders of such views are in need, not of arguments, but of maturity in which to change their opinions'. (*Eudaimonian Ethics* I, 3. I quote from J. L. Ackrill (ed.), *A New Aristotle Reader* (Oxford: Clarendon Press, 1987)) p. 481.

9   Cf. Aquinas, *Summa Theologiae*, 1a2ae,3,2.

10   Robert Nozick, *Anarchy, State and Utopia* (Oxford: Oxford University Press, 1974), pp. 42–5.

11   See Aristotle, *Eudemian Ethics*, 1, 5 (1215b).

12 P. T. Geach, *The Virtues* (Cambridge: Cambridge University Press, 1977), Ch. 1.

13 Alasdair MacIntyre, *After Virtue* (London: Duckworth, 1981), p. 175.

14 See *Summa Theologiae*, 2a,2ae,123.

15 See *Summa Contra Gentiles*, 4, 55.

16 Geach, *The Virtues*, p. 17.

12

Ethics as Language

Man is the linguistic animal. When we say this we are not just pointing to a distinguishing characteristic of man – as if we might say 'giraffes are the ones with the long necks, men are the ones that talk'. Language does not only distinguish man from other animals, it distinguishes his animality from that of other animals. To be a man is to be an animal in a new sense, to be alive in a new sense. This means that even the activities which a man seems to share with other animals are transfigured by the fact that they are part of an animality that finally issues in language. Man does not just *add* speech on to such things as eating and sexual behaviour; the fact that these latter occur in a linguistic context makes a difference to what they are.

Language is a culmination of organic life. In order to give an account of any organism we have to use words like 'relevance' and 'significance'. A structure counts as an organism when the activities of the parts have to be understood in terms of their relevance to the whole – what goes on in the eye is called 'seeing' because of the part it plays in the activity of the animal as a whole. Of course we can talk about very simple organisms without bringing in such notions as relevance, we can talk about them in the same way that we talk about simple machines. Similarly we can talk about sufficiently complicated machines as though they were animals: 'the computer tries out various solutions ... searches through its data ....' It is difficult to say what makes us decide between using 'animal language' and using 'machine language', between regarding this thing as alive or not. It is difficult because there is plainly no single reason; there are a great many considerations to be taken into account. The point is that if we do decide to talk of something as organic, then we employ a whole family of terms that have to do with significance and relevance.

The dog sees the meat as food, as having a certain significance for its life. I do not, of course, mean that the dog says to itself 'this is food', but it shows its appreciation of it as food by trying to eat it. Of course you could describe all that, if you wanted to, in terms of certain successive chemical reactions and physical movements; you could describe it as though the dog were a machine, using chemists' and physicists' language. If you did this you would not use words like 'food', 'trying' or 'eating'. Such a programme would seem forced and unnatural and, in its way, just as whimsical as talking in organic terms about cars and trains: 'she made a heroic effort up the gradient but expired before she got to the top'. There was a time when people assigned a special status to the language of the chemist and physicist, so that it was felt to be somehow more virtuous to suppress our natural way of talking about dogs and grimly to speak of them as though they were machines. This particular piece of prudery – known as 'materialism' – is, I am glad to say, no longer with us. There are, of course, a whole range of borderline cases in which we are not sure whether to use the language of organism or of machine, when we ask 'is this a living thing or not?' Since, however, these are precisely the cases where either language will do equally well, it is hard to see why there should be any fuss about the matter.

To get back to the dog. He sees certain kinds of stuff in the light of food, and he sees various other things in various other lights, as dangerous, or sexually exciting, or repulsive or whatever. In other words he sees signifi-cance in his environment. He is not surrounded by neutral facts but by things that matter to him in various ways. He has a *world*. By a world I mean an environment organized in terms of significance. What we call the senses of the dog are the ways in which this organization takes place. We know a certain amount about the world of the dog; we know that it differs a good deal from our world. Colour, for example, has no significance for a dog, it does not exist in his world. On the other hand, as everyone knows, in comparison with dogs we haven't got noses. The world of a dog may be as exciting or boring in terms of smell as ours can be in terms of colour.

Senses, then, are modes of response to an environment or modes of determining a world. The senses are not eyes and ears and other bits of an animal, they are what the animal is doing with these bits or, if you like, the way in which the behaviour of these bits is relevant to the behaviour of the whole body. Hearing is how my whole body lives through my ears, walking is how it lives through my legs, eating is how it lives through my mouth and stomach and so on. The bodily structure of an animal will determine how it constitutes a world from its environment, but the transaction is not completely unilateral: important environmental changes affect the animal's world and eventually, by natural selection, the bodily structure. But broadly speaking we can say that an animal is an area of sensual life, a point from which a world is organized.

We may ask at this point about the 'environment' which lies behind the animal's world. Is it correct to think of an objectively real environment waiting to be organized into worlds by different animals? The animal is plainly enclosed within its sensual system; it cannot be aware of an environment except as organized into a world by its sensuous life. If we speak of an environment 'behind' the animal's world we are speaking simply of *our* world. We are not, however, just being provincial in giving a special status to our world, because it is created not only by sensuous life but by linguistic life; and language, as we shall see, is precisely a way of not being a prisoner of the sensuous life. The linguistic animal is the one that to some extent creates its own modes of response to the environment, its own modes of constituting a world, and to this extent is not their prisoner.

But to return to the animals. Each animal is the centre of a world, it is an area of sensuous activity that constitutes a world from the environment. Actively sharing a common world is communication. I say 'actively', because any two animals with the same sensory apparatus could be said to share a common world – we have already spoken of 'the world of the dog', which is shared by all dogs – but two dogs are in communication when they are actively engaged together in the determination of a common world. Communication is actively sharing a common life.

Discussion of communication amongst animals is too often confined to the means by which bits of information are conveyed from one to another, but this is simply a piece of anthropomorphism. Amongst men there is an important distinction between the exchange of messages and the other ways of communicating. We distinguish between conversation and choral singing, though both are forms of communication; still more do we distinguish between conversation and common work, though again we have here two kinds of communication. In the pre-linguistic world of the other animals these distinctions have no real place: the bee that dances 'to show the others where the honey is' is no more (and no less) communicating with its fellow bees than when it shares their life in other ways. To single out the dance of the bees or the call of a bird from the rest of its vital activity is to project onto the pre-linguistic world a distinction that only properly has place amongst men.

All shared vital activity is, then, some form of communication. We may speak of the vital response of an animal to its environment as a kind of communication. The animal vitalizes its world and endows it with significance. The world becomes the clothing of the animal and, in a way, an extension of its body. We can see this dramatically in the case of those animals that have a certain personal territory. Here the boundaries of the territory are almost like another skin; the violence with which the animal reacts to penetration of its territory is comparable to the convulsion that occurs when a weapon enters the skin. The space around such an animal has begun to share in its bodily life.

I have spent time on communication and animal life in order to lay a foundation for the use of the word when we come to the linguistic animals. In man communication reaches a new intensity, it becomes language. I think it is important to see language not first of all in terms of the operation that is peculiar to it – the transfer of messages – but to see it as a mode of communication, a sharing of life. With the appearance of language we come, in evolution, to one of those radical changes that I mentioned earlier: a change in which we do not merely see something new but have a new way of seeing, in which something is produced which could not be envisaged in the old terms and which changes our whole way of envisaging what has gone before. The coming of this new kind of communication, this new way of being alive, could not, so to speak, have been predicted before it happened. It is only after it has happened that, looking back in the new terms, from the standpoint of the new kind of life, we can see the continuity of previous life with this. We can then see that, as Aquinas thinks, understanding is a kind of living; it is, indeed, the most perfect kind of living.

We sometimes play with the question 'could we make a machine that talks?' This is to ask whether we could give an account wholly in 'machine language' of something which would then turn out to be a linguistic being – this is what would be required if we were to have a technique for making one. The significant question to ask here, however, is 'what would count as success; what would make us say that we had before us a talking being?' The answer, surely, is that we would say we had a talking being when we recognized that it was talking *to* us. Nothing that we know *about* the thing can compel such a recognition on our part. I think that an important factor here would be irony. We would come to recognize an intelligent response as we detected ironic overtones in the machine's remarks; but the nature of irony and its detection is too complex a subject for us to consider for the moment. We can only say that when the machine begins to talk (when it becomes free and intelligent and enters into human communication) it will announce the fact itself and we will either believe it or not. The change required of us here, from knowing the thing as an object – knowing things about it – to responding to it as another subject, corresponds to the radical change from pre-linguistic to linguistic.

We must now try to characterize the new kind of communication that is language. I think the central point is that with the linguistic animal the media of communication are created by the animal itself. We do not just communicate with each other; we create the means by which we communicate. We do not simply use such tools as we have to make things: we make the tools themselves. The communication of other animals is a matter of shared sensuous life, and the forms of this life are determined by their sensory apparatus, by the kind of bodies they have. A dog has a definite kind of world, which it can share with other dogs, because it has a definite bodily structure. Its life and its world are determined by the constitution of its sensory organs. The human body, on the other hand, is not only more complex than that of other animals but in its extension into its world, in the kind of communication media that surround it, it is to some extent self-determinative. We can communicate in media that we invent ourselves, in language; the media of other animals are genetically determined.

There are several qualifications to be made to that statement: as we shall see, we do not and cannot individually create our own media of expression except in a very marginal sense. Moreover it is not quite true that in other animals the media of communication are unalterably fixed. Konrad Lorenz states quite flatly:

> Of course this purely innate signal code of an animal species differs fundamentally from human language, every word of which must be learned laboriously by the human child. Moreover, being a genetically fixed character of the species – just as much as any bodily character – this so-called language is for every individual animal species ubiquitous in its distribution. Obvious though this fact may seem, it was nevertheless with something akin to naive surprise that I heard the jackdaws in northern Russia 'talk' exactly the same familiar 'dialect' as my birds at home in Altenberg.[1]

H. Munro Fox, however, records a rather charming minor exception to this rule:

The song of the chaffinch in Switzerland is distinctly different from that in England, and the song is slightly different in various parts of Britain. On the Continent chaffinches migrate long distances ... it so happens that a stream of continental migrants passes annually along the Essex coast and from them the native birds acquire a continental accent.[2]

There are of course quite well-known cases of imitative learning by birds and other animals and if, as I have suggested, it is merely an anthropomorphic mistake to treat the 'signal codes' of animals as something specially distinct from the rest of their bodily behaviour, we must include here all sorts of 'learning' with regard to other kinds of activity. It is, in principle, no more surprising that birds should learn new songs by imitation than that the cat should learn to manipulate the door latch; neither more nor less communication is involved.

Lorenz is particularly insistent on the gulf between animal signals and human language. There is, he says, no question of any animal having the conscious intention of influencing another when it makes the appropriate sign. Speaking of some of the most 'communicative' of birds, he says:

Even geese and jackdaws, when reared singly make all these signals as soon as the corresponding mood overtakes them. Under these circumstances the automatic and even mechanical character of these signals becomes strikingly apparent and reveals them as entirely different from human words.[3]

We have then to see language both as the culmination of a developing process of communication, the most intense kind of communication, but also as quite different from all that has gone before, the root of the difference being that other animals are born with their systems of communication, whereas for children the entry into language is a personal matter, a matter of their own biography.

There are, as I see it, three major factors in the growth of human media of communication: nature, history and biography. By nature I mean what we are immediately born with, the structure of our sensory apparatus which is, of course, genetically determined. Our linguistic communication grows out of our sensuous communication. Our linguistic life (human life) is not determined by the structure of our sense organs in the way that the life of other animals is, but it depends upon it. In order to learn the language of a wholly strange people it is necessary to live with them, to share their efforts and disappointments and pleasures, their daily way of life. Then by imitation we come to use their language appropriately: we discover the use of their various sounds. We learn by our mistakes, recognizing a mistake by the fact that it makes a barrier between ourselves and the community, impeding our conformity to their way of life. This, roughly speaking, is how children learn their 'native' language. Now, being able to share a way of life with people depends on a general similarity of bodily structure. In so far as a people differed from us in, for example, the things that gave them pleasure or saddened them, still more if they differed altogether in the bodily expression of such emotions, we should find it hard to live in their community. Learning to live with strangers is, you might say, a matter of adopting the rhythms of their life, like a tuning fork vibrating in harmony with a note on the piano. Our bodies must be more or less tuned to those of the strangers in order for this to happen. It is true that we are, so to speak, self-adjusting tuning forks to a certain extent, but our range of adjustment is not indefinite, our capacity for sympathy (in the literal sense) has limits. This, I think, is why Wittgenstein said 'if a lion could talk, we could not understand him'.[4] He may have been underestimating the extent to which ethologists have succeeded in entering into the lives of lions, but his principle is surely correct: we learn a language only in so far as we can communicate in a sensuous life.[5]

Human communication, then, has its roots in sensuous communication although it is not determined by this. I said earlier that any animal is a centre of significance, a point from which a world is determined. When we come to human life we come to a creature that to some extent creates the significance that it gives to its world, a creature that to some extent creates its world because it creates its language.[6] For a dog, because of the determinate character of its sensuous life, a certain part of the environment will always have the significance of food. With man this is not true even of so sensuous a matter as food. Fashions in what counts as food vary from age to age and from society to society. The significance of human food is very largely created by people. For all animals, eating is a part of the business of communication; for us it is part of language. (The recognition of this, incidentally, lies behind some recent re-statements of Catholic eucharistic theology.)

What counts as food varies between broad limits set by the bodily structure of man; what brings about these variations is the second factor I mentioned, and the most important one: history. Language is the product of the community and not of the individual. In one way this is obvious enough: the English language existed before I was born and I grew into it, just as mankind existed before I was born and I came into existence as the product of it. The process of growing up, of becoming oneself, is a matter of entering into communication in terms of the various media available. This is true at every level. Food, for example, is, at one level, a medium of exchange between my body and its environment; eating is a sensuous response to my world, it is one of the ways in which I constitute my world and, obviously enough, one of the ways in which I continue to live. How I grow up or how I continue to live depends in clear ways on what food is available. Eating is also a social ritual, it is a medium of exchange between members of the community, it has meaning, it is part of language. How I grow into the society, how I am able to realize myself as a part of this society, again depends on the quality of the medium, on the meanings that are available. The question 'what do you eat?' fades into the question 'what does eating mean in your community?' as we bring linguistic communication out of sensuous communication.

Meanings, then, are ways of entering into social life, ways of being with each other. The kind of meanings available in the language of a society – taking 'language' in its widest extent to include all conventionally determined signs and symbols – constitutes the way in which people are with each other in that community. 'To imagine a language', as Wittgenstein says, 'is to imagine a form of life'.

This way of seeing meaning and language has to be contrasted with the very widespread view based on a dualistic theory of man. According to that theory a man inhabits two worlds, an interior private world of subjectivity into which we penetrate by introspection, and an exterior public world of physical objects. These two spheres are variously called 'soul and body' or 'mind and matter' or 'thinking substance and extended substance'. The interior mind is the home of concepts and it is where thinking takes place; actions, however, words and other expressions of my thinking take place in the public world of the body. My words consist of public signs that stand for private thoughts.

This dualism has always had a certain fatal attraction for Christians: partly, I think, because the Christian sees man as in tension, as torn between conflicting poles, and this theory seems to accord well with such a picture. It was deliberately and explicitly attacked from within the Christian church by Aquinas in the thirteenth century, but rapidly re-asserted itself. In our own time it has come again under fire not only amongst philosophers associated with Wittgenstein, but also amongst some continental writers; there have also in recent years been attempts to show that the biblical view of man is non-dualistic. I am not, for the moment, concerned with the dualist theory in general, but only with the theory of meaning associated with it.

According to this theory concepts are generated privately in the mind and then they may or may not have words attached to them as labels. Thus I have used the word 'red' as the sign of my concept of *red*. It is one of the quirks of this theory that, since concepts are private and words are public, a real question seems to arise whether everybody who uses the word 'red' has attached it to the same concept. The empiricist kind of dualist will put the question in the form 'but how do we know that everyone who speaks of red really has the same *experience* of redness?', for to him the concept of red is a kind of experience or arises out of an experience of red things. Since the theory gives rise to a question, which according to the same theory it is in principle impossible to answer, we may question the validity of the theory itself. Such problems dissolve once we recognize that what we call concepts are nothing like experiences but are simply skills in the use of words. My having the concept of *red* is nothing but my ability to use the word 'red' in the English language, in order to communicate with others. If I am satisfied that Fred and I use the word 'red' in exactly the same way, then I have already established that we have the same concept of red. This latter view, however, involves a rejection of the dualistic account. Instead of saying that I have a private mind and a public body, a mind for having concepts in and a body for saying and hearing words, I say that I have a body that is able to be with other bodies not merely by physical contact but by linguistic communication. Having a soul is just being able to communicate; having a mind is being able to communicate linguistically.

The meaning of a word, then, is the purpose it serves in the communication between people in a certain community. The question of meaning is not a question about my secret thoughts but about the public language. This is not to deny that I can have secret thoughts: of course I can. It is just to deny that they have any special position of privilege and especially to deny that thought begins in secrecy. We learn how to think by learning to use the media of communication provided by our society. Besides speaking aloud we can also imagine ourselves speaking without actually making any sound; we can talk to ourselves in our heads or imagine ourselves using other symbols. Just as after learning to read aloud we later learn to read silently, so we learn eventually to think silently. As we grow older we realize that this is quite often the best thing to do.

Meanings, then, belong first of all to the language, to the community who live by this language; the individual learns these meanings, acquires these concepts, by entering into the language, the culture or history of his community. But this, of course, is not the whole story. Communities and their languages change and develop. If we could give no account of novelty in language we should have to regard cultures as something like the fixed species of pre-evolutionary thought, forms of life that had been created from the beginning and which could only change by decaying and disappearing. The difference between a minority language which is 'dead', like Latin, which has to be kept in existence by special preservatives (and in certain schools by physical violence), and one which is alive, like Irish, is, of course, that the latter is in actual use as a medium of creative communication and especially of poetry. It is by this constant creation of new meanings or modifications of old meanings that a language remains alive. Latin, on the other hand, is used only for certain ecclesiastical communications.

Before going on to look at this third factor in the development of language, the creation of new meanings, which I have called biography, I would like to draw attention to the quasi-objective status of meaning. If we reject the dualist view that meanings are secret thoughts in my head, then we must give them a certain status which is, in important ways, independent of my will. I can't just mean what I like by words. I cannot assent to legislation that discriminates between people on grounds of race and secretly make the assent mean that I believe in a racially equal society. I can of course simply tell lies; I can not mean what I say, but I cannot, simply by taking thought, change the meaning of what I say. So meanings are, so to speak, objective, though not in the way that physical objects are. A word has a certain meaning and a piece of metal has a certain temperature and neither of these are immediately changed by anything going on in my head, though the former may eventually be modified through certain things that I do or say. I stress this point since, as will become clearer later, I think that moral values are objective in the same way as meanings and, indeed, are the meanings of behaviour.

I have spoken of the language of the community as though there were simply one society within which a man has his existence. In fact we live our lives in terms of many communities which constantly develop and dissolve. I do not only belong to the English community: I belong to a small community of friends and acquaintances; I belong to a community of people who share certain of my beliefs about political matters, and so on. These communities have each their languages; they are each contexts within which new meanings develop as new forms of relationship are discovered. The poet discovers in his experience – that is, in the community he forms with perhaps one or two others, perhaps many – new forms of communication which he can offer to the larger community who use the language. Such an offer may be accepted or rejected as meaningless. If it is accepted he enriches the whole language, but such marginal enrichment depends on a general stability of meaning, a cultural tradition. Man's creativity is such that no traditional interpretation of the world is final; he reaches always beyond the language he has created, towards a future which, just because its language does not yet exist, can be only dimly perceived. This means that every language is in the end provisional, or at least can be seen by hindsight to have been provisional.

All animal life, then, is a matter of communication, of creating a significant world out of an environment. In the case of man this communication reaches the point of being linguistic, that is to say, man is able to some extent to create the media through which he makes his world significant. These media have their roots in the sensuous life of man and their creation is the history of a community leading into biographies, which are themselves the histories of minor communities.

It is because I have this sort of body, a human body living with a human life, that my communication can be linguistic. The human body is a source of communication; we must be careful not to think of it as an instrument used in communication like a pen or a telephone; such instruments can only be used because there is a body to use them. If the human body itself were an instrument we should have to postulate another body using it – and this, indeed, is what the dualistic theory really amounts to; the mind or soul is thought of, in practice, as a sort of invisible body living inside the visible one. Instead of this we should recognize that the human body is intrinsically communicative. Human flesh, the stuff we are made of, the intricate structure of the human organism, is quite different from wood and stone or even from animal flesh, because it is self-creative. It does not simply produce other bodies which are its children in its own image, it produces *itself* at least to the extent of creating the media, the language and communication systems which are an extension of itself.

It is not just that the human body can produce speech and writing: all its behaviour is in some degree linguistic. The range of bodily activity that we call a man's 'behaviour' consists of those actions which are significant in this way. We would not ordinarily speak of a man's digestion of his food or his tripping over a stone as his behaviour. We call a man's activity his 'behaviour' when it plays a part in his communication with others. A piece of human behaviour is not simply an action that gets something *done*, it also has meaning, it gets something *said*. I do not mean by this that all human activities are gestures. Gestures are visual words and I do not want to suggest that we are constantly talking to each other, in a literal sense, whenever we do anything. When I say that all our behaviour says something, I simply mean that it plays a part in some system of communication.

Now ethics is just the study of human behaviour in so far as it is a piece of communication, in so far as it says something or fails to say something. This does not mean that ethics is uninterested in behaviour in so far as it gets something done, that ethics is not concerned with the consequences of my acts, but its precise concern is with my action as meaningful. The two, of course, are closely related. It is because of the *effect* on you of having a knife stuck into you that my act of knifing you has the *meaning* that it has. But the connection may be quite loose. A mother may smack her child very lightly and almost painlessly and the child will show that he recognizes the act as meaning some kind of rejection; on the other hand, in a game you may hit him much harder and he will be delighted by the sheer physical contact that means the opposite of rejection. The link between physical effect and meaning may be quite loose, but the looser it gets the nearer the action comes to being a gesture whose meaning is conventionally determined in an individual society. A painless smack may be a *gesture* of rejection; cutting a man's throat is a good deal less ambiguous.

It is because human behaviour is intrinsically meaningful that fears of committing the 'naturalistic fallacy' are beside the point. The 'fallacy' is said to consist in moving straight from factual description to value judgement, moving, as the slogan has it, from 'is' to 'ought'. No simple account of what is the case can logically entail anything that ought to be the case; or, as we might say, no account of a situation in a physicist's language can entail an account in a moralist's language. I think that this doctrine is an irrelevance because an account of human behaviour as such is never in a physicist's language. To say that Fred killed Charlie is to say something of a quite different kind from 'this particle moved from point p at time T_1 to point q at time T_2'. To describe an event as a killing is already to describe it in terms of its significance; it is to describe it as having place in a field of communication and not simply in a gravitational or electro-magnetic field.[7] A physicist's account of Fred's action will not entail a moralist's account but neither will it entail that Fred is *killing* Charlie, just as no physicist's account of the activity of the visitor from outer space will entail that it is speaking to me.

Ethics, I have suggested, is the study of human behaviour as communication. I do not mean by this that we are concerned with human behaviour in so far as it bears on the business of talking – a man is not a bad man simply because he speaks or writes badly, for speech and writing are only part of total communication which involves the whole business of living. I am not saying that ethics is an *extension* of literary criticism, but that it is *parallel* to it. Ethics does for the whole of life what literary criticism does for a small part.

Ethics is traditionally and almost universally supposed to be concerned with the difference between right and wrong, between good and bad behaviour. This is, however, a mistake: the same kind of mistake as thinking that literary criticism is concerned with the difference between good and bad poems. It is true that a man may not be thought to have got very far in his literary studies if he does not conclude that some poems are better than others, if, indeed, he does not conclude that some poems are simply atrocious; but this is not the purpose of literary criticism. Its purpose is to enable us to enjoy the poems more by responding to them more sensitively, by entering more deeply into their significance. If we try to do this we shall find that quite a lot of what is offered as poetry will not stand up to being taken as seriously as this; it is these poems that we reject as bad. Now the purpose of ethics is similarly to enable us to enjoy life more by responding to it more sensitively, by entering into the significance of human action. Here too we shall often find behaviour that does not stand up to being taken as seriously as this. There is a kind of case to be made out against literary studies in that the fastidious reader becomes incapable of enjoying certain kinds of sentimental or otherwise feeble writing. There is a similar, and equally invalid, case to be made out against the moralist. In either case the answer is too obvious to be worth stating.

There are, however, at least two important objections to the parallel between ethics and literary criticism. 'The purpose of ethics is to enable us to enjoy life.' The word 'enjoy' may seem peculiarly inappropriate in a world containing, amongst other things, the Vietnam war, but I use the word in the sense in which one can be said to enjoy *King Lear* or, for that matter, St Matthew's gospel. A more serious objection is that the word 'enjoy' might suggest a spectator's attitude; it might suggest that the moralist is one who stands apart from a piece of human behaviour and coolly savours it without becoming himself involved. In fact, it is impossible to appreciate the significance of human behaviour unless one is to some extent involved in it – but then surely the same should be said of our appreciation of a poem or a novel.

There is one extremely important similarity between ethics and literary criticism and this is that neither of them come to an end. I mean that, except in the case of something that can be fairly quickly dismissed as atrocious, you would not claim to have said the last word about a poem. The literary judgement is a matter of continually probing into the depths of a work, seeking a more profound understanding – an understanding which is not just of this poem but of yourself and of your world. You do not at any point say 'well, now I have understood it, there is no more to be said. I see it now precisely as a poem, in the light of literary principles, and my judgement is as follows....' Now it seems to me that the same is true of ethical understanding. We should not expect to be able to say 'now I see this precisely in the light of moral principles, and my definitive judgement is as follows...' We may, of course, say definitively that some behaviour is plainly atrocious, just as we may dismiss some poetry as not worth wasting time on, and in the same way we may say definitively that some action is good. But to say that a piece of human behaviour is 'good' may be as irrelevant a remark as saying that *King Lear* is good.

So I want to say that there is no such thing as *the* moral level. Moral judgement does not consist in seeing something at 'the moral level' or 'in the light of morality'; it consists in the process of trying to see things always at a yet deeper level. Moral judgement does not cease when it arrives at 'the morality of an action', it just is the continuing quest for what we might call greater seriousness or deeper understanding.

I must now try to explain what I mean by the word 'deeper' here. To say that our behaviour has significance is to say that it plays its part in some system of communication, some structure of meaning. Now we live out our lives in terms of many such structures. The quest for the 'deeper' meaning of a piece of behaviour is the quest for the part it plays in structures that are more fundamental to human existence. One might suppose that there is one ultimate structure, one final community to which all men belong and into which all other communities are resolved: membership of mankind. The deepest meaning of an action, on this theory, is the meaning it has in terms of this system of communication. My reason for, in the end, rejecting this view is that if we take seriously the notion of mankind as a structure of meaning, as distinct from a merely biological structure, then we have to admit that it does not yet exist. Mankind is, in a sense, a theoretical construction: we argue 'if all these particular human institutions are all *human* institutions, there must be, behind them all, the institution of simply being human'. We are reminded of the kind of thinking that Wittgenstein attacks: 'if all these are games there must be some concept of game that applies to them all'. In fact, mankind does not form a single linguistic community and this implies a defect of human communication not only in extension but also in intensity. The fact that mankind is split into fragments which are in imperfect communication with each other means that within these fragments, too, full communication is not achieved. Because I cannot express myself to all men I cannot fully give myself to any.

We do not, then, have some ultimate community within which all lesser groupings are contained, but we do have a certain hierarchy amongst the structures to which we belong. We can see that behaviour which makes sense at one level makes less sense as we move down through more fundamental forms of human relatedness or human existence. Men belong to each other (and thereby exist) in trivial ways and in less trivial ways; and even though we have to reject the natural law attempt to describe a *least* trivial way upon which the ultimate judgement of the significance of behaviour is founded, we can say that ethics is the quest of less and less trivial modes of human relatedness. In this quest ethics points towards, without being able to define or comprehend, an ultimate medium of human communication which is beyond humanity and which we call divinity. 'He who does not love does not know God; for God is love' (I Jn 4.8).

Any piece of human behaviour has meaning at some level, however trivial it may be, otherwise we should not call it 'behaviour'. As Aquinas would put it, every human act is done for the sake of some good. We may find an activity quite meaningful at, say, the level of economics – that structure of relationship between men in which the language of money plays a large part – but as we seek to interpret it at other levels we may find it begins to fade into senselessness and non-living. A shallow cliché-ridden piece of journalese is a piece of faded language: the linguistic intensity has slackened, the texture of meaning has worn thin. In a piece of bad writing a man has not lived into his medium, you get no sense of vigorous presence. Now what the literary judgement is to writing, the ethical judgement is to the whole complex field of human communication. In some activities a man has not lived into his medium: his action has made sense at some superficial level of meaning but it does not make full human sense.

Evil behaviour may be colourfully atrocious, it may have catastrophic (and even, incidentally, good) effects on human history, but what makes us call it evil is that its meaning fades relatively soon when we try to take it seriously. The life of the evil man has meaning only at a fairly superficial level. It is entirely appropriate that Hitler's table-talk should have been so boring. Bad, cheap behaviour devalues the structures of human meaning in the way that bad cheap prose devalues the language. There is an appearance of communication concealing a failure to express oneself, to give and realize oneself. If I am right in saying that life is constituted by communication then such behaviour diminishes life or diminishes my existence. The point of evil is that it is a deprivation of reality.

Self-expression is almost the exact opposite of self-assertion. The latter substitutes domination for communication. Through fear of becoming vulnerable to others by opening ourselves to them in communication, we seek to control them so that they fit into our own world. Communication disturbs our present world, lays it open to influence from others, which may involve revolutionary change; we may prefer to tailor others to fit our familiar patterns of living. As so often in morals we can see this pattern most clearly in

the behaviour of political communities. Colonialism, however mildly pater-
nalistic (and very often the missionary activity that accompanies it), is almost
the exact opposite of communication between two cultures.

There is, I think, a quite interesting distinction to be made in almost all
our media of communication between self-assertive behaviour which simply
involves a devaluation of the medium, and the worse behaviour in which
the devaluation of the medium is actually used as a *means* of self-assertion
and domination. It is clear that one of our fundamental media of communication is the human body itself. Indeed it is, as we have seen, not simply
an instrument but the source of all human communication. Certain kinds of
physical violence, and of course killing, mean a devaluing of the body; they
involve treating another's body simply as an object in my world and ignoring
its status as a source of communication. But compare these activities with
torture, in which the body is reduced to object status precisely for the purpose
of domination; we are right, it seems to me, to judge that this is a worse activity
than killing even though in the end it does the victim less harm. We are right,
that is, to think that though killing is worse than hurting, torture is worse than
either. In general I think the direct attack on the medium itself is more sinister
than the incidental devaluation of it: as refusing to tell a man what he has a
right to know is bad, but lying is worse; as theft is bad but forgery is worse ...

Morals in practice, then, is the attempt to live out our lives in terms not
only of the more obvious but also of the deeper forms of communication
with others. Morals as a theoretical study would be the examination of these
media of communication and of the relationships between them, and in this
matter we probably get more help from novelists and dramatists and perhaps
preachers than we do from philosophers.

Notes

1   *King Solomon's Ring*, p. 76.

2   H. M. Fox, *The Personality of Animals* (London: Penguin Books, 1952), p. 28.

3   *King Solomon's Ring*, p. 77.

4   Ludwig Wittgenstein, *Philosophical Investigations* (Oxford: Basil Blackwell, 1968), 223e.

5   The question is sometimes raised, though I think not often enough, about communication between men and beings from outer space who may be supposed to have entirely different bodily shapes. It is sometimes suggested, I think mistakenly, that we could find a common ground for communication on the basis of pure mathematics. This, I think, overlooks the difficulty we should have in knowing whether we were actually communicating with another linguistic being or merely with a computer.

6   'Speech, of course, is the most conspicuous human achievement; speech, that is, as a structure of symbols, which again can be developed, manipulated, interpreted and re-interpreted in an infinity of directions – unlike the code of the bees, which, however marvellously complex and effective, functions as a system of fixed signals. Human language, by contrast, becomes itself a growing world of meanings within meanings, which we not only use for practical ends but dwell in as the very fabric of our being, while at the same time changing it by our participation in it, enacting the history of our language in our history.' Marjorie Grene, *The Knower and the Known* (London: Faber and Faber, 1966), p. 174.

7   'Only by an evaluation do we call the Eroica 'music', not noise, and so assimilate the 'fact' of its composition to the history of music rather than to acoustics. Only by an evaluation do we call the story of Auschwitz or Belsen mass murder and so assimilate it to human history rather than to chemistry or population genetics.' Marjorie Grene, *The Knower and the Known*, p. 160. The whole of this chapter on 'Facts and Values' is of very great interest.

13

Teaching Morals

People engaged in the necessary tasks of the world very frequently find the moralist a nuisance and a bore. It is all very well to sit in your armchair or stand in your pulpit and talk about ideals and all that, but none of this has much relevance to practical affairs. You may succeed in making people feel guilty or complacent but in the meantime the practical questions have to be decided. All this talk of morality is really very abstract and has little to do with the practical affairs of life. People often suspect that moralizing is just a way that the weak, incompetent and impractical man has found for blackmailing the poor fellow who is up to his neck in the real risks and compromises of decision making.

If this is true then it seems probable that we had better not teach morals at all: perhaps all we could do is produce prigs and puritans eager to sit in judgement on their fellows without soiling their own hands with the dirty business of real life. In this chapter, then, since I can tell you absolutely nothing about teaching, I thought I might serve some slight purpose by trying to defend morality against this kind of attack. I want to present a view of morality quite different from the one I have mentioned; and if what I describe is not morality as commonly understood, then I reckon it will do instead.

I think morality is concerned with human behaviour, and its concern is of a special kind: what characterizes morality, as distinct from the many other ways of looking at human behaviour, is first that it is the most practical approach and secondly that it is the least abstract approach.

Let me explain those in turn. First morality is practical. When you learn about morals you are learning not some theoretical truths but how to do something. So learning morality is more like learning music or carpentry than it is like learning astronomy or physics. I'll have more to say about this later but just for now let me explain how Thomas Aquinas saw this matter. He thought that human intelligence is displayed in two broad areas which he called theoretical and practical. It is very important to see that the difference between these is not simply one of subject matter. It is not a matter of whether we are thinking about atoms or about actions. Practical intelligence is displayed not in thinking about actions but in doing them. The sports reporter at the football match is exercising his theoretical reason in describing and analysing the game; the footballer on the pitch is exercising his practical intelligence in playing it. He is playing intelligently, we may hope. Incidentally it is simply because the footballer is playing intelligently (or unintelligently) that the sports reporter can produce the kind of report that he does – basically a critical narrative, or an evaluating story. You cannot report the behaviour of bees or earthquakes in this way. If you are teaching morals your primary aim is to produce someone analogous with an intelligent footballer, not someone analogous to an intelligent reporter. The two have obvious interconnections, but the important thing to see is that the fact that a player is not good as a reporter does not make him an unintelligent player. It is just that if you want to explain how intelligent his play is you have to report it intelligently, or use your theoretical intelligence.

The aim of theoretical reason is to understand the world; the aim of morals is to change it. Understanding the world is much more than being well-informed about what is the case. We understand something when we know not merely that it is the case but the reason why it is the case. Anyone may know that sugar, unlike marble, dissolves in water; it takes a physical chemist to explain why this has to be so given the molecular structure of the materials involved. If the physical chemist has done his job we are able to say: 'Yes, of course, the sugar dissolves.' Science, theoretical understanding in general, deals not in facts but in explanations. And this is one excellent human activity. But if you want to understand human activity as thoroughly as you can, and especially if you want to teach people how to be active as well as they can, you will get more tips from the football coach than from the physics teacher.

Of course things are not as simple as that, for the physics teacher is not just teaching the truths of physics, he is mainly engaged in teaching people how to be physicists, how to do physics, and that, of course, is a practical matter.

What then is the difference between the football coach's concern with the human activity of playing football and the moralist's concern with human activity? This is where our second characteristic comes in: the moralist is less abstract than the football coach. What I mean by this is that the well-doing of football abstracts from a great deal of the complex business of human living. It is not of any direct relevance to playing football well that you are, say, kind, or a good physicist passionately interested in stamp-collecting. The moralist, on the other hand, is concerned not with an isolated abstract feature of human living like football, but with the activity of human living as a concrete whole. He is concerned not just with what it is to be a good physicist or carpenter or footballer, but with what it is to be a good human being. He is concerned with the good life for a human being taken as a whole.

So: first of all I have distinguished between theoretical intelligence, concerned with understanding the reasons why things are as they are, and practical intelligence, concerned with changing the way things are, with human activity. And within this human activity, I have distinguished between acting well in the particular abstract field of endeavour (this is a matter of acquiring skills and techniques) and acting well in the field of endeavouring to be a human being (this, as we shall see, is a matter of acquiring virtues).

It may seem odd to talk of the endeavour to be a human being: are we not simply human by being born as such? Well, yes and no. A human being, unlike, say, a crystal of rock salt, is not a static thing. A human being is a human life which begins and develops. I take it that the whole *raison-d'être* of teachers is to enable people to develop their human lives towards flourishing or maturity. They, and a lot of other people, face the task of helping people through the tricky transition from infancy to a fulfilled instead of a thwarted adult life.

All this is because we are not just human beings but human becomings. Like all other animals and unlike rock crystals, for us to be is to have a life-time, a development; but for us, and unlike for other animals, our life-time is a life-story. The difference is that the characters in a life-story in part make their own development; they make decisions, sometimes crucial ones which determine how the story will go on. Human animals are to this extent in charge of their life-times, their life-stories. That is why the study of human behaviour is ethics, while the study of other animal behaviour is only ethology. When the novel *Watership Down* came out it was reviewed in the *New York Review of Books* and the writer described it as a charming tale about some middle-class English children disguised as rabbits. And so they were. You could not have a story about actual rabbits. Because they do not control their own stories by decisions of the human kind there could be no drama, no comedy, no tragedy. Morality, then, is just the study of human lives considered precisely as life-stories. And what it is concretely to be a human being is to be a character in a life-story.

Whatever extra padding goes into it, the report of a football match is essentially a report on a series of solutions to practical problems, problems that are being solved (or not solved) by the players on the field – not in talking about them to others or to themselves in their heads, but in their intelligent activity. Intelligent activity, whether in the limited and abstract area of a human life, is not a matter, or does not have to be a matter, of first thinking something out in words with your theoretical intelligence and then acting on the conclusion to which you have come. Aristotle compared intelligent activity to a kind of reasoning in which the conclusion you come to is not a proposition but an action.

Of course one big difference between the game of football and the game of life is connected with the abstractness and simplicity of football. It is relatively simple to say what counts as successful activity, well-performed activity in football because the aims and purposes of the players, as players, are easy to understand. They are easy to understand because we invented them. What counts as winning, what counts as good or bad play and also what counts as inadmissible play is decided by the Football Authorities.

This does not seem to be the case with the game of life; nor could it be. I should say immediately that there are a whole lot of twentieth-century philosophers, for example the existentialists in France, and people like Richard Hare in Britain, who thought that the point and purpose of human life *can* be a matter of individual decision, or, as Hare would say, a 'fundamental option'. I think these people have to be wrong because of what decision is. I shall be trying to argue that a decision can only be an incident in the course of a life-story. It is essentially *against the background*, in the context of the story. There cannot be a decision about the story itself. I think these philosophers have been led astray by a mistaken idea called 'free will'. I am not opposing free will to determinism or any mechanistic theory of human behaviour. I am opposing it to what Aquinas calls 'free decision' (*liberum arbitrium*). But more of that in a moment.

So it is quite easy for us to understand that the point and purpose of the game of football is a matter of a decision we make within the game of living; it is not so clear how we come by an idea of the point and purpose of living itself.

To cut a long story relatively short, because I haven't time to argue every-thing, it seems to me that the point of human living cannot be to amuse the birds, in the way in which the point of machines does lie outside themselves:

they are to amuse and be useful to human animals. I think it is true, and very importantly true, that the point of human living lies beyond itself, but not outside itself. This is because I think that in the end the point of human living lies in God who is beyond us but not outside us. God, unlike the birds or any other creatures, cannot lie outside us because he creates us and sustains us all the time, making us to be and keeping us as ourselves. So to say that the point of our lives is in God is not to point to something outside us but to a greater depth within us.

However, before we come to God I would like to suggest that with human animals, as with all the other animals, *the purpose of life is living with each other*. This means that a good and well-functioning animal, a healthy animal, is one that lives well with the rest of its species. Living well with them involves, for example, mating with them, but also competing for mates and, in the case of at least one species, eating your mate after intercourse. We have all been learning from zoologists how extraordinarily diverse and peculiar are the various solutions that different species have found to the problem of surviving. But, whatever the oddity of the set-up, a healthy well-functioning shark or praying mantis is one that fits into the requirements of the species, one that lives well with its kin, according to its kind.

What distinguishes the human animal is the extraordinary new way it has found of living with its kind. What binds the human species together, and what is thus necessary for its flourishing, is not just kinship, blood-relationship, but what we may call culture – that whole area that arises from our capacity to create symbols, centrally of course, to use language (but we have to include music, painting, the building of cities, the development of communications of all kinds, all the technologies, arts and sciences). It is because of all this that our life-times are life-stories, that our lives are in our own hands.

We have a special name for human living with each other. We call it friendship (what Aristotle called *philia*). Friendship is more than people wishing well to other people. It involves what Aquinas calls *communicatio*, sharing, and the New Testament calls *koinonia*, sharing a common life. Friendship is a matter of being *with* others.

Now if the purpose of human living is to live with each other, and if this involves living in friendship, so that the good life for human animals is one in which friendship is fostered and preserved, this is *not* something that we have resolved upon, not a decision or option we have come to, not even a 'fundamental option'. It is something that belongs to us because of the kind of animal we are, the linguistic or rational animal. We are born as players of this game: we do not *decide* what shall be its aim and purpose; we *discover* these things. Of course discovering what kind of animals we are and what this implies takes a very long time and centuries of poetry and drama and critical philosophical thinking, and even then we are likely to make a lot of mistakes. That is why Thomas Aquinas thought it was very decent of God to help us out by giving us an outline of what it is to live in friendship: this is the Ten Commandments. God thought that, after some thought, we might come to the conclusion that friends would not kill each other or seduce each other's husbands or wives or get them falsely convicted of crimes or kidnap them and enslave them or seek to defraud them of their possessions; but all the same it would be a good idea to get all this down in black and white, or better still, on tablets of stone. Well, it wasn't quite like that: the Decalogue is part of God's summons to Israel to be his people, to share in his life and his righteousness. God is telling them that the first step to being God's people is to be human people, and that means living in friendship.

It is, however, important to see that what is provided by such a document as the Decalogue is precisely an *outline* of friendship. That is to say it draws a boundary around friendship to show where it stops: beyond these limits friendship does not exist. This is the characteristic function of *law*. When I was talking about football and saying that it is our invention and that its aims and purposes are decided by the Football Authorities, I said that their decision in the end determined what counts as *good or bad* play, and also what counts as *inadmissible* play. These are two different kinds of stipulation. It is the difference between perhaps not playing football well and not playing it at all, but perhaps pretending to. Someone who commits a foul is seeking to obtain a result which looks like winning a football match, without playing football. It is with such matters that laws are characteristically concerned and they are very important. But you cannot learn how to play football well simply by knowing what such laws are. Learning to play football well is a matter of acquiring skill by practice. For this you need the guidance of a teacher who already knows how to play well, though it may also be useful to read a book written by such a teacher. In either case you do not learn by listening to what the teacher says or by reading what he says. You learn by *practising* in accordance with what he says. If it is a matter of some complicated athletic feat or manoeuvre, you will begin by laboriously following the dotted lines in the diagram and going through the process many times, telling yourself what the next bit is. During the early stages of learning you will be listening to yourself or listening to your teacher and following the instructions. As you carry on you will gradually develop a skill; the thing will become, as they say, 'second nature' to you. This is what Aquinas calls a *habitus*, a disposition. *Habitus* does not mean habit. To be able to drive a car is a *habitus* or disposition. It means you can drive without an instructor, without constantly referring to a manual, without having to tell yourself when it is safe to overtake or when you should use your indicator. You just do these things intelligently and effortlessly. To drive skillfully in this way is not to drive out of habit in the sense that you may have a drink habit or a habit of smoking. A disposition or skill or *habitus* makes it easier for you to do what you want to do; a habit makes it harder for you not to do what you do not want to do.

The dispositions you need to acquire in order to play football well are skills, dispositions towards producing a good *result*, a good solution to a particular footballing problem for example. The dispositions you need to acquire in order to play the game of life well are called virtues. It is because we are not just

human beings but human becomings that we need virtues. We need dispositions that will make it easy for us to make good practical decisions in carrying
on our life-story. So while a skill or a technique is directed to the excellence of
the thing produced, a virtue is directed to the excellence of the producer. The
excellence we are concerned with when we look at human behaviour in the
totally practical, totally non-abstract way that we adopt in moral judgement is
not the excellence of something that *results* from a human action but the very
human action itself. This is going to mean: Is it directed towards or against the
being human (or becoming human) of this human actor? And this is going
to mean in the end: Is it or is it not a preservation and fostering of friendship
– that kind of friendship upon which human community and thus human
existence depends? I say this is what it means in the *end*, because this is what
the good life is for a human animal. But this is not what our immediate moral
judgements are about. You do not criticize a move by a footballer simply by
saying it is bad football, you say in what particular way his actions have failed
in skill, and the skills involved in football are many and various, but nothing
like as many and various as the virtues required for the good human life.

There is one important connection between technical skills and virtues
I'd like to mention because it has to do with learning or acquiring virtues.
Besides individual skills like being able to carve the turkey or play the flute,
there are skills about skills, like being a good host or playing in an orchestra,
which involve coordinating many skills and, most importantly, co-operating
with others. Even learning an individual skill ordinarily involves a relationship
with a teacher; and learning how to work with a team or with an orchestra
involves even more complex relationships with people. It is most commonly
when learning how to engage in large-scale communal projects of this kind
that virtues are developed – even though virtues themselves are not simply
complex skills.

Virtues are dispositions that have to do with practical behaviour. So they
belong to our living, which is a complex interweaving of knowledge and

desire. We share with the other animals desires which arise from our sense-interpretation of our world: things are attractive to us (or not) because of how they feel to us. But being linguistic animals, we also interpret our world in terms of what can be *said* of it. To speak of the world is not merely to express how it makes us feel but how it is and is not. It is our linguistic capacity that makes us able to grasp truth, to escape from the subjectivity and privacy of feeling into objectivity. And this is because linguistic meanings do not belong to anyone in the way that feelings do. Meanings do not *belong* to anyone in the way that feelings do; meanings are in the language, which is, of its nature, public and common. So nobody could have my sensations, only more or less similar ones; but everyone must be able to have my thoughts. It is most unlikely that you have exactly the same sensations as I have in drinking a pint of Guinness, but we all mean exactly the same by the clause 'drinking a pint of Guinness'. As Aquinas sees it, understanding a meaning is transcending our privacy, subjectivity, materiality, to share with each other, communicate with each other in terms of truth, in ways which are not simply bodily, by the use of signs and symbols to express meanings. So to have language is to be able to know the truth about the world, and, of course, by the same token, to make mistakes about it. What we feel is just what we feel and there is no way of 'correcting' it; but what we say of the world is open to discussion with others and within ourselves. Using our intelligence, unlike seeing, is a task, a work of investigation, something we have to do. And we may or may not want to do it. For just as our sense-knowledge gives rise to desires (we are attracted or not by what we sense) so does our rational knowledge, our linguistic way of interpreting the world. And the thing about this linguistic interpretation is that it isn't simply there like a sensation. A hungry dog seeing a juicy steak, unless it is sick, cannot but desire it. It can only be aware of the steak under the aspect of its smell and pleasant appearance. But we are aware of things not just in terms of their sensible appearance but also under a description, in fact under an indefinite number of descriptions. We are not only attracted by the smell, etc.; we also recognize the steak as, for example, belonging to somebody else, being produced by the slaughter of harmless beasts, high in cholesterol, extremely expensive, and so on. All these are thoughts or considerations about the steak, and plainly they could go on indefinitely. How much we will think about the matter is in part a matter of how much we want to. For considering something is a human activity and human activity is done because we want to do it, because we find it attractive, or at least not repulsive, to do it.

Suppose that my neighbour's wife and I are extremely attracted to each other and wish to go to bed together. Of course I know quite well that she is my neighbour's wife. But there is a difference between knowing something and considering it, bringing it before my mind: just as you knew five minutes ago who was the President of the United States but you were, I like to think, not paying any especial attention to this piece of knowledge. Now it is quite possible for me to find the thought of my beloved as my neighbour's wife an unpleasant one to contemplate, and so I push it to the back of my mind where it does not provide a motive for action (or inaction). In this way I will be motivated to do what I know quite well to be irrational and wrong and which on later consideration I will acknowledge to be such. It is our linguistic capacity to understand things and situations under an indefinite number of descriptions that in St Thomas's view is the root of human freedom, the root of our capacity to make actions really our own, flowing from our own decision, and also of course our capacity to deceive ourselves and behave irrationally.

In the story I have been telling about my alleged sex life, what was missing, of course, was a good education. If I had only acquired by education certain elementary virtues, things would have appeared differently. What I needed was, for example, the virtue of temperateness in my emotional life so that I would not be simply overwhelmed by sexual attraction but keep it in its proper place amongst many other aspects of human living. I would also need the virtue of justice so that I just naturally took account of what was owing both to my beloved and to her husband; I would be reluctant to exploit her affection for me, and reluctant to deceive him and make their marital life even more difficult than most marital lives are. The result of acquiring such virtues would be that I would have had a truer view of the situation, I would be considering the important things about it and not the relatively trivial good to be attained by going to bed with her, or anyway not concentrating exclusively on this trivial good.

But above and beyond such virtues as temperateness and justice, I would need to have acquired the virtue of good sense, or *prudentia*. This is not reckoned by St Thomas among the moral virtues because it has not to do directly with desires but with understanding. He says it is an intellectual virtue, but since it is concerned with the practical intellect it is all tied up with the virtues that govern desires, and without it there can be no true moral virtues. Good sense is the virtue or, rather, the cluster of virtues that make it easy and second nature to us to make good decisions. Good sense is a kind of clear-sightedness about our problems which enables us to put them in proper perspective, to see what is more important and what is less so. It also, and most importantly, involves a certain clear-sightedness about my self.

Moralists from the late middle ages onwards, and particularly since the sixteenth century, have seen the characteristic human act as one flowing from the free will, viewed as a separate faculty from intelligence. For Aristotle and for Aquinas, the characteristic human act is one done for a reason, the product of practical intelligence. In such practice, desire and understanding interact at all stages: we desire what we consider good, and we consider when we want to.

The pattern of moral thinking for the later thinkers consisted of two sharply divided stages: first the understanding assembled all the facts and worked out what would happen if we did and worked out what was in accordance with moral law and presented all these findings to the will. At this stage you know what is right and proper to do. Then comes the crucial question. After all the reasoning has been done, we still have to find out whether you will act on these findings or not. This is the sacred province of the free will: your will to go one way rather than the other.

This is the theory of decision making that is satirized in the BBC comedy show *Yes Minister*. Humphrey, the civil servant, is supposed to be a pure intellect and fact-gathering machine with no policies of his own; when he has delivered his findings, Jim Hacker, the minister, will exercise his will and action will follow. The point of the programme, of course, is to show that it is actually Humphrey who makes the policy decisions, for there is no such thing as pure will. How you act depends on how the facts are presented and this itself comes from an interplay of desire and understanding. Once this is done, Jim Hacker's alleged decision is a foregone conclusion. This is as true of individual personal decisions as it is of politics. There is no practical intelligence standing neutrally above the fray. How you think about a situation, even how you identify a situation, crucially depends on your policies or, as we say in the personal case, your virtues or vices.

The consequence of the sixteenth-century 'voluntarist' view of the moral life was that the work of the intelligence was seen as something that could be detached from the actual moments of decision. You could think of a solution to moral problems in the abstract, in the quiet of your study, and you could write your conclusions in books – thus we got the handbooks of so-called moral theology giving you the solution to each problem. Of course it was recognized that in the concrete no two moral problems are exactly the same, so as time went on more and more complicated qualifications were added, and the science of casuistry was born. In the face of conflicting reasons for thinking an action lawful or not, principles of decision called systems of casuistry were devised – 'It is OK to follow the most probable view', or even 'any probable view', and so on. I will not deter you with these. The important point is that when with the aid of your handbooks and your casuistry you had seen the light, there then remained the decision for Jim Hacker, your free will.

It is, as always, a relief to turn from all this muddle to the sanity of Aristotle and Aquinas. For them, acting in terms of reasons is *of course* free because thinking is free. The way you interpret the world through language and concepts is not determined by your bodily structure, your nervous system and brain, as is the way you and other animals interpret it through your senses. Thinking is creative interpretation. But how you interpret your world will depend on what kind of person you are, what virtues or vices you have developed. In what, in this tradition, is called the 'practical syllogism', an *action* follows from premises in a way parallel to the way a *conclusion* follows from premises in a theoretical syllogism. Practical reasoning is not just thinking about what means are the best way of achieving this end; it is much more crucially thinking what sort of action follows from the kind of person I am.

As Aristotle said, in a remark which has puzzled modern moralists, you have to have a *character* in order to make a decision. To make a decision is to make an action *your own*, one that really flows from you, flows from the dispositions that have made you the person you are. Just plumping for one thing rather than another, as a child might, just being persuaded by the handsome canvasser on the doorstep or threats from the pulpit, is not to make a decision of your own. Of course when it comes to praise and blame, when it comes to deciding whether you are engaged in leading the good life, carrying on your life-story in a human way, not making a decision may be as blame-worthy as making a bad decision.

The basic point is that teaching morality (or anything I could recognize as morality) must be a matter of enabling people to make good decisions which will be their *own* decisions. And this is done by helping them to acquire dispositions both of heart and mind. I suppose this might sometimes be done by story-telling – not telling moral tales, but entering imaginatively into the life-stories of interesting people, and also by imaginative dramatic reconstruction of situations of decision and so on. That is just a suggestion I throw out. I am, however, sure that the task is not to be achieved by getting people to read handbooks of moral theology.

But perhaps the most important conclusion of all follows from the recognition that morality is about doing and making and not first of all about explaining. The modern philosopher who has done more than anyone else in recent years to re-habilitate the Aristotelean idea of morality as based in virtue is surely Alasdair MacIntyre. For him all philosophical thinking is a kind of traditional craft that has to be handed from generation to generation, so that if the sequence is broken certain disastrous results follow. Whether or not this is in general true it seems to me quite obviously true of moral philosophy. Of its practical nature it must be traditional, that is to say deriving from and criticizing and modifying a tradition. If your aim is to teach the craft of making violins, you do not give your student some wood and some tools and tell him to get on with it. You show him how violins have been made – and this is part of showing him what a violin is. He will copy the work and techniques of skilled men of the past, and after several years or nearly a life-time of this he may be ready to add to and modify the tradition into which he has been introduced. And now I leave it to you to consider whether the craft of making human beings, or human becomings, is likely to be any quicker and easier to acquire than the making of violins. For me, I think to imagine you can read it all up in a book (*Teach Yourself Human-Making* as it might be named) must be crazy; though that is what they sometimes call being traditional. It is just as crazy to imagine that the beginner is somehow automatically competent to decide or even understand or even recognize what human decisions are, off his or her own bat. Learning morality is, it seems to me, learning to be free; and doing that in any depth has to take most of a life-time, most of a life-story.

PART THREE

ESSAYS ON AQUINAS

14

A Very Short Introduction to Aquinas

I

A friend of mine claims that once in a restaurant he overheard one waiter saying to another waiter: 'He's eaten it.' When you catch a snippet of conversation like that you begin to be puzzled about its context. It's going to be a little like that with what follows. We are going to overhear fragments of talk, and I am going to try to fit them into a context.

Imagine you are passing the open window of a lecture room in the University of Paris one autumn in the thirteenth century. The room is crowded with young men who are going to be teachers or preachers (or both), and their lecturer, a Dominican Friar called Thomas Aquinas, is starting his course of lectures by telling them that if they are going to teach or preach they must first of all be taught themselves by God.

God has destined us for a goal beyond the grasp of reason – *No eye has seen what you have prepared for those who love you* – and since we must set ourselves this goal and pursue it we needed teaching about it beforehand. We even need revealed instruction in things reason can learn about God. If such truths had been left to us to discover, they would have been learnt by few over long periods and mingled with much error; yet our whole well-being is centered on God and depends on knowing them. So, in order that more of us might more safely attain him, we need teaching in which God revealed himself.[1]

Aquinas treats theology as a practical matter. He is not interested in spinning theories about angels and the points of a pin. He is concerned with human well-being. Behind what he says is the image of people going somewhere: we have a 'goal', and (more mysteriously) a goal 'beyond the grasp of reason'. Human well-being, he thinks, is a kind of journey, but a journey into the unknown, towards a destination we only dimly perceive by faith. I think here of the medieval folk-tale of the youngest son going out to seek his fortune. I used to think that he was going out in search of a fortune, a whole lot of money, but of course he wasn't: he went to seek his *fortuna*, his luck.

For Aquinas the goal is already partly with us in the journey itself. For him the world is good – but not good enough. For him there is no evil in this material creation. Everything that is, is good. Every being has God within it holding it in being. It is just that some goods are greater than others. Evil comes in when we neglect some great good for the sake of some trivial good: when we sacrifice, say, being just and loving for the sake of being rich. Evil, for Aquinas is a purely spiritual thing. It belongs to the world of minds and policies and decisions – and even there it is not a positive thing but a failure, a failure to want the good enough. The material world, however, is innocent, and more than innocent; it is the scintillating manifestation of the love of God.

All the more important, then, that we get our priorities right, and, to a certain extent, we can get them right if we keep our emotions in order and exercise ordinary good sense. We can try to use maps, but, in the end, ours is a journey without maps because it is a journey beyond the human horizon, a journey towards living with God himself. We are fortunate enough, lucky enough, to be personal friends of God – this good luck is what Thomas calls 'grace'. So our journey is really more like a treasure hunt – we are guided only by certain clues. But God, Aquinas is telling his students, is generous even with the clues. He tells us not only things we couldn't know of ourselves. He even tells us some things that we might have found out for ourselves if we were clever enough. And he does this, says Aquinas, because the journey to human well-being is not just for intellectuals, not just for an elite, the well-educated, the perceptive. God has distributed his clues to all of us, showing us how our lives can be more human, showing us how we can become divine, because he loves all of us.

II

Thomas Aquinas thought that theologians don't know what they are talking about. They try to talk about God, but Aquinas was most insistent that they do not, and cannot, know what God is. He was, I suppose, the most agnostic theologian in the western Christian tradition – not agnostic in the sense of doubting whether God exists, but agnostic in the sense of being quite clear and certain that God is a *mystery* beyond any understanding we can now have.

He was sure that God *is* because he thought that there must *be* an answer to the deepest and most vertiginous question: 'Why is there anything instead of nothing at all?' But he was also sure that we do not know what that answer is. To say it is God who made the whole universe, and holds it continually in existence from moment to moment (as singers hold their songs in existence from moment to moment), is not to *explain* how the universe comes to exist. For we do not know what we mean by 'God'. We use this word just as a convenient label for something we do not understand. For Aquinas, only God understands what God is. Aquinas thought that in the Bible God has promised us that one day he will give us a share in his self-understanding, but not yet. Until that day, although God has begun to reveal himself in his Word made flesh, we grasp his self-communication not by coming to know, but only by faith. Faith is an illumination that appears as darkness: we come to know that we do not know.

Aquinas thought that we know of God only by trying to understand the things he has done and does for us – the marvellous works of his creation, the even more marvellous works of his salvation, God's personal love for creatures who have rejected him by sin – the whole story that he tells us in the Bible. But none of these works are adequate to show us God himself – no more than you could come to understand the mind of Shakespeare or Beethoven by hearing them ask you to pass the salt.

> Our natural knowledge starts from sense-perception and reaches only as far as things so perceived can lead us, which is not far enough to see God in himself. For the things we sense, though effects of God, are not effects fully expressing his power. But because they do depend on him as their cause, they can lead us to know that he exists, and reveal to us whatever is true of him as first cause of all such things, surpassingly different from all of them … God's gracious revelation … strengthens our natural light of intelligence … Although in this life revelation cannot show us what God is in himself, but joins us to him as unknown, nevertheless it helps us to know him better, showing us more and greater works of his.[2]

For Thomas Aquinas, our proper and reasonable response to God is not one of exact analysis, but of prayer. People who think they have no belief quite often say that they want to pray but do not know who or what they could be praying to. Aquinas would *not* say to such people, 'Ah, but you see, if you became a believer, a Christian, we would change all that. You would come to understand to whom you are praying.' Not at all. He would say to such people, 'If you became a Christian you would stop being surprised by or ashamed of your condition. You would be happy with it. For faith would assure you that you *could not* know what God is until he reveals himself to us openly.'

Praying without knowing, or expecting to know, to whom you are praying is the normal and natural way for a Christian. For now what matters is not knowledge; what matters is faith and confidence in the love of God for us, and the courage to share in that love and pass it on to others – until the time when God's promise is fulfilled. 'For now we see in a mirror, dimly, but then we will see face to face. Now I know only in part; then I will know fully, even as I have been fully known.'[3]

III

According to Thomas Aquinas, if God is the cause of *all* that is, we can at least be sure that nothing can be the cause of God. This, says Aquinas, makes a radical difference between the way we love and the way God loves. For our love is caused by the goodness and attractiveness of what we love, but this cannot be the case with God. He does not love things or people because they are good; on the contrary, they are good and attractive because God loves them. God's love is creative; it brings about the goodness of what he loves. When, as it says in the beginning of the Book of Genesis (1.31), 'God saw everything that he had made, and indeed, it was very good', God was not discovering its goodness. He was not struck with admiration by its beauty. Its goodness and beauty were his doing, the work of his love. For Aquinas, the entire universe, from each single raindrop to the furthest galaxies, exists because at every moment it is known and loved by God. The reason why God cannot love sin and evil is simply that 'sin' and 'evil' are not the names of things. They are defects, failures, non-being in otherwise good things. If I am sinful it is because I am failing to live up to what my humanity demands of me. I am failing to be just, kind, gentle or loving. I am failing to have that intense, passionate love for God's creation and God himself that would make me a fully developed human being. So God does not make sin and evil any more than he makes the elephant that is not in my garden. He makes all that does exist, and makes it by love.

> Everything that exists is, as such, good, and has God as its cause. Clearly then God loves all things, willing them every good they possess; yet not as we do. Our love doesn't cause a thing's goodness; rather the thing's goodness, real or imagined, evokes our love, and enlists our help in preserving and furthering that goodness. But God's love evokes and creates the goodness in things … God loves sinners as beings he has created, but he hates their sinning, which is a way of not being and is not God's doing. God loves everything with the same simple uniform act of will; but just as we love those persons more to whom we will greater good, even when we will it with no greater intensity, so too with God. God causes the goodness in things, and one thing would not be better than another unless God loved it more.[4]

So God's love is at the centre of every existing thing, the deepest reality in every existing thing. The special point about human beings, however, which is not shared by other animals, is that we can lay hold on ourselves, on the centre of our being, by knowledge and love. Of course, other animals can know and love too, but not in the very profound sense in which we are able to do so by our capacity for symbolizing and articulating our world in language. Because we have this capacity to understand and to love, God can give us the capacity to respond to his love at the centre of our being. God strengthens our understanding by the gift of faith and strengthens our loving by the gift of charity, so that we share in *his* self-understanding and in *his* loving. It is true that our share in God's self-understanding does not yet make God clear to us – that is something we are promised for the future. For the present, faith is more like a darkness. But we walk confidently in this dark, for we have learned not to put our trust in the specious and beguiling lights which fall short of the truth of God.

Faith is only the beginning of our sharing in God's self-knowledge, in God's Word, and, as St Paul tells us, it will pass away as it is transformed into the vision of God.[5] But our sharing in God's loving, in that creative love in which he makes all things, our *charity*, will not pass away. The power to love as God loves, the power to share in his creativity, is the life we shall share for eternity.

IV

Thomas Aquinas thought that God created a world with its own order, with its own natural causes within it. So we can explain the characteristic behaviour of one sort of thing by referring to the behaviour of another kind of thing within creation. Magnetic needles point to the north because of the earth's magnetic field, and in its turn a magnetic field is caused by the behaviour of subatomic particles.

These are not, of course, Aquinas's own examples, but, like most of us, he thought that there were causes in this world, and causes of these causes – a sort of hierarchical order of causes (like a chain of command). And this whole explanatory order, he thought, was created and sustained in being by God. He also thought it was the business of the natural sciences to trace this order of natural explanations (to show how the universe explains its own character). For this reason, he thought that there was no need for scientists to bring God into their scientific explanations. God is simply presupposed to be at the heart of the existence of the whole world that the scientist studies. It is quite true that God causes the kettle to boil, as he causes everything, but the scientist is interested in the natural created causes that God uses to bring about this effect. Physicists may well be driven to ask, 'What is the explanation of there being anything at all instead of nothing at all?', but if they ask this, they are no longer doing physics. Aquinas would have been surprised and amused by the idea that in studying what seems to have happened in the first moments of the Big Bang we are somehow studying the act of creation. The creative act of God is not, for him, something *unique* to the beginning (if there was, indeed, a beginning), but to the continuing existence of anything at any time. In fact, he thought that God could easily have created a world which never had a beginning. For him the creative act of God is at work within the working of every creature all the time.

What, then, does he think about miracles? He says that God's activity is deep within everything and that nature's activities are to be attributed to God working within nature. But Aquinas also thinks that, if he wants, God can override created causes so that he himself produces their normal effects or effects beyond their power.[6] So Aquinas didn't see miracles as God intervening to interfere with the world. God, cannot literally intervene in the universe because he is always there – just as much in the normal, natural run of things as in the Resurrection of Christ or in any other miraculous event. A miracle, for Aquinas, is not a special *presence* of God; it is a special *absence* of natural causes – a special absence that makes the perpetual presence of God more visible to us. Since God is there all the time, and since he doesn't need to be mentioned when we are doing physics or biology, or doing the shopping, we may be in danger of forgetting him. So a miracle, in Aquinas's view, is an exuberant gesture, like an embrace or a kiss, to say 'Look, I'm here; I love you', lest in our wonder and delight at the works of his creation we forget that all that we have and all we are is the radiance of his love for us.

V

What is it to be a good person? What is it to live well rather than badly? We might say: 'It is to act in accordance with some true moral code.' If we are Christians or Jews, we might mention the moral code of the Ten Commandments. If we say this, however, we will find at least one person who disagrees with us, and that is Thomas Aquinas. He did not think that living well consists in acting in accordance with the commandments. This is not because he thought (as some modern Christians do) that the commandments have been superseded by the law of love. He thought the Ten Commandments were just a common-sense account of what loving behaviour is like (and especially what it is *not* like). He thought that any society which was indifferent to whether you broke the commandments or not couldn't be a community of friends. He thought these commandments were one of those things given to us by God in his revelation which we could have worked out for ourselves if we thought hard and honestly enough about what a society based on friendship would be like.

But although Aquinas holds the moral code of the commandments in high esteem, he would still disagree with you if you said that living well is simply acting in accordance with the commandments. Why? Because, he says, living well is not *just* a matter of doing good things instead of bad things. It is a matter of doing them *well*, and that means doing them from the depths of your real character.

You may do an act of kindness, you may send a donation for the relief of famine, say, in Africa, because you have been momentarily swayed by television reporting or whatever, and that, of course, is a good thing to do. You may do it because you have been told that it is the right thing for a Christian to do. You may do it because you fear that God will punish you if you don't, and it is still a good thing to do. But Aquinas would say that this is still not what living well means. Living well means doing good because you *want* to do it, because you have become the kind of *you* that just naturally wants to do this. Then you are no longer just doing kind *acts*. You are a kind *person*.

Living well is not only doing good things, but doing them well, choosing them in a right way and not simply acting on impulse or emotion. Right choosing involves having a right goal and suitably acting to achieve that goal. The dispositions to right goals are the moral virtues in the appetites; the disposition to act suitably to achieve the goal must dispose reason to plan and decide well, and that is the virtue of prudence. Doing something good on another's advice rather than one's own judgment is not yet a perfect activity of one's own reasoning and desiring. One does the good but not altogether well, as living requires. Thinking in a theoretical way seeks the true match of mind to things ... Thinking practically seeks the true match to right appetite, and that can only happen in ... matters we have power to influence ... So the virtues concerned with contingent matters are dispositions of practical thought: skill for making, prudence for doing. In the case of doing, man's practical reasoning makes plans and decisions just as his theoretical reasoning explores and arrives at conclusions, but then goes on to issue commands to do things, and that is its special role. If men made good decisions and then didn't implement them properly, reason's work would be incomplete.[7]

So Aquinas thought we become good, we live well, by acquiring a *character*, a complex set of dispositions which incline us, first of all, to want good things (and to want greater goods more than lesser goods), and then to think well in a practical way (to be wise) about how to achieve these goods. These dispositions are *virtues*, and we acquire them normally by *practice*. First, we do good things because we want to please our parents or others, or because we want to follow some moral code. But, gradually, such behaviour becomes second nature to us, and then and *only* then do we have the virtues. Then we are grown up. Then when we do good actions they are our *own*, springing from the personality we have created for ourselves with the help of others. That's what education is, or ought to be.

But, of course, Aquinas thought that we are not simply called by God to live well as human beings, but to live the life of God; and this is the sheer gift of God. So God, besides giving us clues to guide us on our way to him, also gives us the power to make the journey. He begins to share his own live with us and so gives us the virtues we need to live well both humanly and divinely – and gives them as a free grace, by-passing the laborious educational process.

VI

That great English Tory, Dr Johnson, declared: 'I have always said the first Whig was the Devil.' That great English Whig (or liberal), Lord Acton, said: 'The first Whig was not the Devil, but Thomas Aquinas.' I am not sure that Aquinas would have been altogether pleased with that compliment. Certainly he had no time for liberal free-market economics and unrestrained competition. He thought that it was the business of the state to care for all the people, especially the poor, and in some cases to intervene to decree maximum prices and minimum wages. He thought that the purpose of law was not just to protect people from each other, but to help them all to be virtuous and, therefore, most likely to be happy in this world. He would undoubtedly have welcomed the Welfare State.

He would have disagreed strongly with Margaret Thatcher when she said: 'There is no such thing as society, only individuals and their families.' He was more subtle than that. He said that the individual is essentially a part of society, and that the good of the whole society is greater than the good of the individual. But he also thought that the whole society exists for the sake of the good lives of its individuals.

Aquinas was a Whig or liberal in that he had no time for any notion of the 'divine right of kings', or the divine right of the Party, and would rejoice at the collapse of dictatorships. He said that the authority of rulers and their laws comes only from the consent of the governed, and he said that 'planning for the general good belongs to the people as a whole, or to those who represent them' (*Summa Theologiae*, 1a2ae,90,3). He thought that a legitimate representative of the people, ruling with their consent and making laws for the common good (and not just for the good of this or that class or section within society), was ruling justly. Insofar as he or she ruled justly, he or she ruled with the authority of God, but *only* insofar as he or she ruled justly.

> Humanly enacted laws can be just or unjust. To be just they must serve the general good, must not exceed the lawmaker's authority, and must fairly apportion the burdens of the general good amongst all members of the community. Such just laws oblige us in conscience since they derive from the eternal law. Laws however can be unjust: by serving not the general good but some lawmaker's own greed or vanity, or by exceeding his authority, or by unfairly apportioning the burdens the general good imposes. Such laws are not so much laws as forms of violence, and do not oblige our consciences except perhaps to avoid scandal and disorder, on which account men must sometimes forego their right. Laws can also be unjust by running counter to God's good, promoting idolatry say; and nobody is allowed to obey such laws: *we must obey God rather than men.*[8]

Aquinas thought that an unjust society which discriminates against some section of the people on grounds of racism or ideology or religious bigotry, or any other grounds, is already a society of violence rather than law – long before any dissidents seek to overthrow it. Law, says Aquinas, is only just, and only genuine law, if it is an expression of morality. On the other hand, however, Aquinas did not think it the business of law to repress every immorality, for, he believed, this may often do more damage to the common good than tolerating a wicked practice. Here, said Aquinas, rulers must use their common sense, their wisdom, to decide whether or not some particular human behaviour should be a crime. Aquinas, for instance, thought that abortion was sinful and a great human evil. But, when you have said that, you have not yet decided whether and how it should be forbidden by law. That is something Aquinas would think open to discussion amongst people all equally committed to the sanctity of all human life. Yes, perhaps he was the first Whig.

VII

It would be quite generally agreed that the foundation of Christian morality is that people should love each other. Thomas Aquinas, interestingly, did not agree. Of course, it depends on what you mean by 'love'. You can love your mother, good wine, your country and your boyfriend – each with a different kind of love. When it comes to love in its most fundamental sense, however, Aquinas thought that the author of the first letter of John had got it right: 'In this is love, not that we loved God but that he loved us and sent his Son ...'[9] Love is, first of all, what *God* has for us; indeed this love *is* God. God loves us so much that he lets us share in his own power of loving. We have a special name for our sharing in God's power to love: we call it *charity*.

This divine charity of ours, says Aquinas, is first of all our response to God's love for us. So first there is the mutual love which makes us friends with God, sharing in his life and joy. This is the foundation of Christian morality: not a code of conduct but our friendship with God, or sharing in his Spirit, which shows itself in our love for God's friends and creatures. But our friendship with God, says Aquinas, surprisingly but profoundly, does not first overflow into love of others. First of all, he insists, we must love ourselves. If we do not love ourselves, we cannot love others.

There is a kind of fake altruism in which we can busy ourselves with others because we fear that, if we really considered ourselves, we would hate what we see. But charity means that we are able to take a clear look at ourselves, warts and all, and yet love ourselves in charity as God does. This is not selfishness. Selfishness comes from loving not our whole selves but just that part of ourselves that is our bodily life and our bodily possessions (in which we can be in competition with others). In charity I am concerned for the flourishing and happiness of my whole self, including the health and strength and liveliness of my body, but not excluding even more important things like my attitudes to others.

> Strictly speaking we don't have friendship for ourselves but something more: a love of self which is at the root of all friendship, since in friendship we love others as we love ourselves. But charity is friendship first with God and secondly with all who belong to God including ourselves. So we love ourselves with charity, inasmuch as we too are God's. When we blame people for self-love it is because they love … their bodily natures, not loving what is genuinely good for themselves as rational beings … Our bodies were created by God, not … by some evil principle. So we can serve God with our bodies, and should love them with the charity with which we love God. What we shouldn't love is the taint of sin and the damage it has wreaked in our bodies; we should rather long with charity for an end of all that. Our body helps us to happiness, and that happiness will overflow into our bodies, so that they too can be loved with charity.[10]

Thomas Aquinas is a very long way from those people, including some Christians, who think that the body, and especially our bodily pleasures and emotions, is to be feared and avoided. He thought that we must learn to love and take delight in our bodily life (as God does) – giving it its due place and dignity. For God loves our bodily selves not only as creatures, but as personal friends. Aquinas says in one place that separation from God by sin has so distorted our emotional life that we do not enjoy sex enough.[11]

For Aquinas, it is only heretics who dislike and despise the body. For him the Word of God to us is not, first of all, words in a book. It is the Word made flesh, through whose body and blood we are brought back to friendship with God, so that at the resurrection of the body the divine life will overflow into our bodies in eternity.

VIII

Not very many people can claim to understand just where physics is going nowadays, but sixty or so years ago we were hearing that the behaviour of things depended on their atoms, and that atoms consisted of rings of electrons spinning around a nucleus. Each atom was a bit like a tiny solar system, and the familiar visible goings on in the world were more or less determined by the structure of these revolving systems of particles.

Remembering this may help us to understand how Aquinas, in the thirteenth century, saw the physical world. His picture was remarkably similar, except that the spinning objects that determined the laws of physics and chemistry, instead of being very much smaller than our familiar objects, were very much bigger. He inherited the ancient belief that the revolutions of the stars and the planets played much the same part as the modern spinning of subatomic particles: they accounted for the regular, predictable behaviour of physical objects. Aquinas was quite wrong, of course, but his ideas about how far the stars determine happenings on earth remain, perhaps, relevant when we ask how far the mechanisms studied by modern scientists determine what goes on.

Medieval people were almost as superstitious as modern people, and fascinated by 'what the stars foretell'. But Aquinas was very sceptical about all that. He thought that the stars could affect us physically, and so, like tranquillizers, or alcohol, or lack of sleep, could affect our emotions and feelings, and incline us to certain kinds of behaviour. *Incline* us, but not *determine* us, for we can stop and think, and we can deliberately cultivate patterns of reasonable behaviour (virtues), so that we won't be dominated by the feelings of the moment. In this way we can escape slavery to the stars (so Aquinas thought).

Nevertheless, because a great many people don't bother to think, or to learn how to be reasonable, they are swept away by their feelings and prejudices. That, Aquinas thought, is why astrologers can often be right statistically about majority behaviour – rather like sociologists predicting (or at least explaining) trends or voting patterns.

> Clearly events which happen necessarily can be predicted with the help of the stars, in the way astronomers predict eclipses. But the stars neither signify nor cause future chance events ... Nor can the stars cause free acts of reason and will; bodies cannot directly affect our mind and will, which are neither bodily nor functions of bodily organs. The stars can cause changes in human bodies, and so influence our sensual desires which are functions of bodily organs. So the stars can incline us to certain behaviour. But since ... our sensual desires obey reason, man still has a free will to act against the influence of the stars. So, trying to predict chance events or human behaviour from an inspection of the stars is pointless ... This doesn't preclude prediction of things which are truly effects of the stars, like drought and rainfall and suchlike. Moreover, the stars cause changes in our bodies and influence our emotions, and since most men follow their emotions without controlling them, astrologers often get things right, especially when predicting group behaviour.[12]

For Aquinas, the constant movement of the stars, and the regular behaviour of nature governed by this, is the work of God the creator. But the works of human intelligence are an even greater manifestation of God's power. The things we do because we decide to do so for our own reasons (and not because we are the playthings of physical causes), these *free* acts, are not brought about by any created things, but are directly created by God.

So Aquinas did not think that our freedom makes us independent of God's creative energy (nothing that exists could be that). But it makes us independent of other creatures. For Aquinas, we can stand over against all the forces of nature because of the creative work of God within us. We are free not *in spite of* God, but *because of* God. So human freedom, human creativity, is the greatest manifestation in the world of God's creative love – except for that most free of all human beings, who was himself God's love in the flesh amongst us.

Notes

1   Thomas Aquinas, *Summa Theologiae*, 1a,1,1. All translations of Aquinas here come from Timothy McDermott (ed.), *St Thomas Aquinas, 'Summa Theologiae': A Concise Translation* (London: Eyre and Spottiswoode, 1989). For the present passage see McDermott, p. 1.

2   *Summa Theologiae*, 1a,12,12 and 12,13 (McDermott, p. 29).

3   1 Corinthians 13.12.

4   *Summa Theologiae*, 1a,20,2 (cf. McDermott, pp. 156f.).

5   1 Corinthians, 13.

6   Cf. *Summa Theologiae*, 1a,105,6.

7   *Summa Theologiae*, 1a2ae,57,5–6 (McDermott, p. 236, with slight alterations).

8   *Summa Theologiae*, 1a2ae,96,4 (McDermott, p. 291). The biblical reference is to *Acts* 5.29.

9   1 John 4.10.

10   *Summa Theologiae*, 2a2ae,25,4 and 5 (McDermott, p. 355, with slight alterations).

11   Cf. *Summa Theologiae*, 1a,98,2,ad.3.

12   *Summa Theologiae*, 2a2ae,95,5 (McDermott, p. 413, with slight alterations).

15

Aquinas on 'God is Good'

When we ask ourselves whether God is good we are inclined to think along these lines: God is some kind of person, so to ask whether God is good is to ask whether he is a good person, to ask whether we can attribute to him the characteristics of good people. Is he kind and considerate and just and honest?

Aquinas, to whom I am much indebted when it comes to the topic of God's goodness, decides that some of the words we use in describing good people can be applied to God. But not for reasons as simple-minded as these. He thinks it makes sense to speak of God as just and truthful and loving, and to deny that he is unjust or untruthful. But words which designate moral virtues in human beings do not in the same sense refer to the morality of God. God is not, in this sense, morally good – not, of course, because like tigers and tables he is below the moral level, but because he transcends it. God could not be morally good; still less could he be morally bad, as he could not be physically strong or feeble, healthy or sick. Moral goodness and badness belong to beings which consciously and freely attain, or seek by rational choice to attain, their perfection – a perfection they might or might not have had. Plainly, Aquinas cannot think of God in this way. For according to him there is no potentiality in God, no unfulfilled possibility, or even fulfilled possibility. It never makes sense to say that God might not have been what he actually is. Nor of course could God be rational or irrational or make choices: these things belong to material animals which understand by the use of language or other material symbols. So what *does* Aquinas mean by saying that God is good?

He begins by asking what 'good' means. In its most general sense, he thinks, following Aristotle, that what is good is what is aimed at or sought. It is connected with appetite or tendency, or desire. As truth is what is known, goodness is what is wanted. What is good is what is wanted, to be good is to be attractive. Thus a good bicycle is a bicycle that someone would want if he wanted a bicycle and wanted it simply for being a *bicycle*. You might want a bicycle for very special purposes – for example, as a weapon, or as an object in an artistic composition. And then you might not necessarily want a good bicycle. But if you want it for what bicycles are characteristically for, for *cycling*, then, other things being equal, a good one is just what you will want.

It follows, of course, that goodness is not some common property of things, like roundness or redness, but a function of the nature or role of a thing. The features that make a bicycle a good one are not the features that make an elephant or a glass of whiskey a good one. For this way of thinking, a good X is an X which has whatever features are desirable in that *kind* of thing, an X-kind of thing. A bad X would be an X which lacked some such features. For Aquinas, to say that something is bad is always to indicate that it lacks some feature required for its goodness. Being bad, like being *deaf* or *absent* or *fake* or *neutral*, is always *not* being something. Aquinas thought that we become very confused about the so-called 'problem of evil' if we overlook this elementary logical point, if we imagine that badness is a positive feature of things. He does not mean that what is bad always lacks some bit or part, as though a bad X were always *smaller* than a good X. For a thing may be bad, it may lack desirable features, through having unwanted extras as well as through having bits missing. A bad washing machine, one that fails to wash the clothes, may be so because it doesn't have enough bits (driving belts) or has too much (someone has filled it up with glue). A bad human being, one who fails in, say, the virtue of temperateness, may be so through being filled with strange passions and energies. But more of this later.

Aquinas now considers the notion of perfection. The perfect means, literally, the 'thoroughly made' (from *per* and *facere*). I could botch together something that would be recognizable, and even viable, as a bicycle, but only if I go on to make it *thoroughly*, to give it all the features desirable in a bicycle, does it begin to approach perfection. Other things being equal, if I want to make a bicycle, I will necessarily want to make a good bicycle. The good bicycle will be just what I am aiming at, even though I may not make it thoroughly enough to achieve this aim. Of course, there may be special circumstances in which what I want is precisely to make a bad bicycle (for my enemy, let us say, so that the brakes will fail at a sharp bend when going downhill). But the point is that these are always *special* circumstances. There do not have to be special circumstances for me to aim at making a good bicycle. It is sufficient that I simply want to make a good bicycle.

If you were to watch a bicycle being made, and if you understood the process, you would see the bicycle approaching perfection. To understand the process just is to see it as a making, a movement towards being thoroughly made. This process is at one and the same time the fulfilment of the aim of the bicycle-maker *as* bicycle-maker, and fulfilment or perfecting of the bicycle itself. *The thing before us becomes a perfected and good bicycle just insofar as it attains the end set for it by its maker, which is also the aim set by the maker for himself.* It is a characteristic difference between Aristotelians (like Aquinas) and Platonists that for the Platonists the ideal or model of a thing by which we judge it (and to which it never fully attains) is a form or pattern already existing in an immaterial world apart, laid up in heaven so to say, while for the Aristotelian it is a form or pattern in the aim or intention of the maker. Of course, this is easy to see with human-made artefacts; it is the makers who decide what they are aiming at, and it is by their success or failure in attaining it that they judge their artefact to be good or bad.

Aquinas, however, seeks to apply the same sort of language to natural things: a horse is a good horse in that it attains the aim intended by the maker of horses. Now what does this mean?

In the first place, the maker in question can't be simply the parents of some particular horse (a defective horse is not simply a disappointment to its parents), for the parents of a horse simply produce a repetition of themselves, they are not the makers that determine what *sort of thing* a horse is – in, for example, the way that a bicycle-maker does determine what sort of thing a bicycle is, and so determines what would count as a good, successfully made bicycle. The parents' actions simply determine that there shall be another individual horse. They do not bring it about that there should be horses at all. For evidently the parents themselves are horses already, as were their grandparents and great-grandparents, indefinitely, and they could not bring it about that they themselves are horses. The maker in question, by whose aims the goodness or badness of a horse is to be assessed, must be the second-order maker who determines *what it is to be a horse* in the way that the bicycle-maker (who is not himself a bicycle) determines what it is to be a bicycle.

Suppose that I were to construct a computerized machine, and suppose I were to program it to collect together materials and to shape them into another computer of exactly the same kind, which would, of course, *eo ipso*, be programmed to make yet another. And so on. There does not seem to be anything incongruous or logically odd about this, and, indeed, it seems to be rather like what we see around us in the plants and beasts. Each of these computers could be seen as aiming at replicating another identical computer, though, of course, this does not imply any conscious purpose or choice in them. It is simply *what they tend to do,* being the kind of things they are. This tendency itself is built into them by the manufacturer who determined that they should be *this kind* of machine, having *this* design. Such a manufacturer could be called a *second*-order cause of each computer in the series. The *first*-order cause is the machine immediately before it in the series which brings it about that there shall be another identical individual machine. The second-order cause would be the manufacturer who determined, perhaps chose, the design and programming of the computers, and thereby determined what operations they perform and what they would be (so to say) 'aiming at'. Such a computer would be a good (non-defective) one if it fulfilled this aim of the manufacturer, *qua* manufacturer, who determined the design and, thus, determined what would count as a good computer.

According to the strange cosmology of Aquinas's day, the second-order causes that determined which species of plants and animals there should be reproducing themselves in the world, what designs the terrestrial computers would have, were the 'heavenly bodies'. In some unexplained way the sun and the stars, circling the heavens with an absolute regularity (like the later laws of physics), were supposed to be at the origin of species. This determined that a giraffe would be generated in the image of its parents (its *first*-order cause – the immediately preceding computer) and, at another level, by the sun, its *second*-order cause. It is because of the second-order causal action of the sun that the first-order actions of the parents produce another identical giraffe; just as, in our example, it is the second-order action of the manufacturer which brings it about that the action of the computer brings about the next identical computer in the series. All this appeal to the 'heavenly bodies' was simply the ancient attempt to explain the origin of species. A better answer to the same problem was provided by Charles Darwin who noted that the offspring were sometimes (by chance mutation) *not* exactly identical with their parents and that, in some rare cases, this gave them an advantage in changed circumstances. This meant they lived longer and had more offspring identical with themselves than other less advantaged relatives had, and finally outbred them. We should notice that the difference between Aquinas in the thirteenth century and Darwin in the nineteenth is entirely within the study of biology and need have no theological significance. The Christians who became hot under the theological collar about Darwin were those who did not think that God could creatively bring about random or chance or free occurrences, and who also held that the first chapter of Genesis answered questions in biology and cosmology. Aquinas and his brethren, for the most part, would not accept either of these premises.

Anything made, then, in Aquinas's way of thinking, of its nature (because it is this kind of thing) tends toward or aims at what is intended *for* it by its *second-order cause*. In the case of living things that move themselves this is an active tendency and, in the case of animals, an appetite, a desire. Thus he says that each thing aims at, or has by nature an appetite for, its own perfection and good, and this perfection is to be found in the intention of the maker which determined that it shall have that nature. In seeking its own perfection it is, *eo ipso*, seeking what is in the intention of the maker. In being attracted to its own perfection it is being attracted to its maker precisely as its maker, as having *that* intention.

Thus, for this Aristotelian thinking, the notion of good (aim or final cause) and the notion of efficient, explanatory cause come together. For Aquinas, Kant's dichotomy between truth and value is nonsensical. The good is the object of tendency and, in the case of higher animals, of appetite or desire. What it is that things tend towards is due to (and to be found in) their makers. To be a second-order maker is, as such, to be desired by what it has made as the thing made desires its own perfection. And, with all this in mind, and since God is the ultimate Nth-order maker of everything, Aquinas concludes that each thing, in seeking its own perfection, is seeking (is oriented towards) God. In explaining the activity of any substance we need to look at not only the first-order cause (e.g. the parents of the giraffe whose activity results in there being another individual of the species), nor simply the second-order cause (e.g. the stars or the process of evolution) which determined that there should be *this* species instead of some other, but ultimately the cause in virtue of which there is anything instead of there not being anything, not the origin of the species but the origin of the origin of the species, the cause which Aquinas says we all call God.

So God is the ultimate maker, and, as such, the ultimate desirable, the ultimate good. Every creature, just in naturally tending to its own goodness, is seeking God as what ultimately intends it, as its maker. And this is what, for Aquinas, the goodness of God is first of all about: it is the goodness, the attractiveness or desirability inseparable from being Creator. God is the *omega* because he is the *alpha*, the end because he is the beginning. God is good because he is Creator; not, first, in the moral sense that it was very good of him to create us and we should be grateful, but in the metaphysical sense that, being Creator, he must be the ultimate object of our desire without which we would have no desires. Aquinas puts this by saying that each creature tends to its own natural perfection, but God 'contains the perfections of all things', meaning not that he *is* all things, but that, as maker, he intends their perfections. God has these perfections, says Aquinas, 'in a higher way' in the way that they are in the intention of the *maker* before they are in the *thing made* – not before in time, but in the sense that the presence of these perfections in the made things *depends on* them being in the intention of the maker.

It is because the Creator necessarily contains in this higher way all the perfections that are desired by creatures that we can apply to God words that signify such perfections. Thus we can say that God is wise because he contains (in a higher way) the wisdom that he has intended and created amongst creatures. Just because the wisdom exists in God in a higher way it exceeds what can be signified by our word 'wisdom', and, thus, although we know there is wisdom in God, we cannot understand what it is like for God to be wise – in the way we *can* understand what it is like for Solomon or myself to be wise. Aquinas points out that words like 'wise' are used quite literally of God. They are not used metaphorically. We mean that it is quite true that God is wise and quite *untrue that he is not* wise. Nevertheless, although used literally, these terms are used 'analogically', rather as, say, the word 'good' is used analogically when you say you love wine and you love your mother. The important difference, however, is that whereas we understand just as easily *both* the analogically related uses of 'good' or of 'love' in these cases, we do not understand what the word 'good' or 'wise' refers to when it is used analogically of God.

Aquinas points out that not all words signifying perfections can be applied in this literal (though analogical) way to God, for many of them signify perfection within a context of creatureliness, or even of imperfection. Thus it is a perfection in human beings to be courageous or, in appropriate circumstances, sorrowful and contrite. To say of people that they are courageous is to presuppose that they encounter enemies or dangers, and obviously God cannot literally be threatened like that. So if we were to use such a word of God we would be speaking metaphorically, not literally. And a mark of this would be that it would be quite legitimate both to assert that God is courageous and to deny it – something that would be nonsense if we were speaking literally. Similarly, we must be speaking metaphorically if we say, as one of the authors of Genesis says, 'God was sorry that he had made humankind'.[1]

It will now, perhaps, be clear why Aquinas thinks that we can apply to God words like 'just' and 'truthful' and 'merciful', which amongst us signify moral virtue, human virtue, without thereby intending to say that God is in our sense morally good. Such words (which do not have in their meaning any necessary reference to creaturely limitation) can be used of God literally. But because the perfections exist in him in a higher way than in us (for he is the Creator of our justice and our mercy, and so on), we can only use them analogically, recognizing that we do not understand the justice of God or comprehend the mystery of his mercy.

Nevertheless, to speak of the justice or the mercy of God, however incomprehensible it may be, does seem to qualify God's *activity*. It is hard to see how justice could belong (even in a higher way) to what has no activity at all. There is, however, a problem about God's activity and, in particular, God's voluntary activity – for, surely, only activities which are in some sense voluntary can be in any sense just or merciful.

I think that it never makes any sense to say that God might not have been what he actually is. There could be no potentiality in God, no 'what he might have been but is not'. Now this seems to exclude voluntary activity from God, for a voluntary act seems to be one which an agent might not have done had he or she chosen otherwise. Pagan neo-Platonists saw the world as a necessary emanation from God – given his nature and goodness (*bonum est diffusivum sui*). For Jews, and hence Christians, however, creation was an act of love, hence a voluntary act. God might not have been creator, and yet he actually is. How can this be?

In dealing with this problem Aquinas distinguishes between different kinds of predicates used of God. Some, particularly those implying change or temporality, are applied to God not because of *his* nature, but because of what is the case about *other* things. So, on the one hand, we say that God is wise as one way of speaking about his nature, for God *is* his wisdom. And thus there could be no occasion when God is not wise. But, on the other hand, if we say God saved the soul of Peter, what we say was clearly not true before Peter existed or stood in need of salvation. Thus we are able to say that God became the saviour of Peter's soul. But, says Aquinas, these new predications become true not because of any change in God, but because of a change in *Peter*, of a (sort of) change in the whole universe. I say 'sort of' because, of course, creation is not a change – without it there is nothing to change. This depends on Aquinas's view that activity does not of itself necessarily involve a change in the agent, but only in the subject of the change. Thus, I can be said to teach you if and *only* if because of me a certain change – enlightenment, learning – takes place in you. Whatever energetic activities and changes take place in me, however much I talk or write or gesture or shout, however many hours I spend polishing my lectures, the activity of teaching has not occurred unless there is a change in you. It is merely a limiting condition of my nature that I can only bring about this change in you by, as a matter of fact, changing myself, working at it. There is nothing in the notion of teaching itself that involves such an effort and sweat in the teacher. There is thus no logical reason why God should not teach you or create you by bringing about something in you without in any way changing himself. In such a case there is a change in the relational propositions we can make about God but these new true propositions are founded in what happens to us, not in anything happening to God – as a tree which is now on my right can be truly said to become anew on my left without any change in the tree itself.

The corollary of this is that though God is what he is necessarily and from eternity (there is nothing that he is that he might not have been), nevertheless there are things that he has done that, from the point of view of creatures, he might not have done – not because God might have been different, but because the subjects of his action might have been differently related to God. Peter's soul might not have been saved (if, for example, like St Philomena, Peter had never existed), and hence God might not have been truly called the saviour of Peter's soul.

Thus, the fact that God exists necessarily and that with him, as the Bible puts it, there is 'no variation or shadow due to change' does not entail that the creation or anything within it necessarily happened.[2] We can intelligibly say that God in unchanging eternity freely chose to save Peter's soul at the time when the contingent fact of Peter's soul being saved occurred. But this temporal action was the playing out in time of a will which is unchangeable and from eternity.

We can say that from eternity God willed that Peter should be saved in the twentieth century. But it is only in the twentieth century, and from then on, that we can call God 'saviour of Peter', not in the eighteenth or nineteenth century; so we can say that God *became* saviour of Peter – as, of course, we can say that, in Jesus, God became man (without there being thereby a change in God). Indeed God became man in order that by having also a human nature God might be able to change, to suffer, to die.

It follows, of course, that for Aquinas God cannot change his mind or be motivated to act by anything that happens amongst creatures. It cannot be true that God has decided to save Peter and that he has so decided because of what Peter has done (because he has repented, for example). It can, however, be true from eternity that God has decided to save Peter because of his repentance (that is how he shall be saved) just as he has decided from eternity to boil the kettle because of the fire underneath it (that is how it shall be boiled). The notion of petitionary prayer is unintelligible if we interpret it as putting pressure on God or seeking to *change his mind*. It is intelligible if we see it as the means God has chosen from eternity to bring about some outcome. Aquinas reminds us that my freely uttered prayer is as much a creature of God as is the 'answer' to my prayer. My prayer does not bring it about that God does something; God brings it about that it is my prayer that does something.

We can, then, speak of God's voluntary actions. We can speak of him as doing things that he might not have done. And so the stage is set for the problem of evil. If God might have made a world different from the one we live in, why did he not do so? Is he the voluntary cause of evil and misery in the world? And, if so, what content is there left to notions like God's justice and mercy? These are serious questions, but ones which would take me beyond what I want to say in the present chapter.

Notes

1   Genesis 6.6.

2   James 1.17.

16

Aquinas on the Trinity

That God is one and three is, of course, for Aquinas a profound mystery which we could not hope to know apart from divine revelation, but we can only begin to understand what he has to say about it if we recognize that for him God is a profound mystery anyway. There are people who think that the notion of God is a relatively clear one; you know where you are when you are simply talking about God whereas when it comes to the Trinity we move into the incomprehensible where our reason breaks down. To understand Aquinas it is essential to see that for him our reason has already broken down when we talk of God at all – at least it has broken down in the sense of recognizing what is beyond it. Dealing with God is trying to talk of what we cannot talk of, trying to think of what we cannot think. Which is not to say that it involves nonsense or contradiction.

This similarity is sometimes obscured for us by the fact that Aquinas thinks we can prove the existence of God by natural reason whereas such unaided natural reason could tell us nothing of the Trinity. This, however, does not, for him, make the latter a mystery where the former is not, for he thought that to prove the existence of God was not to understand God but simply to prove the existence of a mystery. His arguments for the existence of God are arguments to show that there are real questions to which we do not and cannot know the answer. He seeks to show that it is proper to ask: 'Why is there anything at all instead of nothing at all?'; he seeks, that is, to show that it is not an idle question like 'How thick is the equator?' or 'What is the weight of Thursday week?' It is a question with an answer but one that we cannot know, and this answer all men, he says, call 'God'. He is never tired of repeating that we do not know what God is, we know only *that* God is and what he is *not*, and everything we come to say of him, whether expressed in positive or negative statements, is based on this.

After his arguments for the existence of God, for the validity of our unanswerable question, he says in the *Summa Theologiae*:

> When we know that something is it remains to inquire in what *way* it is so that we may know *what* it is. But since concerning God we cannot know what he is but only what he is not, we cannot consider in what way God is but only in what way he is not. So first we must ask in what way he is not, secondly how he may be known to us and thirdly how we may speak of him.

This, at the opening of Q.3, is his programme for the next ten questions and beyond. And none of the hundreds of questions that follow in the 4 parts of the *Summa* marks a conscious departure from this austere principle. Indeed he constantly comes back to it explicitly or implicitly.

God must be incomprehensible to us precisely because he is creator of all that is and, as Aquinas puts it, outside the order of all beings. God therefore cannot be classified as any kind of being. God cannot be compared or contrasted with other things in respect of what they are, like dogs *can* be compared and contrasted with cats and both of them with stones or stars. God is not an inhabitant of the universe; he is the reason why there *is* a universe at all. God is in everything holding it constantly in existence but he is not located anywhere, nor is what it is to be God located anywhere in logical space. When you have finished classifying and counting all the things in the universe you cannot add: 'And also there is God.' When you have finished classifying and counting everything in the universe you have finished, period. There is no God in the world.

Given this extreme view of the mysteriousness and incomprehensibility of God we may well ask Aquinas how he thinks we have any meaning at all for the word 'God'. Surely if we do not know what God is we do not know what 'God' means and theology must be a whole lot of codology. To know what a daisy is and to know the meaning of the word 'daisy' comes to much the same thing. Aquinas replies that even amongst ordinary things we can sometimes know how to use a name without knowing anything much about the nature of the thing named. Thus the businessman may quite rationally order a computer system to deal with his office work without having the faintest idea of how a computer works. His meaning for the word 'computer' is not derived precisely from knowing what a computer *is*; it is derived from the effect that it has on his business. Now Aquinas says that with God it is like this but more so. We have our meaning for the word 'God', we know how to use it, not because of anything at all that we know about God, but simply from the effects of God: creatures. Principally that they *are* instead of there being nothing. But the businessman is better off because knowing what a computer is for is a very large part of knowing what it is. Whereas God does not exist in order to make creatures. So the meaning of 'God' is not the same as the meaning of 'the existence of things instead of there not being anything'; we have the word 'God' because the existence of things instead of there not being anything is *mysterious* to us (and, Aquinas argues in the five ways, *ought* to be mysterious to us).

What we say of the word 'God' has also to be said of every other word we use of God. If we speak of God as good or wise it is not because we under-stand what it is for God to be good or wise – we are wholly in the dark about this – we use these and similar words because of certain things we know about creatures. When we do this, we take words which have at least a fairly clear sense in a context of creatures and seek to use them in a different context. This, in Aquinas's terminology, is to use them *analogically*. Certain words, of course, simply cannot be taken out of their creaturely context because this context is *part* of their meaning. Thus we could not, even speaking analogically, say that a mighty fortress is our God, because mighty fortresses are essentially material things and God could not be a material thing. We could only say that metaphorically not analogically.

Thus when we say that God is maker or cause of the world we are using 'maker' and 'cause' outside their familiar contexts in senses which we do not understand.

So it should be clear that for Aquinas the existence of God at all is as mysterious as you can get. The Trinity for him is no less and no more mysterious. To say that there is Father, Son and Holy Spirit who are God is for him no more mysterious than to say there is God at all. In neither case do we know what we are saying, but in neither case are we talking nonsense by contradicting ourselves. This latter is, of course, the next point to consider.

Aquinas holds that although we do not know what it is for God to be maker of the world it is not *nonsense* to say this of God in the way that it would be nonsense to say literally that God is a mighty fortress or a cup of tea. It is frequently the case that we find we have to apply several predicates to God, and because we do not understand them in this context we cannot see *how* they can be compatible with each other; but this is very different from saying that they are *in*compatible. It is one thing not to know how something makes sense and quite another to know that it does *not* make sense. Aquinas's task is to show that while we do not see *how* there can be Father, Son and Spirit who are all one God, we can show that it is not nonsense.

The thought may (at least at first) appear to be simpler if we look at the mystery of the incarnation. Here Aquinas holds that we do not understand how anyone could be simultaneously divine and human in the way that, for example, we *can* understand how someone could be simultaneously Russian and human. But he holds that we can understand that for someone to be both divine and human does *not* involve a contradiction in the sense that for something to be both a square and a circle *would* involve a contradiction.

Now similarly he holds that we cannot understand how God could be both Father, Son and Spirit as well as utterly one and simple, but we do understand that this does not involve the kind of contradiction that would be involved in saying, say, that God is three Fathers as well as being one Father, or three Gods as well as being one God.

What we have to do in this case is to see how we are compelled to say each of the things but not try to imagine them being simultaneously true or even try to *conceive* of them being simultaneously true; we should not expect to form a concept of the triune God, or indeed of God at all. We must rest content with establishing that we are not breaking any rules of logic, in other words that we are not being intellectually dishonest.

There is nothing especially odd or irrational about this. It only seems shocking to those who expect the study of God to be easy and obvious, a less demanding discipline than, say, the study of nuclear physics. In physics we are quite accustomed to the idea that there are two ways of talking about the ultimate constituents of matter, both of them necessary and both of them internally coherent, and yet we do not know how to reconcile them: one in terms of waves and the other in terms of particles. It is not a question of choosing between them; we have to accept them both. We do not, however, *need* to conceive of how anything could be both wave and particle; we simply accept that, at least for the moment, we have these two languages and that the use of them does not involve a contradiction although we cannot see *how* it avoids contradiction. It is true that most physicists would look forward to some future theoretical development in which we will devise a single language for expressing these matters but they do not see themselves as talking nonsense in the meantime. This too is rather similar to Aquinas's position, for he also looks forward to a theoretical development by which we will come to see, to understand, how God is both one and three, but this he thinks can only come by sharing God's own self-understanding in the beatific vision. But meanwhile we are not talking nonsense.

To take another parallel: the square root of a number is that which when multiplied by itself yields that number. Since any number whether positive or negative when multiplied by itself yields a positive number, what could be made of a notion like the square root of a *negative* number, the square root of minus 2 for example? There is plainly no way in which we could conceive of the square root of minus 2 but this does not faze mathematicians; they are content to use it in a rule-governed way and find it a very useful device.

Aquinas, then, is faced with a situation similar to the physicist's. We have on the grounds of revelation to say two quite different kinds of things about God: that God is altogether one and that there are three who are God. We cannot *see* how they can both be true but that need not faze us; what we have to do is to show that there are no good grounds for saying that they are incompatible. We have to show in fact that the conditions which would make them incompatible in other cases do not and cannot apply to God – remember that all we know of God is what he is not, what he cannot be if he is to be God, the reason why there is anything instead of nothing.

One of the basic principles which Aquinas employs in considering the Trinity is the principle quoted, I think, from Augustine that *everything that is in God is God*. This is again something we cannot understand, we cannot see *how* it could be true but we are forced to assert that it is true. It follows, in Aquinas's view, from the fact that there can be no passive potentiality in God. This means that there is nothing in God which might not have been in him; there is never anything which he might be but is not or that he is but might not have been.

This in its turn follows from the fact that God cannot be changed by anything. If God were the patient or subject or victim of some other agent he could not be the source of the existence, the reality of everything that is. Rather, there would be something (this other agent) who would be a source of something in God. If God were not the source of the existence of all that is he would not be what we use the word 'God' for. Now Aquinas holds, surely reasonably, that it makes no sense to speak of what does not exist as acting or doing anything or bringing anything about. Hence what is merely potential – what might exist but does not – cannot act to bring itself about nor can it bring anything else about. What is potential can only be brought into existence by something that is actual. We must not confuse potentiality in this sense with power, an active capacity to do something; we mean simply what might be but isn't. Thus if there were any potentiality in God in this passive sense, he would need to be acted on by some other agent and thus, as we have seen, would not be God. God is thus, in Aquinas's phrase, *actus purus*, sheer actuality. He does not become, he just is. He cannot become because then there would be something he might be but is not. It is for these reasons that Aquinas says that God is totally unchanging and timeless.

Because of this, Aquinas argues that there can be no 'accidents' in God. Let me explain that. It is accidental to me that I am giving this lecture. This means that I would still be me if I were not giving it. Similarly it is accidental to me that I am wearing these clothes and that I am 6 feet high. I am still *me* in bed, and I was the same me when I was 4 feet high. What is accidental is opposed to what is essential. Thus it is not accidental but essential to me that I am an animal or that I am a human being. If I ceased to be an animal I would cease to exist, I would turn into something else – a corpse. By what is essential to a thing we mean what it takes for it to exist. What it takes for me to be is my being human; just as what it takes for Fido to be is being a dog; but both Fido and I have many other things about us which are not essential in this sense, many things which we could lose or gain without ceasing to be. This is what 'accidents' means.

Now it is clear that if giving this lecture is accidental to me I might not have been giving it – I mean I would still have been me if I had gone down with flu or simply been too scared. To have accidental features then is to be potential in some respect. Fido is eating a bone but he might not have been; he is not barking but he might be. To have accidental features as distinct from essential ones is to have some potentiality. Hence a being, God, with no potentiality can have no accidents. Every feature of God must be of his essence, essential to him.

Now please notice that all this argument is based not on any knowledge or understanding that we have of God; it is simply what we are compelled to say if we are to use the word 'God' correctly, i.e. to mean whatever unknown mystery is the source of the being of all that is. Whatever would answer the question: 'Why is there anything rather than nothing at all?' Whatever 'God' refers to, it could not be anything with potentiality and hence it could not be anything with accidental features.

This means that whatever is in God *is* God. My giving this lecture is not my being me, it is accidental to me, whereas my being human *is* my being me. Now with God *everything* he is is just his being God.

So if we say that God is wise or omnipotent we cannot be referring to two different features that God *happens* to have over and above being God. The wisdom of God just is his being God; so are his omnipotence and his goodness and whatever else we attribute to him. Now of course we cannot understand what it would be like for something to be its own wisdom. The wisdom we understand is always an accidental feature of persons, and so is power or goodness. When we use such words of God we must be using them analogically, outside the context of their first use, and we do not understand what we mean by them. We have no concept of the wisdom of God; for that matter we have no concept of God.

So every feature we attribute to God just is God, it is the divine essence or nature. But now we come to a complication because not everything we *say* of God attributes in this sense a feature to him. I mean not every sentence beginning 'God is ...' or 'God has ...' is intended to attribute some real feature to him. This is because some of the things we say about God are relational. Let me explain that.

Suppose that next week I shall become a great-uncle. At the moment it is, we shall say, not true that I am a great-uncle; next week it will become true. Are we then to say that a potentiality in me to become a great-uncle has been fulfilled? Not so, because my becoming a great-uncle involves no change in me at all; it is entirely a matter of a change in my niece Kate and what is in her womb. So although a sentence like 'Herbert is becoming a great-uncle' sounds just like 'Herbert is becoming wise' or 'Herbert is becoming a Dominican', we should not be misled by the grammar into thinking we are talking about a change in what is named by the subject term. The fact that there really is a new thing to say of me does not have to mean there is a new reality in me. Relational expressions are quite often like this. For example: 'You are on my left but you used to be on my right' doesn't have to imply any change in you; I may simply have turned round. You have not fulfilled any potentiality in yourself to become on my left. There would be only a *verbal* change – something new to *say* about you. Similarly 'you are farther away' or 'you have become richer than I' may or may not be true because of changes in you; they may be, for you, merely verbal changes.

Now consider the profoundly mysterious truth that God sustains Margaret Thatcher in existence. This was not true of God in, say, 1920 because in those far-off happy times Mrs Thatcher did not exist and so God could not have been sustaining her in existence. So God began to sustain her, he *became* the sustainer of Mrs Thatcher. But, Aquinas says, this does not entail any change in God any more than becoming a great-uncle entails any change in me. Thus becoming the sustainer of Mrs Thatcher is not a real happening to God, in our sense, although it becomes true of him. It is true of him not because of some new reality in him but because of some reality in Mrs Thatcher – that she began to be alive. Of course that she is alive is *due to* a reality in God: his profoundly mysterious eternal will that she should come to exist at a certain date. But this eternal will is not something that comes about at a date so this does not imply any real change in God.

So when Mrs Thatcher was conceived there was something going on in her, but on God's side the change is merely verbal: we have a new thing to say about God, but it is not a new thing about God that we are saying.

So there is a great deal of logical difference between saying that God is *wise* and saying that God is the *sustainer of Mrs Thatcher*, or in general saying that he is creator. In the first case we attribute a real feature to God, wisdom, which (because there can be no accidents in God) must therefore be identical with being God. In the second case the reality is in the creature; there is merely a verbal change in God – a change in what has to be said of him. For this reason we are rescued from the appalling fate of suggesting that being creator and sustainer of Mrs Thatcher is essential to God, that he would not be God had he not created Mrs Thatcher.

So being creator of the world is not part of what it is to be God. God did not become God when in, say, 4005 BC he created the world. Indeed he did not change at all. Although saying he *became* creator sounds like attributing an accident to God it is not in fact attributing any new feature to him at all; we say it in order to say something new about the world. (Strictly speaking even the world itself did not *change* when it was created because until it was created it wasn't there to change. But that is another question.) We should remember, of course, that when we say God does not change, we do not mean God stays the same all the time. God is not 'all the time'. God is eternal. To attribute stasis to God is as mistaken as to attribute change to him.

The main point is this: that what we say of God because of his creative relationship to creatures does not attribute any new reality to God and thus does not speak of God's essence.

James Mackey in his interesting book *The Christian Experience of God as Trinity* (1983) (the title ought to be enough to warn you) has a generally hostile account of Aquinas's treatment of the Trinity; and he finds the notion I am trying to explain especially unlovable. He says:

(Aquinas) is quite clear in his insistence that the Trinity cannot be known from creation – the principle *opera ad extra sunt indivisa* is by now sacrosanct and he further distances from our world all discussion of real divine relation by stating quite baldly 'there is no real relation in God to the creature'. Creatures, that is, may experience a real relationship of dependence upon and need of God, but God experiences no such real relationship to creatures.[1]

I'm afraid this is a dreadful muddle. Whether a relationship in me is real or merely verbal has nothing whatever to do with experience. The fact that the relationship of being a great-uncle is not a real one in me in no way makes it something I do not experience; it in no way makes me less aware of my great-niece nor less concerned about her.

God, of course, for Aquinas does not experience anything in the world. He has no need to. He does not, as I do, have to learn about the world from outside. He is at the heart of absolutely everything in the world, holding it in existence and bringing about everything it does.

The principle that whatever is in God is God, then, does not apply to such relational predicates as being creator or being sustainer of Mrs Thatcher. It *does* apply to non-relational predicates like 'is wise' and 'is good' and 'is merciful'. God's wisdom, goodness and mercy are all identical with his essence and there is no real distinction in God between his goodness and his wisdom. On the other hand there *is* a real distinction between God sustaining Mrs Thatcher and God sustaining me, but it is not a real distinction in God but a very fundamental one between myself and Mrs Thatcher, one for which I thank God every day.

It is indeed a great mystery that the wisdom of God is God, and the power of God is God, and the goodness of God is God, and all three are the same God – we cannot understand how this can be, but it is not like the mystery of the Trinity because we cheerfully admit that (in some way we do not understand) all three are in fact identical, there is no distinction between the goodness and the power and the wisdom of God.

In the case of the Trinity, however, we want to say that the Father is God and the Son is God and the Spirit is God and all three are the same God but never-theless they are *not* identical. There *is* distinction between Father, Son and Spirit.

What we have got to so far is that when we are speaking of *what is real in God* we are speaking of what is God's essence and all our predicates refer to one and the same identical essence of divinity, not to a number of accidents; our different predicates do not mark real distinctions in God. When, however, we are speaking of God's *relationship to creatures*, our different predicates *do* mark real distinctions but not in *God* because they entail no reality in God.

Aquinas's next move is to speak not of God's activity with regard to creatures, his creative act, but of God's activity within himself. And here we have to notice a difference between transitive and intransitive verbs. Aquinas points out that not all our acts are actions upon something else, acts which make a difference to something else. Carving and writing and teaching are all acts whose reality consists in what happens to some subject, and so is creating. Carving can only be going on if some stuff is being carved; writing can only be going on if some words are being written; but what about the act of, say, growing? You can of course grow in a transitive sense as when a gardener grows begonias, but growing in the intransitive sense is not an activity that does something to something else, nor is boiling or collapsing. To use Aquinas's phrase, it remains within the agent. Still more clearly the act of understanding is not an act which does anything or makes any difference to anything else. It is a kind of growing or development of the mind itself, not an operation on what is understood or on anything else. Of course there are philosophers who, partly for this reason, think it a mistake to talk of under-standing as an *act*, but we cannot pause here to argue with them. For Aquinas, at any rate, it is an act performed by the agent but not passing outside the agent to alter or influence or change anything else. Aquinas occasionally calls such actions 'immanent' acts as opposed to 'transient' ones.

Now can we speak of *God's* act of understanding? It would take much too long to give an account of Aquinas's general theory of understanding. You will just have to take it from me that for him both understanding and being intelligible have to do with not being *material*. To understand a nature is just to possess that nature immaterially. To possess the nature of a dog materially is to *be* a dog; to possess the nature of a dog immaterially (to have it in mind) is to *understand* a dog, to know what a dog is or what the word 'dog' means.

For Aquinas, you might say, the *norm* for being is that it should be intelligent, understanding, *immaterial* being; the exceptional ones are those whose being is curbed and restricted by matter: matter not thought of as some special kind of stuff but as the limitedness and potentiality of things. For Aquinas *we* can understand because we are just about able to transcend our materiality. While almost all our vital operations are operations of the body, circumscribed by matter, in the act of understanding we have an act which, although it is heavily involved with bodily activity and cannot ordinarily take place without concomitant bodily working, is not of itself an act of the body, a bodily process. Beings which are not material at all, quite unlimited by matter, angels for example, would understand much better than we do, without the tedious need for bodily experience, for what he calls the sense power of the *imaginatio* or *phantasmata* and for the use of material symbols and words.

For Aquinas, then, it follows simply from the fact that God cannot be material that he cannot be non-intellectual: he cannot fail to be understanding. This is part of our negative knowledge of God, our knowledge of what God is not.

We should, however, be quite clear that in saying that we know that God is not impersonal, not lacking in understanding and knowledge, we are laying no claim to knowing what it means for God to understand. Aquinas will go on to speak of God having an understanding of himself or forming a concept of himself but it is clear that we have so far no warrant for saying this. There is no reason to suppose that God's act of understanding is so much like ours. But on the other hand we have equally no warrant for saying that it isn't. I mean we *do* have warrant for saying that God does not *hear* or *see* anything just as he does not chop down trees, for all these are operations of a material body; the idea of God forming a concept of himself is not excluded in *that* way. It is simply that other things being equal we would have no reason to assert it. Aquinas, however, thinks other things are not equal for he interprets the Logos theology of John's gospel as suggesting just this.

When we understand a nature – say, what an apple is – we form a concept of what an apple is and this concept is the meaning we have for the word 'apple'. (When I speak of understanding the nature of an apple I do not mean some profound grasp of the essence of apples; I just mean the situation of someone who knows what apples are as distinct from someone who has never come across them or heard of them.) The concept is not precisely *what* we understand; what we understand is *what apples are, the nature of apples,* but the concept is what we have in mind in understanding this nature. It is the meaning for us of apples, the meaning expressed in the word 'apple'. So when you learn, say, what peevishness is, you do so by forming a concept which is the meaning of the word 'peevish' or 'peevishness'. It is not exactly that you learn the word itself, for you may not know that useful word and you may express the meaning you understand by some complicated circumlocution, and again a Frenchman who comes to the same understanding of what peevishness is will form the same concept which for him will be the meaning of the word 'maussaderie'. The concept, then, is what is conceived in the mind in the act of understanding and because it is the meaning of a word it was called by the medievals the *verbum mentis*, the word of the mind. This does not commit them to any doctrine that we can have concepts before we have any words in which we express them; indeed Aquinas clearly thought we could not, but it is plain that many different words or signs may express the same concept: that is what we mean when we say that this word or phrase means the same as that one.

Now let us return to the understanding of God. God's understanding of me or of any of his creatures is not something other than his creating and sustaining of them. God, you may say, knows what he is doing and what he is doing is keeping these things in their being and everything about them. God's knowledge of me, then, like his creating of me is a relational predicate true of God because of a reality in me. Just as I will be a great-uncle because of the reality of my great-niece. God knows me not by having a concept of me distinct from a concept he has of you; he knows me by knowing himself and thus knowing himself as creator of me and you. Thus that God knows me and also knows you does not imply that there are two different concepts, two different realities in God, any more than when I become a great-uncle three times over there will be three different realities in me.

But what, asks Aquinas, about God's understanding of *himself*. Here he will form a concept of himself. The concept, remember, is not *what* is understood but *how* something is understood, what is produced, brought forth, conceived, in the understanding of something. *What* God understands is himself, identical with himself, but *in* understanding he conceives the concept, the *verbum mentis*, and this because *produced, brought forth* by him is not him.

Let us remind ourselves again that there is no 'must' about it. Aquinas is not trying to deduce the Trinity from God's intellectuality. We do not understand God's understanding, and apart from the revelation about God's Word we should not be talking about God forming a concept. However, given this revelation, it seems reasonable to interpret it this way.

Notice the importance of the switch from looking at God's activity that *passes outside him* to creatures, to looking at his *immanent* activity of self-understanding. In the former case there is no reality in God on which the relationship of being created or being understood is based: it is a reality in the creature and a merely verbal thing in God, a change in what is to be said of him. In the latter case, however, there is a reality, a concept, in God himself. A reality distinct from God in God.

And now comes the hammer-blow of that principle we established at the beginning: everything that is real in God is God. We cannot see the concept in God (as we can see our own concepts) as an accident distinct from the essence. In us our concept is a reality distinct from us. It is an accident. Our concepts come and go, and we remain what we are; this cannot be true of God. If God has formed a concept it is not an accident of God, it is God. This is quite beyond our understanding; we are merely forced to it by our reasoning. We are not, of course, forced by our reasoning to say that God forms a concept of himself, but we are forced to say that *if* he does so it cannot be merely accidental, it must be God.

The act of creating brings about a relationship between God and his creature. They are *distinct* but *related* to each other as creator and creature. But the basis of this relation is real only in the creature, just as the basis of the relationship of being a great-uncle is real only on one side. The act of God's self-understanding which involves the bringing forth of a concept, *a verbum mentis*, also brings about a relationship between God and the concept. They are *distinct* but *related* to each other as conceiver and what is conceived, meaner and meaning. But the basis of this relationship, unlike the relationship of creation, is real at *both* ends. The mind and the *verbum* it produces are really distinct as the opposite ends of a relationship. And whatever is real in God is God.

St Thomas shifts, as does St John himself, from Logos language ('In the beginning was the word and the word was with God and the word was God') to the language of Father and Son. He argues that these come to the same thing: there are two essential requirements for the act of generation – firstly that A should have been *brought forth* by B and secondly that it should have the *same nature* as B. I did not generate *you* because, although you have the same nature as I have, I did not bring you forth. On the other hand, I did not generate my nail clippings or my thoughts, although I brought them forth, because they are not themselves human beings. I would generate only my children which are both brought forth and of the same nature. The *verbum mentis* of God, however, is *both* brought forth by him, conceived by him, and *also* is of the same nature, for, being real in God, it is God. Thus the language of generation, of Son and Father, is here applicable.

It does not in any case seem fortuitous that the language of mental activity parallels that of sexual generation. The word 'concept' itself belongs primarily to the context of generation. Of course all this fits much more easily into an Aristotelian and biblical biology according to which fathers generate their sons merely in the environment of women. Nothing was then known of the splitting of chromosomes and sharing of genes; women were not thought to contribute actively to the generative process. From our more knowledgeable point of view it would make more sense to speak of God the Parents rather than God the Father. (The plural of 'parents' would be no more misleading than is the sexual connotation of 'Father'.) However, that of course is not in Aquinas.

So for Aquinas, as indeed for the Catholic faith, Father and Son do not differ in any way (*homo-ousion*). In each case what they are is God and they are nothing except that they are God. The Father has no features or properties which the Son has not. The only thing that distinguishes them is that they are at opposite ends of a relationship. The Father *generates* the Son, the Son *is generated by* the Father. Being the Father just is standing in that relationship to the Son; being the Son just is standing in that relationship to the Father. The Father *is a relation*. It is not that he *has* a relation. Just as in creatures wisdom is always an accident, wisdom of some subject, so in creatures 'a relation to ...' is always an accident supervening on some already existing subject. It is the lectern that is shorter than I am, that *has* the relation of shorter than to me; relations supervene upon what is already something in its own right. But of course, as we have seen, nothing supervenes on God. In him there are no accidents. Whatever really is in God is the essence of God. So the Father does not *have* a relationship of Fatherhood to the Son; he *is* that relationship subsisting as God. And the Son *is* the relation of being generated by the Father, subsisting as God.

Need I say that the notion of a subsisting relation is mysterious to us, we do not know what it would mean or what it would be like, but (to repeat) we do not know what subsisting wisdom would mean or what God would mean or what God would be like.

We see then that the only distinction in God is that of being at opposite ends of a relationship due to an act or 'process' within the Godhead. Nothing that is said non-relationally about God makes any distinction between Father and Son, and nothing that is said even relationally about God in virtue of his dealings with creatures refers to any real distinction in God at all. God turns to creatures, *as his creatures*, the single unified face of the one God, the unchanging, the eternal, the single source of all that is. It is only with God's own interior life, his own self-understanding, that there is a basis for distinction. And of course that interior life is of vast interest to us because we are called on to share it. God does not look upon us human creatures simply as creatures; he has invited us by our unity in Christ to share in Christ's divine life within the Trinity, to share in his Sonship. And this of course brings us, perhaps a little belatedly, to the Holy Spirit, for it is by receiving the Spirit through faith in baptism that we share in the interior life of the Godhead.

The main principles for Aquinas's treatment of the Spirit are already laid down in his discussion of the Father and the Son. This indeed is one of the major difficulties with his treatment. He is, however, quite conscious and explicit about what he is doing. He says that it is necessary to consider the Holy Spirit on the same lines as we consider the Son. His reason for this is that the only possible distinction in the Godhead is the distinction of two opposite ends of a relationship, and the only possible basis for relationship in the Godhead is the relation of origin to what is originated, a relation set up by some *procession* such as the conception of the Word, the generation of the Son.

So the Holy Spirit too must be distinct in its relation to its origin and its origin, says St Thomas, lies in that other immanent operation of the intellectual being, the operation of the will, the operation of love.

This, however, is where the difficulties begin. It is not too difficult to see how in understanding himself the Father forms a concept of himself which being real in God is itself God; it is much less easy to see how anything is formed in the operation of the will. This is especially so if we remember Aquinas's own often repeated doctrine that while truth is in the mind, goodness is in things. The act of understanding is a taking into the mind of the form or nature of things and this is the formation of a concept; but the act of loving is a going out towards the thing, a being attracted to it or an enjoyment of it. It is not at all clear what it is that is originated in this act of the will. Remember that the Holy Spirit is not *what* is loved, any more than the concept or word or Son is *what* is known; what is known and loved is the divine nature itself; it is a question of *self*-knowledge and *self*-love; the Word is what is formed in this self-knowledge and the Holy Spirit is what is formed in this self-love.

Well, says Aquinas, we ought not to think of the Holy Spirit as a likeness of what is loved in the way that the concept is a likeness (in this case a perfect likeness) of what is known; rather it is a tendency towards, a nisus or impulsion towards, even a kind of excitement – an enjoyment. This, Aquinas thinks, is formed in the act of loving. This is the term of the act of what he calls *spiratio*, breathing forth. It becomes, then, difficult to speak of the Holy Spirit as a 'thing' that is formed, and I remember Victor White always used to regard this as one of the great strengths and glories of Aquinas's teaching on the Trinity. With the Holy Spirit, at least, we are in no danger of seeing God as a 'person' in the modern sense. Here God is a movement, an impulse, a love, a delight.

It is essential to Aquinas's doctrine that the Holy Spirit proceeds from *both* the Father and the Son, and not merely from the Father. The reason for this is that the only distinction admissible in the Trinity is that of being at opposite ends of a relation based on a procession of origination. If the Holy Spirit does not proceed from the Son there is no such relation between them and therefore no distinction between Son and Holy Spirit.

Thus in Aquinas's account there are two *processions* in God, one of the intellect, God's knowing himself, which is generation, and one of the will, God's enjoying himself, which is spiration. Each of these gives rise to a relationship with two (opposite) ends, the origin and the originated. There are thus four of these *relations*. This does not, however, result in four distinct persons, for in order to be distinct a person must be at the opposite end of a relation from *both* other persons. The Father is opposed to the Son by generating and to the Spirit by spiration. The Son is opposed to the Father by being generated and to the Spirit by spiration. The Spirit is opposed to both the Father and the Son by being spirated, or *processio* (in a new sense).

This does not commit Aquinas to the 'filioque' in the sense in which it is found objectionable by the Eastern churches. The root of their complaint, as I understand it, is that the *filioque* seems to take away from the Father as unique source or principle of the Godhead. However, the Greek Orthodox theologians who in 1875 came to an agreement with the Old Catholics[2] expressed their faith by saying, 'We do call the Holy Spirit the Spirit of the Son and so it is proper to say that the Holy Spirit proceeds from the Father *through* the Son'. But that last clause is an exact quotation from Aquinas:

> *Quia igitur Filius habet a Patre quod ab eo procedat Spiritus Sanctus, potest dici quod Pater per Filium spirat Spiritum Sanctum; vel quod Spiritus Sanctus procedat a Patre per Filium, quod idem est.*

Because the Son owes it to the Father that the Holy Spirit should proceed from him, it can be said that the Father through the Son breathes forth the Holy Spirit, or that the Holy Spirit proceeds from the Father through the Son, which is to say the same thing.

I think it will be clear that Aquinas's doctrine gives us no warrant for saying that there are three persons in God, for 'person' in English undoubtedly means an individual subject, a distinct centre of consciousness. Now the consciousness of the Son is the consciousness of the Father and of the Holy Spirit: it is simply God's consciousness. There are not three knowledges or three lovings in God. The Word simply is the way in which God is self-conscious, knows what he is, as the Spirit simply is the delight God takes in what he is when he is knowing it. If we say there are three persons in God, in the ordinary sense of person, we are tritheists.

For Aquinas the key to the Trinity is not the notion of person but of relation, and in fact in my account of his teaching I have not found it necessary to use the word 'person' at all. Aquinas quotes with ostensible approval Boethius's definition of a person as 'an individual substance of rational nature'. But, as speedily emerges, the 'persons' of the Trinity are not individuals, not substances, not rational and do not *have* natures. What Aquinas labours to show is that in this unique case 'person' can mean relation. This he does out of characteristic *pietas* towards the traditional language of the church. But of course even in Aquinas's time *persona* did *not* mean relation, and most emphatically in our time 'person' does not. For our culture the 'person' is almost the opposite of the relational; it is the isolated bastion of individuality set over against the collective. Even if we criticize this individualism, even if we try to put the human being back into a social context as a part of various communities, the notion of person does not become relational enough to use in an account of the Trinity. Aquinas could have made better use of the original sense of *prosopon* or *persona* as the player's mask; and his doctrine of the Trinity might be more easily grasped if we spoke of three *roles* in the strict sense of three roles in a theatrical cast – though we have to forget that in the theatre there are people *with* the roles. We should have to think just of the roles as such and notice how they each have meaning only in relation to and distinction from each other. We could speak of the role of parenthood, the role of childhood and the role of love or delight. This is not to speak of the Trinity as a matter simply of three aspects of God, three ways in which God appears *to us*, as Sabellius is alleged to have taught, for essential to this whole teaching is that God turns only one aspect to us, *opera ad extra sunt indivisa*; it is in his immanent activity of self-understanding and self-love, delight, that the roles are generated.

These roles, firmly established in the life of the Godhead, are then reflected (I prefer the word 'projected', as on a cinema screen) in our history in the external missions of the Son and the Spirit by which we are taken up into that life of the Godhead. In this way the obedience of Jesus is the projection of his eternal Sonship and the outpouring of the Spirit is the projection of his eternal procession from the Father through the Son. It is because of these missions in time that the life of the Trinity becomes available to us: I mean both in the sense that we know of it, believe in it, and in the sense that we belong to it. These are of course the same thing. It is because we share in the Holy Spirit through faith and charity and the other infused virtues that we are able to speak of the Trinity at all. It is not therefore adequate to speak of God's redemptive act as an *opus ad extra*. It is precisely the act by which we cease to be *extra* to God and come within his own life.

Notes

1   James Mackey, *The Christian Experience of God as Trinity* (London: SCM Press, 1983), p. 182.

2   *The Christian Experience of God as Trinity*, p. 186.

17

Aquinas on the Incarnation

In *Summa Theologiae* 3a,16, Aquinas looks at the things that can truly be said of Christ in virtue of the union in one *esse*, one *persona*, of the nature of God and of man.[1] For Aquinas, the nature of a thing governs what can be said of it. To know the nature of a thing is to know how to talk about it, thus the union of two natures in Christ means, for Aquinas, that we have two ways of speaking about him – only one of which we understand. In virtue of his human nature we speak of him in exactly the same way that we would speak of any other human being. In virtue of his divine nature we can also say more enigmatic and mysterious things such as that he forgives sins or is our redeemer.

In order to understand Aquinas's treatment of such statements it is first necessary to remind you of his theory of the proposition in general. Aquinas did not hold what has come to be called the 'two-name' theory of the proposition: this is the theory that in a proposition a subject and a predicate are linked by a copula. The subject stands for one thing or class of things, and the predicate stands for another, and the copula shows how these classes overlap: 'All men are mortal' in this view says that the class of men is wholly included in the class of mortal things. I only mention this absurd theory because at one time it used to be found in logic textbooks called 'scholastic' and even 'Aristotelian'. In fact it has nothing whatever to do with Aristotle and had its origins, I think, amongst the Jansenists of the school of Port Royal. Aquinas's own view is altogether different. For him a simple proposition consists typically of two parts, not three: a subject and a predicate (roughly speaking, a noun and a verb). The so-called copula is just the verb 'to be' when it is used to construct the predicate. If instead of saying 'John sings' you prefer to say 'John is singing' then you have a copula. But there is no logical virtue in doing so. If, instead of saying 'All men are mortal', you say 'All men die', you have just as perspicuous a logical form (not to mention a better English sentence).

Now for Aquinas the words in the two parts of a proposition function in quite different ways. (For the 'two-name' theory, they function in the same way – to denote classes.) Terms in the subject place, he says, are to be taken 'materially', and those in the predicate place are to be taken *formaliter*. Without going too far into this, what he means is that the subject words are there to stand for, to identify what you are talking about, to refer, while the words of the predicate are there to say something about it, they are taken as to their meaning (*formaliter*). For Aquinas, identifying something is not the same as saying something about it. If you say 'The President is in the White House' you are, for him, enunciating the same truth as when you say 'George W. Bush is in the White House', even though to be President of the USA and to be George W. Bush are not the same thing. In those two propositions 'the President' and 'George W. Bush' are fulfilling the same function of identifying the one you want to talk about. When you identify Bush as the President you are not asserting that he is President. You are just taking for granted that people know who the President is. The thing you are asserting is that he is in the White House. And this can be just as well asserted by saying that George W. Bush is in the White House. Any word or phrase will do in the subject place provided it makes clear what you are talking about. Very often this will be because the words you use in the subject place could be predicated of the subject. For example, 'the President' serves to identify George W. Bush because the proposition 'George W. Bush is the President' is true (in 2001, anyway). But this proposition is not being enunciated when you say 'The President is in the White House'. It is just part of the background.

Now the relevance of all this to talk of the Incarnation is this: since the one person (Jesus) is both divine and human, we can identify him either with divine or with human terms. So long as what we are doing is simply identifying Jesus it makes no difference whether we call him son of God or son of Mary. As far as words in the subject part of the sentence are concerned, it makes no difference whether we use identifying phrases derived from Jesus' divine nature or his human nature.

Thus we might say 'The friend of Peter and Andrew sat down by the well'. Or we might say 'The son of God born of the Father before all ages sat down by the well'. And these are exactly the same proposition. They are both simply asserting that Jesus sat down by the well. (They are the same proposition in that one is true if and only if the other is true.) They are the same proposition because 'The friend of Peter and Andrew' and 'The son of God born of the Father before all ages' are both simply being used to identify Jesus. The first proposition does not include the assertion that Jesus is a friend of Peter and Andrew. The second does not include the assertion that he is son of God, etc. These assertions are not included in what is said. They are simply taken for granted.

For Aquinas, what is formal to a proposition, what makes it the proposition it is, is the predicate not the subject terms. It doesn't matter much what you use to identify the subject, but if you change the predicate then you have a new proposition. So to say 'Jesus is son of God' is to say something quite different from saying 'Jesus is son of Mary' because here 'son of God' and 'son of Mary' are in the predicate place. But to say 'The son of God died on the cross' is to make the same assertion as is expressed by 'The son of Mary died on the cross'.

We now come to the word '*qua*' or 'in virtue of being'. If you say 'Mr Tony Blair *qua* Prime Minister chairs the meetings of the cabinet', you mean that it is just because Mr Tony Blair is Prime Minister that he does this. You mean that his being Prime Minister is a condition of his chairing the meetings. So your proposition is a complex one; it asserts (1) that Mr Tony Blair chairs the meetings, (2) that he is Prime Minister and (3) that it is because of being Prime Minister that he chairs the meetings (which seems an enormous lot to unpack out of the little word '*qua*', but there it is).

What is important here is that what follows the *qua* is part of the predicate of the proposition. It is part of what is being asserted.

Now consider the proposition 'God sat down by the well'. This for Aquinas is a perfectly proper and true utterance since 'God' is one of the ways in which you could identify Jesus; 'God' here, is in the subject place and is being used to identify what is being talked about.

But if you said 'Jesus *qua* God sat down by the well' it would be very different. This would assert (1) that Jesus sat by the well, (2) that Jesus is God and (3) that it is because of being God that he sat by the well.

Now since the third of these is false the original proposition is false. The word '*qua*' is important because we are to be concerned with natures, and a nature is that in virtue of which things are true of a thing, or can be said of a thing. To say that Jesus has two natures is to say that he has, as it were, two *qua*s. He does some things *qua* human and others *qua* divine. This does not mean that he had two sources of power and could switch from one to the other, like having an emergency engine on a sailing boat. It means that there are two levels of talking about him, or that he exists at two levels.

Another little phrase of importance in talking about the incarnate word is 'as such'.

'God sat by the well' is fine, but 'God *as such* sat by the well' is the same as 'God (that is, Jesus) *qua* God sat by the well', which is false.

Similarly, 'This man created the world' is fine. But 'This man *as such* created the world' is false.

But let us look at Aquinas's own examples.

3a,16,1: Is this statement true, 'God is a man'? Aquinas replies that 'God is a man' is true because 'the person of the son of God, for whom the term "God" here stands (*pro qua supponit hoc nomen Deus*) is a subject (*suppositum*) subsisting in human nature' and since 'the term "a man" may [therefore] truly and literally be predicated of the term "God" when the latter stands for the person of the Son of God'. Aquinas is of course speaking loosely here; it is not the word 'man' that is predicated of the word 'God', but what the word 'man' means is predicated of what the word 'God' stands for or identifies.

The first objection to this is that the proposition 'God is a man' is *in materia remota*. A proposition *in materia remota* would be, for example 'Thursday is green' – when, as Aquinas puts it, 'Two forms cannot come together in the same *suppositum*'. The kind of thing that is Thursday just isn't the kind of thing that could be green. The thing seems to depend on the meaning of 'Thursday' and of 'green'. Now the objector argues that the meaning of being God is so totally different from the meaning of being man that the kind of thing that is God just couldn't be the kind of thing that is man. But when you have a case of two forms, even quite different and unrelated forms, that can come together in one *suppositum*, then you have not got *materia remota*: for example, if the same man is both white and musical you can sensibly say 'the white is musical', even though being white and being musical are quite different. Such a proposition is said to be in *materia contingenti*.

Aquinas points out that *au fond* it is not precisely the difference of forms or of meanings that make for nonsense. It is their not being able to come together in one *suppositum*. And he argues that, although to be divine and to be human are totally different (*maxime distantes*), this is not the important thing; the significant thing is that through the mystery of the Incarnation they do come together in one *suppositum*. But it is not just as with 'the white is musical', for, in the case of the Incarnation, we have not simply an accidental conjunction of forms. Neither the being divine nor the being human belongs to the *suppositum* 'per accidens' but 'secundum se'. Being human is a matter of what Jesus is as Jesus; and being divine is a matter of what Jesus is as Jesus. So, says Aquinas, the proposition 'God is a man' is neither in *materia remota* nor in *materia contingenti*. It is in what Aquinas calls *materia naturali*. He means by this that it belongs to the same class of propositions as, for example, that a man is rational. 'Being a man' is predicated of God not *per accidens* but *per se*, not however by reason of the form signified by 'God' (the meaning of 'God') but by reason of the *suppositum* which becomes the *hypostasis* (the subsisting subject, the independent, concrete, substantial reality) of the human nature. Thus 'God is a man' is *per se*, but not in quite the same way as 'A man is rational' is *per se*. 'A man is rational' is *per se* and not *per accidens* because a man as man (because of what it means to be human) is rational. But 'God is man' is *per se* and not *per accidens* not because of the meaning of 'God', not because God as God (because of what it means to be divine) is a man, but because God as this person, this *hypostasis*, is the *hypostasis* of the man.

Aquinas, you see, is here steering his way between (a) saying that God is a man because of some merging of the natures of God and man (a matter of the meaning of being God and the meaning of being man) and (b) saying that the union of divinity and humanity is accidental, like the union of whiteness and musicalness in one man. The union is non-accidental, but not non-accidental in the way that other unities are (e.g. man and his rationality).

What Aquinas is here saying is that it is not merely a contingent fact that God is man. It is not a contingent fact like the fact that John is singing. It is non-contingent much the same way as the statement that John is human is non-contingent. Of course 'John is human' might not be true, but only if John doesn't exist; John cannot cease to be human in the way that he can cease to sing; he can't take it or leave it alone. In the same way, it might not have been the case that God became man, and for a long time it was not the case that God became man. But when it happens it is not a contingent fact. God did not take on humanity like John might take on singing.

Aquinas, naturally enough, argues that just as you can say 'God is a man' so you can say 'A man is God' (3a,16,2). But then he comes to consider two other propositions: 'God was made a man' (3a,16,6) and 'A man was made God' (3a,16,7). The first of these he allows, but the second presents problems.

Aquinas points out, of course, that the truth of the first proposition, 'God was made a man', does not entail any change in God. All that it says is that whereas previously it was not true of God that he was man, it became true about 2,000 years ago. What happened was that a new relationship was set up between God and human nature, but this relationship, so Aquinas argues, is not based on any change in God but on a change in human nature which becomes the human nature of the Son of God. God does not change by becoming man any more than I change by becoming an uncle.

'A man was made God' would be fine, Aquinas says, if it meant simply 'It became true that a man is God'. But, so he adds, this is not the natural meaning of the sentence. The natural meaning is that the *suppositum* that 'this man' stands for (the *suppositum* that is identified by this term in the subject place) became God. But the *suppositum* that it stands for is the Second Person of the Trinity and it cannot be the case that the Second Person of the Trinity became God. So we can't say, says Aquinas, that a man became God or that he began to be God, or that he was made God (*factus est Deus*), even though we can say that God became man or that God began to be man, or that God was made man. It is just this logical point that Aquinas is referring to when he speaks of Christ not having a human *personalitas* or human 'existence'. It has nothing to do with Christ not being a human person.

In 3a,16,8 Aquinas asks whether we can say that Christ is a creature. It will be clear from the principles that we have already established that we can, for 'Christ' in the subject place simply identifies what is being talked of. So it is legitimate to say that Christ is a creature, just as we can say that he suffered and died and was buried. We mean of course that Christ, *qua* human, is a creature. But as a matter of fact Aquinas is not keen on saying that Christ is a creature. He says that it would be misleading to do so and that its most natural meaning could sound Arian. He says it would be as misleading as to say that the Ethiopian is white. Technically you could say this because of his teeth. But it would be misleading.

With better reason Aquinas (3a,16,9) disallows 'That man (pointing to Christ) began to exist', for 'That man' in the subject place stands for the *suppositum* (*terminus in subjecto positus non tenetur formaliter pro natura sed magis materialiter pro supposito*), and the *suppositum* in question is the Second Person of the Trinity, who did not begin to exist. Aquinas is, of course, aware that you can use the same sentence to mean different things, and he allows that someone might use the sentence 'This man began to exist' to mean 'This man, as man, began to exist' (or 'This man, as such, began to exist'), which would be fine. But, as with respect to 'Christ is a creature', he advises against 'This man began to exist' (said pointing to Christ) on the grounds that it is a sentence which would be used with an heretical meaning by the Arians.

Finally Aquinas asks whether you can say 'Christ as man is a subject (*hypostasis*) or person'. And he says clearly that, if you are asking whether Christ is a human person, then the answer is 'Yes' since 'whatever subsists in human nature is a person' (*omne enim quod subsistit in humana natura est persona*). But, Aquinas adds, 'Christ as man is a subject or person' could mean that 'the human nature in Christ ought to have its own personality, having its causal origin in the human nature'. And, so Aquinas continues, 'in this sense, Christ, as man, is not a person; for his human nature does not exist by itself apart from the divine nature, as would be required if it were to have its own personality'. This is a point to which I referred above. Aquinas's meaning is that Christ's human nature does not define his existence (*esse*) in such sense that there would be an existence of Christ according to his humanity and another according to his divinity. For Aquinas, Christ is one existence: divine and human.

He puts this very nicely in 3a,17,2 (my translation):

In Christ whatever pertains to the nature is twofold, whatever pertains to the *hypostatis* is single. Now to be (*esse*) pertains to both nature and *hypostasis*: to the *hypostasis* as *that which has* being, to the nature as *that by which* something has being. For we speak of a nature as we speak of a form – as 'being' in the sense that by it something is (*by* whiteness something *is* white; *by* humanity something *is* a man).

A form or nature that does not pertain to the being-a-person of some subsistent *hypostasis* does not simply speaking make that person be; it only makes him be in some respect: to be white is indeed a being that Socrates has, but not insofar as he is Socrates, just insofar as he is a white thing. In this (accidental) sense of being there is no reason why one person should not have many 'beings': Socrates can *be* white and *be* musical, and these 'beings' are different. But the being that belongs to the *hypostasis* or person *as such* cannot be multiplied like this, for it is impossible that one thing should have more than one existence.

If therefore the Son of God acquired human nature not hypostatically or personally but accidentally, as some have held, we should have to say that in Christ there are two existences, one as he is God, the other as he is man. Just as in Socrates there is one being in that he *is* white and another in that he *is* a man, for being white is not part of being Socrates as this person.

Contrast this with *being* equipped with a head, or *being* corporeal or *being* alive. All these in fact make up the one being, the person Socrates. So from these there is but one being in Socrates. Now suppose that after Socrates is constituted as a person he acquires hands or feet or eyes (like the man born blind); from these he would not acquire a new being but only a new relation to these things in that he would now be said to be in respect of these and not just in respect of what he had before.

Now human nature is joined to the Son of God hypostatically or personally and not accidentally. Consequently with his new human nature he does not acquire a new personal being, but simply a new relation of the personal being that is already there to human nature, so that this person is now said to subsist not only in respect of a divine nature but also of a human nature.

Aquinas is looking for something that might be acquired and yet not be accidental, something that once acquired simply contributes to the *esse* that is already there. There is a difference between, let us say, becoming a postman and becoming sexually mature. Being a postman is accidental to you, and so it is by two separate acts of being that you are a postman and are human. Being sexually mature, although it is something you acquire and grow into, once acquired is part of you. It is not by two acts of being that you are grown up and are human. You do not just happen to be grown up, as you happen to be a postman. Being grown up is a new way in which you are yourself. Now in the Incarnation the Son of God has acquired a new way of being himself; it is as though he had grown up or achieved sexual maturity (in fact he did achieve sexual maturity).

Of course Aquinas is not here trying to fit the mystery of the Incarnation into our own categories of thought. He is not saying that becoming a man is for God just like a man born blind acquiring the sight that belongs to him, or a child becoming a man. For one thing, of course, any such example must begin with something imperfect receiving the perfection that belongs to it, and this is hardly the case with the Incarnation. Aquinas is not saying this is just how the Incarnation was, rather he is rejecting any attempt to force the Incarnation into other categories, to say that the humanity must be accidental to the divinity, or the divinity must accidentally have supervened on the humanity.

The Incarnation remains a mystery. But, perhaps, Aquinas can help us to see that we don't therefore have to talk nonsense about it.

Note

1 In what follows, and except as indicated, English translations of *Summa Theologiae* 3a,16 are taken from vol. 50 of the Blackfriars edition of the *Summa Theologiae*.

18

Aquinas on Good Sense

Elizabeth, Anne and Emma

I am concerned here with the virtue which Aquinas calls *prudentia*. But, as is almost always the case with Aquinas's technical vocabulary, the nearest English word to the Latin one would be a mistranslation: *prudentia* does not mean what we call prudence. Prudence suggests to us a certain caution and canniness, whereas *prudentia* is much nearer to wisdom, practical wisdom.

Fortunately, however, we have a nearly perfect English equivalent in Jane Austen's phrase 'good sense'. I take Jane Austen to be centrally concerned not with presenting the ethos of the new respectable middle class but rather with the failure of the new bourgeoisie to live satisfactory lives because of the inability of the older 'aristocratic' tradition to transmit to them a certain outlook and way of behaving and education that came down to the author via the remains of a Christian morality. The eighteenth-century ideal of civilized living collapsed because it involved the loss of this tradition, a tradition which (as Gilbert Ryle and others have pointed out) is, broadly speaking, Aristotelian.

Of course, no novel is a philosophical treatise, but much of Jane Austen's writing can usefully be seen as an exploration of this tradition and in particular of the notion of *prudentia*. Elizabeth Bennett is shown as having and growing in good sense, in contrast both to the silliness of her younger sisters, who think of nothing beyond present pleasure, and, on the other hand, to the pedantry of her elder sister Mary, who thinks that book-learning is enough. She also stands in contrast to her witty and perceptive but almost purely voyeuristic father, who uses his intelligence to survey a life in which he refuses to become involved. Finally, there is a contrast with her friend Charlotte, who succumbs to worldly wisdom and marries the dreadful Mr Collins for 'prudential' reasons. All these people are presented as morally inferior (and thus ultimately unhappy) because they lack good sense. Anne Elliot is, of course, centrally concerned with what Aquinas regards as a major constituent of *prudentia*: making proper use of the counsel of others. And one aspect of the education of Emma is even more interesting, because this is not completed until at the end of the book when Mr Knightley, who in part represents an alien imposed morality, is integrated into her life – he marries her and goes to live in her house together with the totally undisciplined father. The scuffles between the super-ego and the libido are being resolved in what begins to look more like virtue.

Conscience

Anyway, it is with good sense that we are concerned. A prominent part has been played in post-renaissance moral thinking by the notion of conscience, and people are often shocked to discover that this plays so small a part in Aquinas's moral teaching. Like the notion of the sheer individual in abstraction from social roles and community, and like the idea of 'human rights' attaching to such an abstract individual, it was a notion for which nobody has a word in either classical or post-classical antiquity or in the Middle Ages. Aquinas does use the word *conscientia*, but for him it is not a faculty or power which we exercise, nor a disposition of any power, nor an innate moral code, but simply the judgement we may come to on a piece of our behaviour in the light of various rational considerations. Usually it is a judgement we make on our past behaviour, but it can be extended to judgement on behaviour about which we are deliberating. Plainly such judgements happen, and they are important when they do; but what is meant in modern talk by conscience is normally something quite different. Nowadays we speak of someone 'consulting her conscience', rather as one might consult a cookery book or a railway timetable. Conscience is here seen as a private repository of answers to questions, or perhaps a set of rules of behaviour. Someone who 'has a conscience' about, say, abortion or betting is someone who detects in herself the belief that this activity is wrong or forbidden and who would therefore feel guilty were she to engage in it.

To have a conscience, then, in this way of thinking is to be equipped with a personal set of guide-lines to good behaviour, and to stifle your conscience is not to pay attention to these guide-lines. Since following the guide-lines is often inconvenient or difficult, it is necessary to exert our will-power to do so. The moral life, in other words, is an awareness of your rules of behaviour coupled with a strong will which enables you to follow these rules.

For most of those who think in this way, the verdict of conscience is ultimately unarguable. If someone says honestly 'My conscience tells me this is wrong', she is thought to be giving an infallible report on the delivery of her inner source of principles which must call a halt to argument. It is believed that the reason why violating the consciences of others – i.e. coercing them to do what is contrary to their conscience – is a very grave evil, is that there can be no rational appeal beyond conscience. For this reason there are 'conscience clauses', and for this reason a tribunal for conscientious objectors to war-service is essentially concerned to determine whether a person who claims to have a conscientious objection is telling the truth about the delivery of his conscience. Such a tribunal is not expected directly to consider the validity or otherwise of the objector's position: what matters is simply that it is the decision of his conscience. This concern for conscience as such is admirably

expressed in Robert Bolt's play about Thomas More, *A Man for All Seasons*,
though it is not an attitude that would have been shared by an old-fashioned
thinker like St Thomas More himself. For this modern way of thinking there
exists a *prima facie* right for individuals to follow their consciences, and hence
societies in which, for example, there is no such provision for conscientious
objection are seen as necessarily unjust and tyrannous.

In the tradition with which I am concerned, there exists no such right, for
rights have a quite different foundation. On the other hand, there is a principle
of good sense in legal matters that even activities thought to be anti-social
are not to be prohibited by the apparatus of the law if this will cause more
social harm than tolerating them. A society that legally tolerates any number
of devious and peculiar sexual or financial practices is not proclaiming its
belief that these are harmless (still less that they are possible options for the
good life); it is proclaiming its belief that, whatever harm they do, sending
in the police or opening the way for blackmail would be immensely more
disruptive and dangerous to the general good. Similarly, much more harm
would be done by imprisoning or forcibly conscripting people who genuinely
believe that war (or this war) is unjust than by tolerating them. It is for this
reason, and not because of the alleged absolute rights of conscience, that it is
a bad thing not to respect conscientious objectors. It is not the strength and
sincerity of my conviction that the use of nuclear weapons must always be evil,
but rather the grounds for this conviction that make it morally right for me
to refuse any co-operation with such use. Obviously, no tribunal could accept
these grounds without becoming conscientious objectors themselves; short of
this they can only make a sensible, and therefore just, decision to tolerate me.

The truth of this can be seen, I think, if we ask ourselves whether there
should be tribunals to judge whether a man really holds as a matter of
conscience that he should strangle all Jewish babies at birth or that his
children's moral education is best served by starving them or burning them
with cigarette ends. It is, I think, a mark of the confusion that has prevailed in

moral thinking that intelligent people can find it quite hard to give a reasoned answer to such questions. So let us turn from this to the Aristotelian tradition as developed by Aquinas.

Prudentia

In this view we come to decisions, the 'deliveries of conscience', by practical thinking, and such thinking, like so many human activities, can be done well or badly, 'conscientiously' or sloppily, honestly or with self-deception. The virtue which disposes us to think well about what to do is *prudentia*, good sense.

We should notice that, like most thinking, this would normally be a communal activity. We would ordinarily try to get the thing right by discussing the matter with others, by asking advice or arguing a case; we would have a background of reading books or watching Channel Four, of listening to preachers or parents or children, of criticizing the views and behaviour of others, of attending to things for which we could appropriately be blamed, and this shows that to be disposed not to behave like that is to have a virtue. We may on particular occasions pity the credulous, foolish or stubbornly unreasonable person, just as we might pity the coward or drug-addict, but ordinarily we would think it also proper to blame such people (and therefore, of course, proper to forgive them).

Unreasonableness, pig-headedness, bigotry and self-deception are all in themselves blameworthy, and they are constitutive of the kind of stupidity that is a vice. That is why no stupid person can be good. In case anyone should think that this gives academics and intellectuals a moral advantage over ignorant peasants, let us remember that what is in question is not theoretical thinking and the handling of concepts and words, but the practical shrewdness and common sense in matters of human behaviour. In this matter

I think the 'ignorant' peasant may often have the edge over the professor. One of the hindrances to acquiring the virtue of good sense is living too sheltered a life. There is, of course, a sense of 'education' (rather different from the one in common use) in which the educated person does indeed have a moral advantage over the uneducated; if this were not so, education would not be a serious human activity. It will be clear that in this Aristotelian view, conscience, the moral judgement I have come to, is in no sense infallible. For what I have called the modern position, the delivery of conscience is a base-line: moral questions concern simply whether and to what extent you follow your conscience. For the older point of view you can be praised or blamed for the moral principles you hold. People who have come to the conclusion (who have convinced themselves) that torture can be a good and necessary thing and who thus carry it out cheerfully without a qualm of conscience would, in accordance with the older view, be not less but more to blame than those who recognize that torture is evil, who do not want to do it, but nevertheless do it out of fear of reprisals should they fail in their 'duty'.

Concerning judgements of conscience, Aquinas asks two interesting questions in succession. Is it always wrong, he asks, not to do what you mistakenly think is right? (Is it always wrong to go against your conscience?) He says that it is always wrong to flout your judgement of conscience in this way – he holds, for example, that someone who had come to the conclusion that Christianity was erroneous would be wrong not to leave the Church. But then he asks the following question: Is it always right to do what you mistakenly think is right? (Is it always good to follow your conscience?) This is where he departs from the modern view: he says it is not necessarily right for you to do what you think is right, for you may have come to your decision of conscience carelessly, dishonestly or by self-deception. He holds, in fact, the disturbing view that you can be in the position of being wrong if you do not follow your conscience and also being wrong if you do. But, he argues, you can only have got yourself into this position through your own fault. It is only by continual failure in virtue, by the cultivation of excuses and ration-alizations, that you have blinded yourself to reality. It is not at all uncommon for individuals through their own fault to have put themselves in positions in which the only courses left open to them are all bad. Then they simply have to choose the lesser evil, which does not on that account become good. Suppose, for example, that a government has established in a remote and desolate area a large set of factories for the wicked purpose of manufacturing nuclear weapons. Unemployed people from distant parts of the country get on their bikes and flock to this place to get jobs. Once this has happened the government may continue its genocidal activity or else it may throw these thousands of people out of work with no hope of work. It has put itself in the position where all its options, for which it would rightly be held responsible, are bad.

Thus, for Aquinas, a clear conscience is no guarantee of virtue. We should always, he says, fear that we may be wrong. We should have what he calls *sollicitudo* about this. As Oliver Cromwell (not always an assiduous disciple of St Thomas) said to the General Assembly of the Church of Scotland: 'I beseech you, gentlemen, in the bowels of Christ, to bethink you that you may be mistaken.'

Good sense is the virtue that disposes us to deliberate well, to exercise our practical reasoning well, and it presupposes that we have some good intention, that we intend an end that is in itself reasonable. The *intentio finis*, intending the end, is an *actus voluntatis*, a realization or actualization of the power we call the will, the power to be attracted by what we intellectually apprehend as good. (We should be on our guard against translating '*actus voluntatis*' as an 'action' or performance of the will: that primrose path leads to the dualistic notion of an interior performance of the will, an intention, accompanying the exterior action. The *actus voluntatis* here is the condition or state of being attracted to some good, which is *actus* in that it fulfils the potentiality of the will as the oak fulfils the potentiality of an acorn, not as the kick fulfils the potentiality of the leg. It must be said that Aquinas's own language is not always as guarded as it might be on this important point.)

It is in and by the will that we are in a state of intending an end; it is by the will, that is, that we find this end attractive as an end. The will is being actualized or exercized because we present the end to ourselves rationally (in language or other symbols). This is to be distinguished from being attracted to some good that presents itself to us simply as sensually apprehended. The latter attractions and appetites we share, more or less, with other non-linguistic animals. Such animals can, of course, in Aquinas's view be moved by an end or purpose in what they do, they can act willingly (*voluntarie*); but they cannot be said in his technical language (which I believe he invented) to *intend* that end. In modern English I think we would say that the dog intended to chase the rabbit, but all that we would mean is that the dog's seeing of the rabbit, its sensual apprehension of it as desirable, is the reason why it is chasing. We do not mean that the dog *has* this reason, for this would only be possible if the dog were able to *analyse* its situation in language, to see, as Aquinas puts it, 'the *end as end* to be pursued by these or those means'. So while we may certainly say the dog is willingly (*voluntarie*) chasing (as opposed to unwillingly, involuntary, or without willing, *non-voluntarie*) we cannot say that the dog has the intention, *intentio*, of chasing it. Although it is acting willingly, *voluntarie*, it is not acting in terms of a state or condition of willing. Because it has no language it can have no will.

Synderesis

So, for Aquinas, good sense, good deliberation, does not concern itself with the *intentio finis*, the wanting of the end, but with the adjustment of the means to the end. The intellectual presentation of the end that we find attractive (which we want or intend) is not in the field of practical reasoning but of an intellectual disposition that Aquinas calls *synderesis*. This is a very peculiar word for a very peculiar and interesting concept. It is, for one thing, a piece of fake Greek that seems to have been invented by Latin-speaking medieval philosophers and does not occur in any classical Greek text. The clue to understanding it, I believe, is to see that, for Aquinas, in the sphere of practical action *synderesis* is related to deliberation in the way that, in the theoretical sphere, *intellectus* is related to reasoning.

Aquinas thought that in any kind of true knowledge, any *scientia*, there must be certain first principles that are simply taken for granted: they are not part of the subject of the *scientia* itself. Keynesians do not argue with Milton Friedmanites about whether $1 + 1 = 2$; economists take for granted truths that are argued to by philosophers of mathematics. The statistical study of economics is permeated by the truths of arithmetic, but it is not about them. Economics is done in terms of arithmetic; it does not seek to establish these truths. The economist needs the arithmetical *habitus* or skill, but what he is engaged in is something different. Now, as I understand him, Aquinas would think of the economist as having *intellectus* with regard to the arithmetical principles he takes for granted but exercising his *ratio*, reasoning, about his own particular topic. We should notice that the arithmetical truths are not premises from which truths of economics are deduced; they are terms within which, in the light of which (to use Aquinas's own metaphor), the argument is conducted. Aquinas frequently says that *intellectus* is the *habitus* of first principles, while reason, *ratio*, is concerned with how to draw conclusions in the light of these principles in some particular field.

'First principles' must be a relative term, for what are the first principles of one science (economics or chemistry) will be the conclusions of another (mathematics). Aquinas did not think there could be an infinite regress of sciences, each treating as arguable what the one below it took for granted. We must, he thought, eventually arrive at some first principles that nobody could think of as arguable, as the conclusion of a reasoned argument. He instances the principle of non-contradiction: that the same proposition cannot simul-taneously be both true and false. And indeed this cannot be argued since any argument, to be an argument at all, must take this for granted; it must be conducted in terms of, in the light of, this. (This principle must not be confused with the principle called the 'excluded middle', which says that a proposition must be either true or false: this can be rationally denied and all multi-valued logics start from rejecting it.) So the absolutely ultimate first principle in theoretical reasoning, the principle in terms of which any reasoning whatever must take place, is something like the principle of non-contradiction, and *intellectus* in its ultimate sense is the *habitus* or settled disposition to conduct argument in terms of this principle: that is, the disposition simply to conduct argument, to use definite meaningful symbols, at all.

Now Aquinas sees *synderesis* as parallel in practical reasoning to *intellectus* in theoretical reasoning. Practical reasoning begins with something you want; it takes for granted that this is wanted and deliberates about the means of achieving it. The intellectual grasp of the aim as aim (not the attraction to it and intention of it, which is the actualization of will, but the understanding of it) is *synderesis*. The deliberation takes place in terms of this end presented to us as understood by *synderesis* and found attractive as an end, intended by us in virtue of our being able to want rationally (because we have a reason), and it concludes to an action or decision to act.

But, of course, what might be the starting point of one deliberation may be a conclusion come to in a previous one. We do not, says Aristotle, deliberate about aims; but what we aim at, what we have *synderesis* of intellectually and intend as a matter of will, may be the result of a previous deliberation. In each bit of practical reasoning, if we take them separately, it is by *synderesis* that we intellectually grasp what by the will we intend, find attractive (i.e. good), and it is by practical reasoning (preferably disposed by good sense) that we decide what we will do about it.

Now, just as with a hierarchy of sciences in theoretical reasoning we get back to some ultimate first principles that we simply grasp by *intellectus* (principles which cannot be the conclusion of any previous reasoning) like the principle of non-contradiction, so in practical reasoning there is *synderesis* not only of relative first principles but also of some ultimate first principle such as that the good is what is to be wanted (which could not itself be the conclusion of some previous practical reasoning), just as all theoretical reasoning is conducted in terms of, in the light of, the practical principle of seeking what is in some respect good (which lies at the root of all meaningful human action – what Aquinas calls an *actus humanus* as distinct from a mere *actus hominis*). Practical reasoning is practical reasoning because it is conducted in this light, just as theoretical reasoning is theoretical reasoning because it is conducted in the light of non-contradiction.

Synderesis, then, in its ultimate sense is the natural dispositional grasp of this ultimate practical principle; and we should remember that in neither the theoretical nor the practical case is the principle a premise of some syllogism, although it can be stated as a proposition. It is rather the principle in virtue of which there is any syllogism at all.

Practical Reasoning

Another way of putting this is to say that just as the *intellectus* of the ultimate first theoretical principle is the natural (and unacquired) disposition to be 'truth-preserving' in reasoning, so the *synderesis* of the ultimate first practical principle is the natural (and unacquired) disposition to be 'satisfactoriness-preserving' in deliberation. I owe these terms to Dr Anthony Kenny and what follows draws heavily on his *Will, Freedom and Power* (Oxford: Blackwell, 1975), especially Chapter 5. Kenny notes that theoretical argument has a truth-preserving logic: its concern is that we should not move from true premises to a false conclusion. Now he suggests that practical thinking is to be governed by a satisfactoriness-preserving logic which will ensure that we do not move from satisfactory premises to an unsatisfactory conclusion. Take the thinking: 'I want to get this carpet clean; the Hoover vacuum cleaner will do it; so, to the Hoover!' We should notice that the first clause expresses an intention (the *intentio finis*) and the last, in the optative mood, may be replaced simply by the action of using the Hoover. This action as the conclusion of a piece of practical reasoning (that is, done for a reason) is itself meaningful. It has become an act of cleaning the carpet because of the intention with which it is being done. What, to a less informed observer, might seem to be the same act, might have had other meanings and been a different human action if, for instance, I used the Hoover because I wanted its noise to irritate my hated neighbour. In that case there would be a different piece of practical reasoning exhibiting the meaning of my action, exhibiting, that is, the intention with which it is being done.

The intention with which it is done centrally defines a human act as the sort of human act it is. Thus, if you accidentally drop a five pound note and I pick it up, I may do so with the intention of keeping it for myself or with the intention of giving it back to you. The first intention specifies my action as one of stealing, and the second as one of restitution. My intention or motive in picking up the note is not an occurrence inside my head which causes me to pick up the money in the way that an agent brings about an event (as 'efficient cause'); it is what Aquinas calls a 'final cause' in virtue of which I, the agent, do the action and in virtue of which the action has its 'form', its specification. It is the practical reasoning, exhibiting the intention with which the action is done, that shows what, in human terms, the action counts as or is. Nobody, of course, suggests that whenever you act meaningfully you go through some particular chain of reasoning in your mind. That would be no more true of practical thinking than it is of theoretical thinking. We can act or think quite reasonably without going through syllogisms or other arguments.

But in both cases it is possible to spell out the thought in some such way in order to show whether it is really a valid piece of reasoning or a muddle; a muddle in practical thinking can lead to your being mistaken; a muddle in practical thinking can lead to your not doing or getting what you want, what you intended.

Some philosophers, Alasdair MacIntyre, for example *After Virtue* (London: Duckworth, 1981), Chapter 12, hold that the conclusion of a practical syllogism is always a meaningful action (or meaningful inaction) rather than a proposition, but this seems unnecessarily restrictive. It is clear that the conclusion is not a theoretical proposition (in the indicative mood) but it may well be not simply an action but (in the optative mood) a plan of action or, as Aquinas prefers to see it, a command addressed (in the imperative mood) either to others or to oneself.

The logic of practical reasoning differs from that of theoretical reasoning most evidently in being based not on necessity but on sufficiency. Its conclusion is an action or proposal of action which will be sufficient to attain the aim expressed in the major premises: one that will sufficiently preserve the satisfactoriness of the original aim; what will be excluded are practical conclusions which do not thus preserve satisfactoriness. In theoretical reasoning, on the other hand, the conclusion will be what is necessarily entailed by the premises; what will be excluded will be conclusions which are not thus necessarily entailed, which may be false when the premises are true.

Thus one common form of theoretical reasoning goes like this: 'If p then q; but p; therefore q.' 'If he's from Blackburn, then he's from the north; but he's from Blackburn; so he's from the north.' One form which would be excluded would be: 'If p then q; but q; therefore p.' 'If he's from Blackburn, he's from the north; but he's from the north; so he's from Blackburn.' Plainly this is not necessary, for he may be from Stockton or Carlisle.

Now contrast this with a piece of practical reasoning: 'If I use the Hoover the carpet will be cleaned; but I want the carpet clean; so I'll use the Hoover.'

This provides a practical conclusion sufficient for my purposes. It is not however necessitated. There may be many other practical conclusions which would attain my aim, which would preserve the satisfactoriness of getting the carpet clean. The shape of this valid practical reasoning resembles, however, the shape of invalid theoretical reasoning. We seem to be arguing: 'If p then q; but q; therefore p.' But such a form of reasoning is only invalid if we are seeking a necessitated conclusion; in practical reasoning we are never doing this; we look simply for an action which will be sufficient for our purposes.

One very important contrast between theoretical and practical reasoning is that if we have a valid piece of theoretical reasoning no number of extra premises will render it invalid. Thus I may argue as follows: 'All clergymen are wrong about the meaning of life; but all bishops are clergymen; therefore all bishops are wrong about the meaning of life.' This conclusion remains valid however many other things I may find to say about clergymen or bishops: it makes no difference whether or not they play the piano nicely or have long furry ears and prehensile tails or are (some of them) my best friends or whatever. In this argument, so long as the original premises are true the conclusion is necessarily true. This does not go for practical reasoning. Take the argument: 'If I take this train it will get me to London; but I want to go to London; so I'll take the train.' This conclusion is practically valid so far as it goes but it ceases to be so if we add: 'I am always sick on trains' or 'This train is about to be blown up by crazed fascists'. In such a case the meaning of the action of boarding the train is no longer to be seen simply as going to London but also as becoming sick or being killed, which I may not want at all.

Thus the logic of theoretical reasoning can provide us with formulae which tell us what it is reasonable and what it is unreasonable to think, given certain premises. Practical reasoning, concerned with what it is reasonable to do, is not closed off by any such formulae. If we are to think well practically we must have an eye to all relevant additional premises which may serve to invalidate a conclusion. Actions done for reasons can be done for an indefinite number of reasons. And no single reason necessarily compels you to the action: there could be others dissuading you. It is just this multi-facetedness of actions done for reasons that, in St Thomas's view, lies at the root of our freedom. No particular reason, no particular good that is sought, can necessitate our action; only the vision of the ultimate infinite good, God, can thus necessitate us.

Good sense, then, for St Thomas, as the disposition to do our practical reasoning well, involving a sensitive awareness of a multitude of factors which may be relevant to our decision. It involves, he says, bringing into play not merely our purely intellectual (symbol-using) powers but our sensuous apprehension of the concrete individual circumstances of our action. In his view, since our rather limited form of intelligence can only deal in the meanings of words and other symbols (for him our thinking is conceived on the model of our talking), and since no concrete individual can be the meaning of a symbol, we grasp the particular individual not by our intelligence but only by our sense powers. Thus, for him, you cannot identify a particular individual simply by describing it in words (any such words could be referring to another individual); in the end you have to point at it or single it out by some such bodily act. He concludes from this that if we are to be good at practical decision making, if we are to have good sense, we need to exercise well our sensual, bodily apprehension of the world; so we need to be in good bodily health as well as clear in our ideas. The depression (tristitia) which for him comes principally from not getting enough fun out of life is likely to impede the virtue of good sense just as it impedes the sensual virtues of courage or chastity.

Aquinas's treatment of the ancillary dispositions that attend on the virtue of prudentia is one of the most interesting and, I think, original parts of his treatment, but I cannot discuss it here. I will conclude with a glance at one important topic: What is the difference between good sense and cunning?

Cunning and Good Sense

The logic of practical reasoning is neutral, as between good and bad ends; the same canons of argument apply to thinking about how to get your uncle his Christmas present and thinking about how to murder him. But, in Aquinas's view, practical reasoning is directed towards good ends. The cunning practised by the one seeking apparently good but actually evil ends is not misdirected prudence but a degenerate form of practical reasoning, a false prudence. There are more ways of being unreasonable than being illogical.

Aquinas gives us a clue to the difference between cunning and good sense in one of his many comparisons between practical and theoretical reasoning. It is like the difference between dialectical argumentation and *scientia*. By true *scientia* we know that something is true and really why it is true. The characteristic cry of the one with *scientia* is: 'Yes, I see, of course, that has to be so.' *Scientia* traces facts back to their first principles by argumentation. Now consider this argument: 'All slow-witted people are subjects of the Queen of England; all the British are slow-witted; so all the British are subjects of the Queen of England.' This is a perfectly valid argument and it comes to a true conclusion although both its premises are manifestly false. It is not true that all slow-witted people are subjects of the Queen; nor is it true that all the British are slow-witted. There is nothing logically odd about deriving a true conclusion from false premises; as we have seen, it is deriving false conclusions from true premises that has to be excluded by a 'truth-preserving' logic. But although the falsity of the premises does not make the argument illogical, it does make the argument unscientific. We would be misled to say: 'Yes, I see, the British must necessarily be subjects of the Queen because they are slow-witted.' We would be using the wrong middle term to connect being British and being subject to the Queen. What the correct middle term would be it is a little hard to say – one would need to know something about how the House of Hanover established its legitimacy in Britain.

It is not merely false premises but also 'improper' or irrelevant premises that render an argument unscientific. Thus if we were to substitute going out in the midday sun for slow-wittedness you might, for all I know, have true premises but none the less you will not have truly explained the matter since it is not because of this propensity that the British (or at least Englishmen) are subject to the Queen. If your premises are either untrue or irrelevant or both, but your argument is logically valid and your conclusion true, you have what Aquinas would call a piece of merely dialectical reasoning. *Scientia* is distinguished from dialectical argument by its aim, which is a true comprehension of the order of the world, one the premises of which are both true and 'proper'. Now, in a similar way, good sense is distinguished from cunning by its aim, which is acting well, pursuing ends which constitute or contribute to what is in fact the good life for a human being.

Thus good sense, for Aquinas, is not mere cleverness but presupposes the moral virtues, the dispositions that govern our appetites and intentions, for it is concerned not merely with what seems good to me but with what is in fact good for me; and it is the lynch-pin of humane and reasonable living because without it none of these goods will be attained.

PART FOUR

SERMONS

19

Faith

The letter to the Hebrews tells us that 'Faith is the assurance of things hoped for, the conviction of things not seen' (Heb. 11.1). This is a special way of looking at faith. For the author of Hebrews, faith has to do with what we do not *yet* see, what we hope for. It has to do with what is over the horizon. If you like, it is what lures us on to journey over the horizon to look at what we cannot yet see.

This approach to faith is, I think, very different from, for example, the notion of faith as a kind of test. There was a sort of an idea around when I was a child that God, or possibly the church, proposed to us certain things that were *difficult* to believe or even to understand (that God is both three and one, for example), and we showed our loyalty (our faith) by accepting these propositions. If we were humble enough to accept things we couldn't understand, then we would eventually be rewarded for our devotion. The great enemy was always a thing called 'spiritual pride', which made you always want to understand everything.

That is one way of looking at faith. I don't think it's a very good way, but it's one way. And, when we are dealing with difficult and mysterious things, almost *any* way of seeing them is of *some* help. But this way is very different from the way faith is looked at in Hebrews. Here, faith is all about trying to understand. It is about not being content to understand the things that are obvious, the things we can already see. It is about trying to understand what we do *not* yet see. It is about setting out on the journey to explore what we have not yet seen. We read: 'By faith Abraham obeyed when he was called to set out for a place that he was to receive as an inheritance; and he set out, not knowing where he was going' (Heb. 11.8). Faith, for the author of Hebrews, is seen in terms of a journey, a movement. And not just a commuter's journey, a movement from one familiar spot to another. It is seen as a real journey, the kind of journey you make on a holiday, to see new places and to meet new people. It is a journey of exploration, an adventuring out.

This way of talking about faith is again different from another that you get in the Bible where we hear about the 'household of the faith' (Galatians 6.10). There, the faith is, so to speak, the badge of membership of the community. And we speak of those who are 'sealed with the seal of the faith', as we speak of 'preserving the faith', or 'preserving the deposit of faith'. Here 'the faith' is seen as a kind of treasure we have inherited (we talk of 'handing on the faith'). We are almost talking as though the faith were something we possessed. And this, too, is, of course, a valid way of talking. It brings out one aspect of what we mean by 'faith'. But, again, it is a very different approach from that of the letter to the Hebrews. For this text, the faith is not something we possess. It is all about what we do *not* possess. It is about what we hope for, and do not yet see.

For the author of Hebrews, the first image of faith is the journey of Abraham into the unknown, a journey simply based on a promise: not a planned journey, with all the arrangements made beforehand, but, perhaps; more like modern package tours, where you can't be sure the hotel has actually been built yet, where you are journeying toward the Promised Hotel. But then Hebrews makes things a little more complicated. In a sort of way, Abraham arrives at the promised land. But, even then, it is not something he possesses. 'By faith he stayed for a time in the land he had been promised, as in a foreign land, living in tents, as did Isaac and Jacob, who were heirs with him of the same promise. For he looked forward to the city that has foundations, whose architect and builder is God' (Heb. 11.9-10). The author of Hebrews is here remembering the Old Testament story according to which Abraham arrived as a wandering nomad in Canaan (the promised land) though his family didn't really possess it until 400 years later, until after their time in Egypt (a sort of death), and did not receive the city of Jerusalem from God until many years after that. In Hebrews, that story is being used symbolically of course: we can, in a sort of way, arrive at the promise, at what is over the horizon, at what is hoped for; and yet we do not really arrive until we have gone down into Egypt and returned, until we have been destroyed and remade, died and been brought back from the dead. I think that the author of Hebrews is thinking of the fact that in one way we have received the promise, in one way the kingdom has come. We are no longer simply groping in the dark. In a sort of way, in Jesus Christ the promise is fulfilled, the kingdom is established – in an odd sort of way, mysteriously, in the way we call 'sacramentally'. Sacramentally, we have arrived at the kingdom, just as Abraham arrived as a stranger, a foreigner in the promised land. But he lived there in a tent, a temporary shack. And he didn't make the mistake of thinking that what he built was the real thing. It was just a structure he threw up while waiting for the gift of the real city, waiting for the terrible giving of the city, a giving that involved letting his people be broken and remade.

In a way the whole thing is a bit like growing up, becoming mature, becoming in fact fully human. I'm not saying that adults are always more human than children, certainly not that they are always better than children. But the thing that education, maturing, growing up is supposed to be for is to develop your humanity. Of course children already possesses humanity. But it is also something they are reaching towards, something unknown. They must live in their childhood as in a tent, as in a temporary dwelling. They must not cling to it as a permanent possession. If they do, it becomes a hiding place, a way of avoiding the call to set out and grow up. But obeying that call means not only venturing into the unknown. It means venturing into the unexpected. It means being prepared to let the tent be blown away by the wind of the Spirit.

It means what they call the crisis of adolescence, when you were destroyed and remade (well or badly as the case may be).

Now the Church and any other structures we use on our way to the kingdom, or when we first arrive in the kingdom, are all tents, shacks. But we *can* treat them as permanent. And then they become hiding places, ways of evading the summons to receive the real city from the terrible hands of God, ways of refusing to be taken down into Egypt and remade, ways of refusing death and, therefore, of refusing resurrection.

For faith is about the way we get to the promised land in the most unexpected and least likely way. Not the prudent and reasonable way, but the very opposite. The promised land is like the child Isaac, impossibly born of the barren Sarah and the aged Abraham. It is like Jesus born of the virgin Mary. It is like Isaac given back from the dead. It is like Jesus crucified and raised from the dead. It *is* Jesus crucified and raised from the dead.

Faith is about what is beyond the horizon of the humanly possible. Faith is exploring into what people could never achieve by themselves. Faith is the mysterious *need* in us to get to where we could surely *never* go. Faith, in fact, is about what we call God. Faith is the inkling that we are meant to be divine, that our journey will go beyond any horizon at all into the limitlessness of the Godhead. Faith is not *our* power to set out on this journey into the future. It is our future laying hold on us. It is the crucified and risen Christ gathering us toward himself. Faith is not something we possess. It is something by which we are possessed. It is the Spirit of Christ bringing us to what we are meant for: the eternal love which is the Father.

20

The Genealogy of Christ

The book of the genealogy of Jesus Christ, the son of David, the son of Abraham.

Abraham was the father of Isaac, and Isaac the father of Jacob, and Jacob the father of Judah and his brothers, and Judah the father of Perez and Zerah by Tamar, and Perez the father of Hezron, and Hezron the father of Ram, and Ram the father of Amminadab, and Amminadab the father of Nahshon, and Nahshon the father of Salmon, and Salmon the father of Boaz by Rahab, and Boaz the father of Obed by Ruth, and Obed the father of Jesse, and Jesse the father of David the king.

And David was the father of Solomon by the wife of Uriah, and Solomon the father of Rehoboam, and Rehoboam the father of Abijah, and Abijah the father of Asa, and Asa the father of Jehoshaphat, and Jehoshaphat the father of Joram, and Joram the father of Uzziah, and Uzziah the father of Jotham, and Jotham the father of Ahaz, and Ahaz the father of Hezekiah, and Hezekiah the father of Manasseh, and Manasseh the father of Amos, and Amos the father of Josiah, and Josiah the father of Jechoniah and his brothers, at the time of the deportation to Babylon.

And after the deportation to Babylon: Jechoniah was the father of Shealtiel, and Shealtiel the father of Zerubbabel, and Zerubbabel the father of Abiud, and Abiud the father of Eliakim, and Eliakim the father of Azor, and Azor the father of Zadok, and Zadok the father of Achim, and Achim the father of Eliud, and Eliud the father of Eleazar, and Eleazar the father of Matthan, and Matthan the father of Jacob, and Jacob the father of Joseph the husband of Mary, of whom Jesus was born, who is called Christ.

So all the generations from Abraham to David were fourteen generations, and from David to the deportation to Babylon fourteen generations, and from the deportation to Babylon to the Christ fourteen generations.

(Mt. 1.1-17)

Now I shall fill in the odd quarter of an hour giving you an annotated version of this genealogy. I want to try to put some flesh and blood on the bare skeleton provided by St Matthew. As you will see, there is a good deal both of flesh and blood involved.

The author of John's gospel begins his introduction to Jesus with the cosmos itself: 'In the beginning was the Word, and the Word was with God.' Luke has a narrower but still universalist scope. If you remember, he traces Christ back to Adam. Matthew, however, gets much closer down to earth and puts the family of Jesus in the particular context of the history of Israel. And, of course, the closer you get down to earth, the earthier you get.

One aim of Matthew is to show that Jesus really *was* tied into the squalid realities of human life and sex and politics.

The shape of the thing is fairly simple and based, like so much of Matthew's gospel, on the number seven. Matthew produces twice-seven (fourteen) generations between Abraham and David, when the family receives its kingship; fourteen more until the exile, when they lose it; and another fourteen until Jesus, when the kingship is definitively restored and re-established in a new form. So the whole thing, the Book of Generations, opens the way for Matthew's central theme of the coming of the kingdom.

Well, let us look at the list of ancestors, so far as we know them.

We start with Abraham, the man of faith, because the whole thing starts with faith and depends on the promise to Abraham: initially the promise of children. Then, when Abraham was an old man, Isaac was born, 'out of due time', in consequence of God's promise.

The faith of Abraham meant that, at an early age, Isaac very nearly had his throat cut by his father. But he survived to be the father of Jacob, an unscrupulous but entertaining character who won *his* position in the line that leads to Christ by lying and cheating his old blind father.

He was cheated himself, however. He slept with the wrong girl by mistake and became the father of Judah.

Judah slept, again by mistake, with his own daughter-in-law Tamar, who had cheated him by disguising herself and dressing up as a prostitute (she was a widow; her previous husband had been struck down by the Lord for practising *coitus interruptus*). Anyway, when Judah heard that his daughter-in-law had prostituted herself and become pregnant, he ordered her to be burnt alive. He was disconcerted when he discovered that he himself had been the client and that the child, Perez, was his.

Well, all that is what Matthew was referring to when he said 'Isaac begat Jacob; and Jacob begat Judah and his brethren; and Judah begat Perez and Zerah of Tamar'.

Then we get a list of people we know nothing about. They are just names from the Book of Chronicles: Hezron, Ram, Amminadab, Nahshon, Salmon. But then we come to Boaz. We know about him from the Book of Ruth.

Boaz didn't exactly sleep with Ruth by mistake, but he was surprised in the middle of the night to find her sleeping at his feet. (Though unconventional behaviour by women ought not to have surprised Boaz, for according to Matthew his mother was Rahab, and commentators seem to assume that Matthew must have meant Rahab the prostitute in Jericho, who entertained and hid the secret agents of Joshua and betrayed her city and her people to be massacred.)

The story of Ruth with its fertility symbolism of the barley harvest and of Bethlehem, the House of Bread, is one of the most charming and lovely stories in the Old Testament (though a little obscure because of all the stuff about the law of real estate). But one thing that stands out is that Ruth, a pagan foreigner, is impelled, as Tamar had been, by a strange passionate urge to carry on the line at almost any cost. It was the line that led to David and on to Christ. Ruth's son, Obed, was the father of Jesse, who was the father of David.

The thing, of course, to notice is that God's plan is worked out not in pious people, people with religious experiences, but in a set of crude, passionate and thoroughly disreputable people.

That first section of the genealogy concentrates on sex. From David onwards the accent is more on violence.

David fell in love with a girl he chanced to see bathing naked one evening. He arranged for her husband to be murdered, slept with her and became the father of Solomon, the next in the line of succession towards Christ our saviour.

The whole story of David, the ruthless and highly successful bandit, who, in the power of the Holy Spirit, got control of a whole confederacy of tribes, is, of course, full of intrigue and murder – *successful* intrigue and murder. But Solomon's son Rehoboam lost most of David's gains through high-handedness and greed. The section of territory he was left with, Judah, was badly misruled and, according to the Bible, Rehoboam encouraged pagan cults and sacred male prostitutes.

Abijah, his son, was no better, though his son and grandson, Asa and Jehoshaphat, had some idea of what the call of Yahweh meant.

The Book of Kings at this point concentrates most of its attention on the kingdom next door, the other bit of territory, Israel, where Ahab and Jezebel were having a more colourful and depraved time, in spite of the prophet Elijah.

Meanwhile in Judah, the son of the good Jehoshaphat, the next in line, Jehoram (or Joram as Matthew calls him), tried to reunite the two territories by marrying the sister of Ahab, and he instantly took to Ahab's evil ways. *His* son Ahaziah was (like so many people at that time) murdered by Jehu, a particularly bloodthirsty sort of ninth-century Cromwell: a sadistic mass-killer who did it all to Purify the Land for the sake of Yahweh.

Matthew skips over this, together with the next man, who as a baby was rescued in the nick of time by his aunt while his grandmother, the appalling Athaliah, was systematically murdering his brothers and sisters.

He *was* assassinated in the end though – by a junta of colonels who put his son on the throne. I need hardly say that, when the son was safely established, he had the colonels put to death. And so we move on through Uzziah the leper down the line that leads towards Christmas and the angels and the shepherds and the crib at Bethlehem.

I shall not burden you with further details, but I assure you that it goes on like this through Jotham and Ahaz and Hezekiah (who was a rare good exception), through Manasseh, who used to burn babies alive, and his son Amon (Matthew calls him Amos), who did the same, through Josiah, who tried to reform things too late and invented Deuteronomy, and so on down to the exile and the end of the kingship; and a good thing too, you might think.

After the exile things seem to improve a bit, partly because there aren't any kings, but mainly because most of the names aren't mentioned in the Old Testament at all (and for all I know Matthew made them up, to bring his numbers up to fourteen – Luke mostly has different ones). And so we come down to Joseph, of whom Matthew says that he was 'a just man' – a fact worth noting when you think of the family he came from.

And Jesus belonged to the family of Joseph. Of course, as Matthew himself tells us, Joseph wasn't the physical father of Jesus. But the Jews were not hung up on genetics: people could belong to one family, be brethren, without worrying about the exact biology of it all.

Well, that is the Book of the Generation of Jesus Christ. The moral is too obvious to labour. Jesus did not belong to the nice clean world of Angela Macnamara or Mary Whitehouse, or to the honest, reasonable, sincere world of the *Observer* or the *Irish Times*. He belonged to a family of murderers, cheats, cowards, adulterers and liars. He belonged to *us* and came to help *us*. No wonder he came to a bad end and gave *us* some hope.

21

Jesus and Sanctity

In one way (at one level), you could say that, as knives are for cutting, and pens are for writing, people are for living with each other. Someone might be good at singing, or football, or physiotherapy. But what would make her quite simply good, what would make her a good person, would be a matter of how she lives with others. So the Greek philosophers said that man is the political animal, one who lives in a *polis*, in community with others, in the special kind of community that we call friendship, the special sharing of life with each other, loving each other, that belongs to the animals that talk and think and make decisions freely.

In another way we can say that the aim and purpose of human life is to come to God, who made us for himself, so that our hearts do not rest until they rest in him. All other goods are satisfying, but never completely satisfying. The only complete human satisfaction is to be with God.

What makes the Christian gospel unique is that it proclaims that these two apparently quite different ways of talking are, in the end, saying the same thing. For, as the author of 1 John puts it bluntly: 'Whoever does not love does not know God, for God is love' (1 Jn 4.8). Or, as we sing in Holy Week, 'Ubi caritas et amor ibi Deus', 'Where there is charity and love, *there* is God'.

This is not to reduce the gospel to friendliness – going around smiling at everybody. It is to say that (while friendship and love can mean a thousand things) what we are seeking in our community with each other is, at its *greatest* depth, community with God. In any case, friendship is more than kindness and wishing well to another. It is a way of being with another, of sharing life with another. Friends do not want to be separated. If they have to be apart, they will invent ways of being together. Friendship is a quest for unity.

Jesus tells us that his Father, the one who sent him into the world, the one who laid commands upon him, gave him a mission to fulfil (cf. John 8.18). This Father is doing all this in order that there shall be friendship between Jesus and his disciples just as there is friendship between the Father and Jesus. The aim is that, just as there is one life shared by the Father and Jesus, so there shall be one life shared by Jesus and his followers. Then there will be one life, the same life, shared between the disciples themselves. The Father's command to Jesus is: 'Be in the world and love your fellow men and women.' In his turn Jesus' command to *us* is that we in the same way love each other (cf. Jn 13.34).

So what we hear of Jesus is first of all that he is loved by the Father. And that means that Jesus is a saint. For this is what a saint is: a human being with whom God is in love, with whom God shares his own divine life. What we call grace, or holiness, or godliness is just what it is like to be loved by God, to share in divinity. And Jesus is the *first* saint – not the first saint in history, of course, but the first in the sense that all other saints have their godliness from him. As John says at the very beginning of his Gospel: 'the Word became flesh and lived among us ... From his fullness we have all received, grace upon grace' (Jn 1.14-16). Our grace comes from Christ's grace. We are loved by God because Christ is loved by God.

So sanctity is a matter of being loved. And what *we* are commanded to do, as *Jesus* is commanded to do, is to *abide* in this friendship.

What is it to *abide* in friendship? It is to treat friendship as more important than anything else. We are not abiding in friendship if we prefer something else, if we opt for anything else, even life itself, at the expense of unity with our friend. That is why Jesus goes on to say: 'No one has greater love than this, to lay down one's life for one's friends' (Jn 15.13). Friendship is finding the *sharing* of life more important than carrying on the individual life. This is what Jesus is saying on the cross: 'It is better to die, sharing the last of my life with the Father, than to make my life a little longer in separation from his life.' This is his obedience to the demands of friendship, friendship with the Father.

Friendship is always *with*. It is always reciprocal. When Jesus consummates his friendship with the Father in his death on the cross, the Father reciprocates. And his love for this man Jesus not only brings Jesus from death to a new kind of life but brings all those whom Jesus loves to share in that resurrection and new life. So long, of course, as we abide in Jesus' love; so long as we do not value anything else at all more than this love.

But why should Jesus have to go to these extremes? Why does he have to submit to public torture and execution in order to demonstrate and consummate his loving obedience to the Father? Is this some test that the Father has put him to? No. Jesus goes to the extremes which he does because of the *human* world to which he has been sent, the *less* than human world to which he belongs, which is the *only* human world there is. It is because this human world is one of sin (not just a world with sins in it). It is a world *maladjusted* to the very purpose and point of being human.

The world we have made is one in which what we call 'peace' and 'order' can only be maintained by compromise, by a *moderate* degree of friendship. In this matter Jesus could not compromise, for he bore his mission from the Father. Therefore, to the conscientious administrators who tried to keep a form of peace, or at least tranquillity, in a Roman colony based on exploitation and the fear of violence, and to the priests who wanted to protect the fragile, vulnerable, highly civilized Jewish way of life from the savagery of the barbarian thugs from Rome – to all these people Jesus was an irritation, and a nuisance, and liable to cause a breach of the peace. He had to be removed by what we have learnt to call a 'surgical strike'.

It was because of the kind of world we have made that Jesus could only ultimately show his love by suffering and death. It is also because of the sort of world we have made that our *abiding* in his love also demands on our part death – not always a public execution, but an acceptance of death. Since our baptism we have all lived under sentence of death: the death of Christ, in which we shall die and so come to resurrection.

This is the good news at one level. But John sees much further into it than that. So he writes of Jesus speaking to his Father of his Father's love for him 'before the foundation of the world' (Jn 17.24). Jesus, the saint, sharing by grace in the life of God, Jesus growing in sanctity until God's love for him overflows to take in all his sinful friends, so that they are *incorporated* into him, their bodies united with his risen body: all this is just the tip of the iceberg. All this is but the sacrament of a greater reality hidden and revealed within it.

Of course we must not take the 'before' in 'before the foundation of the world' too literally. Without the foundation of the world there could be no before or after. Jesus is speaking of eternity. And, if we think of that as a long time stretching before and after creation, we are simply making a picture – quite a good one, but one by which we must not be misled. It is useful to balance it with another picture: eternity as a depth within time, creation and history; not more in the same dimension, but another dimension. Though remember that that also is only a picture.

The saintliness of Jesus in our history, the whole saving work of Jesus in our history, his human godliness, his grace, is just a sign, a sacrament, of his Godhead in eternity. In eternity Jesus is not just, as we are through him, given a *share* in the Father's life: his life *is* the Father's life. His unity on earth with the Father in obedience is just a pale reflection of the eternal dependence of God the Child, the Word coming forth from and imaging the Father in eternity. In the Godhead the unity that, for us, love and community and friendship aspire to and reach out for is absolute. 'I and the Father are one' (Jn 10.30).

We speak of God the Father and God the Son. But their unity is far beyond that of parent and child. The parent brings forth a child like herself, of the same human nature as herself and resembling herself. But, evidently, they are not *one*. They are two separate individuals of the same kind; they are two people, two distinct centres of consciousness, each with her own understanding, her own will, her own point of view. Although we speak of Father and Son as two 'Persons' we certainly do not mean two people. In the Godhead there is but one understanding and one will. There are not different centres of consciousness, different subjects with their own lives to lead. The understanding of God, the will of God, the life of God, are all the one mystery which just is God. Those who love *seek* to be *of* one mind and one heart. The Father and the Son *are* quite simply one mind and one heart.

Jesus, the Word made flesh and dwelling amongst us, is of course a distinct individual, a separate person in our modern sense of the word, a distinct centre of consciousness, with his own will distinct from the will of God, a will that needs to grow in conformity to the will of God. 'My Father, if it is possible, let this cup pass from me; yet not what I want but what you want' (Matthew 26.39). But God the Son, coming forth in eternity from the Father, is not a different person in that sense.

God the Son is the Word, the concept, coming forth from God in his eternal contemplation of the divine life – as the Holy Spirit, coming forth from the Father through the Son, is his eternal delight in contemplating that divine life. This eternal word and this eternal joy go together. Where the Word is, there is the Spirit. And that is why, in living out the sacrament of this eternal life, Jesus says to his faithful disciples: 'I have said these things to you so that my joy may be in you, and that your joy may be complete' (Jn 15.11). The joy Jesus refers to here is not just the human reassurance that all things will be well, that the suffering and death of Christ will be life-giving for the whole world, a joy in the fulfilment of God's loving design for humankind, the joy that comes from hearing the word of the gospel. No, not just that: this joy is the eternal joy which is the Holy Spirit, the joy that God has; not just his joy in loving us, but the joy he has in *being God*. That's what we share.

So, at its greatest depth, the *word* we receive is not just the good news of our liberation, our *salvation*; it is not just the forgiveness of our *sins*; it is the *eternal* Word that was in the beginning with God, the Word that was God. And the *joy* that we are given is not just the joy of release from bondage, from evil, the end of the world of violence and domination and killing. It is the incomprehensible mystery of the joy of *God* in being God that was before the foundation of the world.

When the eternal Word of God is fully spoken in our world (and, as I have said, that had to mean the cross), when that Word is heard throughout the world, then the eternal joy bursts out in all the world; the Holy Spirit of God's delight is poured out. And that is why the final feast in our celebration of our salvation, our release from slavery to sin through the cross of Christ, will be the feast of our divinity, our beginning to live the eternal life of the Trinity, the feast of Pentecost.

22

A Sermon for Easter

We do not gather at Easter to celebrate a doctrine, the doctrine of the Resurrection. We come here to rejoice in the presence of one we love, in Jesus who was lost to us and has been found. Jesus went into the ultimate absence which is death. Human love and friendship is a bodily affair; every separation is being out of *touch*: when someone we love is away we cannot touch her or him. We can make some kind of second-hand bodily contact by telephone calls or letters or the Internet, and this is better than nothing, but it is a lot less than being in the bodily presence of your friend. Every separation is a being out of touch, and that is why we rightly say that separation is a kind of little death. Being dead is being ultimately out of touch. We can remember the dead, we can keep mementos and photographs and relics, but that is a substitute for being with them; it is to ease the pain of total separation.

Jesus really died. The living human body which had been Jesus became no longer a human body but a corpse hanging from the cross and the cadaver was put away in a tomb. There was no longer a man, Jesus of Nazareth: he had lived his short life and was no more. True, his soul was, no doubt, immortal, but a soul is not a human being. We only have an individual human being when that soul is the life of its individual human body. We are animals not ghosts, not even ghosts inside animals. What you are is this living flesh and blood, and when your flesh and blood ceases to live, when your life departs, you cease to be. You are totally absent, utterly not with your fellow men and women.

That is what happened to Jesus. He was lost to us. True, Jesus was eternal Son of God and as God he could not die, could not leave us. If he did we would vanish into nothing, for he is our creator who keeps us in being for every moment as a singer keeps her song in being. As God, Jesus could not die. But neither could he be born, neither could he be with us to share our sufferings and joys. Of course, we can always rejoice in the presence to us of God our creator, but the gospel, the good news, is that God's Son was made flesh and dwelt amongst us and died amongst us. It is Jesus as man, as son of Mary, that was our human friend, Jesus, this Jewish prophet, this living, breathing, human source of astounding acceptance and love. It is this man who was killed, this individual who was loved and who was taken from us.

And today we celebrate: we rejoice because he is alive and with us. 'I am risen and with you.' God has risen him up. What had been a corpse, a cadaver, is now a living human body again, and much more, unimaginably more, humanly alive. His body is closer to us now than he ever could have been to his disciples in Galilee, and he is closer to the whole world. In the sacraments of the Church his bodily presence and contact reaches out to all humankind. Especially in the Eucharist we are united to and in his body. And this is not a metaphor, a poetic image; we are united in a bodily contact of which our familiar bodily touching is just a pale shadow.

The gospel we preach is not about memories or ideals or profound thoughts. It contains all these things, but what it is about is the human person, Jesus, alive and present to us and loving us from his human heart. Our Easter faith is that we really do encounter Jesus himself: not a message from him, or a doctrine inspired by him, or an ethics of love, or a new idea of human destiny, or a picture of him, but Jesus himself. It is in this that we rejoice.

If I met you one day (I mean really met *you*, not a picture of you or a televised three-dimensional hologram, or a truth about you, or a dream about you, but really met *you*) and you said to me 'By the way, it's a rather interesting thing; my bones are in a cave in Palestine', I would be astounded; I would not know what to think, but I would be inclined to say that you or somebody had done a remarkable 'conjuring trick with bones'. This would be the really tricky and puzzling thing: that I should meet you (you, and not a ghost or dream but the actual you) without meeting your body.

There is nothing in the least tricky or puzzling or quaint about God giving back life to the dead Jesus – and not just a resuscitation but a new and greater transfigured life in glory. There is deep mystery here, of course, as there is deep mystery in God's giving us life in the first place, in God's creation of the universe. To believe that God creates the whole universe and holds it in being over against absolute nothing, but to find it tricky and unworthy of belief that he should raise a man from the dead to a human life of glory, seems eccentric. What we might find tricky, though, would be God raising Jesus to glory by doing something for something quite other than Jesus: producing, by sleight of hand, a substitute risen Christ while the body of Jesus is left buried in the grave.

Of course, if you are not a Christian and do not believe that we really meet the man Jesus himself, if you think that Christianity is about being inspired by his memory, then there is no problem: the resurrection is a metaphor. Jesus is literally dead and his body rotted in the grave.

Again, if you do not think that Jesus was (and is) a real human being of flesh and blood, who without his body would be dead (at best a mere soul), if you think he was a god or a spirit disguised in human form, you will not have a problem: Jesus is alive because human beings don't really die; Jesus is alive or 'immortal' just as all those buried in the cemeteries are alive, having shed their mortal bodies. For people who hold any or all of these views, Jesus could be said to live on. But there would be nothing very special or surprising about it, nothing to make a fuss about at Easter, no special cause for wonder or rejoicing.

But if, like all Catholics, you are a materialist in the sense that you think that to be you is to be a living body, and if you believe (as Catholics do) that

Jesus was one of us who was born and died as we do, who left us desolate in his death as all our friends do or will do, if you believe (as Catholics do) that God has mysteriously and wonderfully changed, that by a miracle of new creation Jesus, our human friend, is with us bodily again, and much more with us, and if you also believe (as Catholics do) that because of the new human life of Jesus all our friends too will rise from the dead to a human life of glory, that grieving for the dead, that separation from the dead will come to an end, then, indeed you have something to rejoice about at Easter, a miracle of God's goodness to his creatures. We can celebrate an astounding conquest of human death.

And so on this Easter day we sing with special enthusiasm that great hymn of joy, the Creed: a hymn of joy in life, in the new human life brought back from the grave to share in the life of God himself, brought back from the dead to live as real bodily human beings in the Holy Spirit before the Father through Christ, our risen Lord.

23

Motorways and God

When the M40 motorway comes to the Chiltern Hills, it doesn't really climb them. It slices straight through. And when it comes to the valley of High Wycombe, it doesn't go down to it. It strides across on stilts. It never turns any sharp corners. It goes on in a more or less straight line. And its surface is kept smooth, with no bumps on it to speak of. When they built it they must (cf. Isa. 40.4) have said to themselves:

> Every valley shall be lifted up,
> and every mountain and hill shall be made low;
> the uneven ground shall become level,
> and the rough places a plain.

Think how very different all this is from the old-fashioned kind of road, the winding lane, Chesterton's rolling English road that the English drunkards made. The old road climbs cautiously up the hills with many loops and bends. Then it swoops down into the valley. Often, when it comes to some great property, some important landed estate, it turns and creeps apologetically right round it. It tries to find the most convenient way through the countryside that it encounters. It follows the contours. It responds to the terrain that it has to go through.

Now this old-fashioned sort of road is an image of the way *we* deal with each other, how we *have* to deal with people. With people we don't like

much, it is often an uphill struggle. It is difficult to get to know them, and
we approach them as we climb a hill – with bends and loops and changes of
tactics as we try to respond to them. With our *friends* it is all so much easier:
a downhill run that carries us along. And with *powerful* people that we are
afraid of, we avoid them if we can; we creep right round them and hope we
won't be seen. We often have to make sudden twists and turns, and sometimes
we double back. The going is rough quite a lot of the time. We have to assess
people all the time. We have to judge them to see whether they are friendly,
hostile or uncaring, so that we can measure our best response to them, or
perhaps decide not to respond at all. Are they going to be helpful? Or will they
just make things worse? All this is a bit like the old kind of road, cautiously
picking its way through the terrain, careful to make the appropriate decision.

'My thoughts are not your thoughts, nor are your ways my ways, says the
Lord' (Isa. 55.8). God's way is very much simpler than our ways. He doesn't
have our complications. He is just simply in love with us. Not just with some
of us, not just with saints or people who try to be good, but with absolutely
everybody: with liars and murderers, with traitors and rapists, with the
greedy, the arrogant, the inconsiderate, with prime ministers, and priests, and
policemen. He loves us all. And not in some general way. It is not a question
of some vague warm feeling for humanity, for the human race. You must not
think that because God knows us all, he views us as some lofty bureaucrat
might do, for whom we are each statistics in some great overall pattern. He
loves each of us intimately and personally – more intimately and personally
than we can love ourselves. He is more personally concerned for our good and
happiness than we can be ourselves.

The way of God's love is more like the motorway. It doesn't care whether
it meets easy or difficult, uphill or downhill, good or bad. It doesn't care
how important or unimportant we are. All those careful judgements *we*
have to make, distinguishing friends from foes, working out just the degree
of intimacy that is desirable in particular cases; all that deciding who is

good-hearted and kindly and candid, and who is mean and self-seeking, who is virtuous and who vicious, who is a sinner and who is righteous – none of this counts with God's love. He cuts straight through all the mountains and the valleys, the heights of sanctity and the depths of depravity. He does not turn aside from anyone. His way is smooth and easy and swift. And it reaches to sinners as well as to saints.

God does not *respond* to his world. He does not adjust his reaction to suit good people or bad. You do not have to be good *before* God will love you; you do not have to try to be good *before* God will forgive you; you do not have to repent *before* you will be absolved by God. It is all the other way round. If you *are* good, it is because God's love has already made you so; if you *want to try* to be good, that is because God is loving you; if you *want* to be forgiven, that is because God is forgiving you. You do not have to do anything, or pay anything, in exchange for God's love. God does not demand anything of you. Nothing whatever.

There is just one thing you need: you have to be ready to take a risk. You have to be ready to be destroyed, for all your security to crumble. You have to be prepared to let go of that faith in yourself that you have so lovingly built up, your faith in what *belongs* to you, your possessions of every kind. You have to be ready to be taken into the dark abyss of God's love. You have to have faith in his love; for you face the dreadful danger of becoming good, of becoming yourself as loving as God is loving. And this is a frightening prospect. The motorway can do terrible things to the countryside as it spears through it. And God's love can do terrible things to you. It may make you kind and considerate and loving.

Do you remember how Paul describes the catastrophic effects of love? God's love and forgiveness may make you patient and kind, not jealous or boastful; it may prevent you from being arrogant, or rude, or insisting on your own way, or being irritable or resentful, so that you do not rejoice in wrongs but only in what is right. It may make you bear all things, believe all things, hope all things (cf. 1 Cor. 13.4-7). Well, you know what happens to people like that: they are patronised, taken advantage of, used and despised. If you want an extreme reminder of the risks you take in being forgiven, in being liberated from sin, in becoming loving, just look at the crucifix.

The crucifix shows us that God does not only love us blindly and unconditionally. It also shows us that he was ready himself to take the risks that we take in being loved by God. The Word of God was made flesh so that he could suffer, suffer at our hands because he was a servant of love. God's love does not come from responding to the world. It is his free and gracious gift. But because God became flesh so that *we* could respond to his love, we could take it out on *him* for daring to love us, daring to threaten us with his love, daring to risk transforming us by his love. This is part of the meaning of the season of Advent culminating in Christmas, that God became flesh so that he could suffer. The mystery of Bethlehem is that God began to feel the cold as he was later to feel the torture instruments and the cross. With the insane unthinking directness of love, he blundered into our lives, crashing through like the motorway, so that he could share the price of being loved that this world exacts. He came to *share* our lives and sufferings in time so that we could share his life of love and joy in eternity.

24

Render to Caesar

Broadly speaking, Christians can be divided into two kinds: those who have to try to explain away all those things Jesus says about rich people not being able to enter the kingdom, and how the kingdom belongs only to the poor, and those who have to try to explain away the gospel story about paying tribute to Caesar (Mt. 22.15-22; Mk 12.13-17; Lk. 20.20-26). This story, in all its versions, seems to say that the service of God has nothing to do with rich and poor, nothing to do with class-struggle, nothing to do with politics and all that. It seems to say that all of that belongs to the Emperor, to Caesar. Jesus appears to be envisaging two kinds of service in which we are involved: public life (the things that belong to Caesar, especially things connected with money) and another kind of life (private life perhaps) – the things that have to do with God. He seems to be saying that when it comes to voting, or any other kind of political or economic activity, we can leave God out of it. He also seems to be saying that when it comes to the service of God we can forget about politics and economics.

Many Christians are quite happy about this. For them, the worship of God is essentially a private affair, or, anyway, the concern only of small informal groups who don't interfere with anyone else, who don't want to be interfered with, who just want to be left alone to worship God in their own way. And there are many politicians who would like to be left alone to get on with the pragmatic business of government. These people don't want to interfere with religion. And they don't want bishops and the like to interfere with them. Such people, I think, are especially affected by periods when the mixing of God and politics has produced disastrous explosions, when the church has just been persecuted, when clerics have had their grip on the political process or when sectarian feelings have been exploited for political purposes. People who have been hurt often just want to be left alone.

And you can understand such politicians' point of view. Mixing God with things can be extremely dangerous. God is an unpredictable explosive substance, and when he is around people are likely to get hurt, even crucified. The best thing to do with God is to insulate him carefully inside churches, or, better still, inside small groups of like-minded devout people. And Jesus in the 'Render to Caesar' story really does seem to lend some support to this view. Give to Caesar the things that are Caesar's (on weekdays) and to God the things that are God's (on Sundays).

Yet what of the following?

> In our country one million families live in houses held to be unfit for human habitation. More than double that number are living in sub-standard houses. There is evidence that in the last two or three years the price of moderate sized houses in some areas has doubled. The compulsory increase in the rents of council houses is inevitably reflected in the increased rents of privately owned rented accommodations …

Whose language is this? It obviously has to do with things that are Caesar's. But it comes from a statement issued by British bishops.[1]

Have the bishops got the whole thing wrong? Are they dabbling in politics when they should be looking after the souls of their flocks? They certainly seem to be dabbling in politics. They go on to 'urge Christian societies and parish organizations to … make representations locally to secure some easement or control for the house prices and rents'. If that means anything, it means that some Christians are being urged by their bishops to take part in campaigns against local council authorities.

Well now imagine someone coming to see Jesus asking him: 'Look, should we pay this increased rent or not?' And imagine him replying: 'Show me the rent book. Whose name is here as landlord? The Council? Well render to the Council the things that are the Council's, and to God the things that are God's'. Does that mean 'Yes, pay what you are told to pay, and then go away and pray'?

Maybe, but that isn't what the bishops say. They don't say a word about praying. They first of all try to make sure their own house is in order. They tell diocesan authorities and religious orders to hand over any spare land or buildings they have to housing associations and local authorities (not, of course, to private enterprise) to make homes. And then they talk about putting pressure on local councils and finding ways to reduce what they call 'the hardships and injustices arising from this grave social evil'.

Now most of us, I suppose, want to raise a small cheer when we hear bishops saying things like that. They don't often do this, though they do it a lot more often than they are given credit for, and a lot more often than they used to. But the point is that, if we cheer the bishops, what are we to say about Jesus? Doesn't he teach that bishops as such, people concerned with the service of God, should keep themselves quite separate from the affairs of Caesar? So let's look at our gospel story more carefully just in case this isn't what Jesus is saying.

The first thing we need to do is to question our easy assumption that Caesar stands as a symbol for the political sphere, for the civil power, for the secular world of power and money. Caesar was an actual historical person, and the scene depicted in our story takes place in a definite historical context. If we forget about the context, it won't be surprising if we misinterpret the scene. If we have the idea that Jesus wandered about the peaceful hills of Galilee, or the bustling town of Jerusalem, where people went about their business in an ordinary way under the benign, but strict, rule of Rome and the Herodian family, we have the thing more than slightly wrong.

Jesus lived and preached and died in the run-up to an extremely bloody and unsuccessful colonial uprising. The actual revolutionary war did not take place for another thirty years or so, but already in the time of Jesus there were underground revolutionary movements, illegal armies, acts of terrorism and hideous acts of repression. The country was held down by a large Roman army who, like all armies of occupation, bullied and harassed the people. The Romans maintained as their local puppet ruler (besides their own governor) the family of Herod, who did not come from the culture and background of the natives, and whose power depended on maintaining the union with Rome.

So the Herodians mentioned in this story (they are there in Matthew and Mark's version anyway) were collaborationists with the colonial regime. The Pharisees on the other hand (also mentioned only by Matthew and Mark) were deeply devoted to the national Jewish tradition, to its law and culture. They were profoundly conscious that the Jewish people were called to be the People of God. They believed that the Roman occupation was a blasphemy, and that their fellows belonged, not to Caesar, but only to God. The Pharisees, you might say, identified the kingdom of God with the Jewish people (once it had been liberated and come to its full power). This, indeed, is how the kingdom of God is pictured by some of the Old Testament prophets: Jerusalem ruling the world and spreading its peace and justice to all the nations who flock to her to serve Yahweh.

The Pharisees and Herodians, then, were bitter enemies. They were not merely people who disagreed in an academic sort of way. They were fierce political opponents (at least, the Pharisees were fierce; the Herodians tended to be rather easy-going, as people are when their security and privilege is guaranteed by a large army). The Pharisees tended to be more fanatical and narrow-minded, as subversive groups often are. And it is this fanaticism that we hear most about in the Gospels. But it is not the whole story. On approximately the same side as the Pharisees were the Zealots: various groups of militant revolutionary activists who carried out ambushes and generally harassed the occupying forces. Their ideology doesn't seem to have been very different from the Pharisees. They were fanatical, pious nationalists. The Zealots were an illegal underground movement and, of course, they would not have dreamt of paying taxes to Rome. I expect they intimidated people who did pay taxes, or levied taxes themselves in the villages, as most guerrilla forces do. The Pharisees were, of course, respectable and respected people. However much they might secretly approve of the Zealots' attitude to taxes, they could hardly say so openly. They would have been imprisoned or crucified for doing so.

It is now clear why Jesus calls them hypocrites and says 'Why are you putting me to the test?' (Mt. 22.18; cf. Mk 12.15). The Pharisees have recognized, of course, that the teaching of Jesus is subversive. But it is not only subversive of the political order. It is much more directly subversive of the religious order. The Pharisees see Jesus as putting forward alien and blasphemous ideas that would destroy the national tradition. They view him as a threat to themselves and to everything that makes their lives meaningful. So they propose to betray him to the common enemy: the Roman forces of occupation. That's why Jesus calls them hypocrites. They tacitly, or in private, give support to the Zealot cause. But they are hypocritically asking Jesus to come out and declare support for it in public. And, to make things quite sure, they arrange for some Herodians to be around while he does it. 'We know you are not afraid of anyone, you believe in simply speaking your mind. Come on, stand up and be counted.'

Jesus is in a difficult position. He will either announce his support for the Zealots (and the Herodians will gleefully take this news back to the Roman police), or else he will have to throw in his lot with the upper class Herodians, admit that what he had to say is irrelevant to the struggle going on and lose the young people – people like Simon the Zealot and others who form part of his following – and in fact lose his popular support altogether.

Jesus, of course, is quite prepared to lose his popular support, but not on these terms, not as a collaborationist Herodian. When he does come to die, deserted by practically everyone except his mother, it is at the hands of the Romans and Herodians, betrayed by the nationalists.

This is the difficulty Jesus is in, and we misunderstand his extremely clever reply if we think he simply opts for the Herodian position. If we think that Jesus is simply saying 'My gospel is separate from politics', then he is taking the Herodian side. But this is not what he says at all. This wouldn't account for the conclusion of our gospel story: 'They were amazed' (Mt. 22.22); 'They were utterly amazed at him' (Mk 12.17); 'Being amazed by his answer, they became silent' (Lk. 20.26). It would not have been particularly surprising if Jesus had taken the side of the collaborationists. It would merely have been a little dull. What he, in fact, does is extricate himself with a witty phrase. And the point of the phrase is that it could be understood either way.

It *could* be a revolutionary Zealot slogan: 'Let Caesar take what is his, but this people belongs to God. Let Caesar have his petty little empire in the rest of the world, but this land and this people is to be ruled by no one but God himself and his law, given directly to us.' This reading, of course, is emphasized by the coin of the tribute that has a representation of Caesar on it (the kind of graven image that was strictly forbidden by Jewish law). The Jews were forbidden to make images of the human form. The coins of God's tribute are the living coins stamped with God's image. The only image of God for the Jews is man. Let Caesar lay claim to his human possessions, but not to this people. Let God claim what is his and smash the power of these blasphemers who dare to tread on the Holy Ground of Israel. In other words: 'Romans Go Home, where you belong.'

On the other hand, Jesus' phrase *could* be read as a Herodian slogan (in the way that we have so often been taught to read it): 'Pay your taxes and keep religion out of public life; keep it as a private personal indulgence.'

But, of course, Jesus is not just extricating himself neatly from a trap. After all, in the final showdown he doesn't bother to extricate himself at all. He allows himself to be betrayed by the nationalists to the colonial power. He is not just wriggling out of a difficult situation with a kind of 'No Comment'. He wants to say that the question he is put is the wrong one. The quarrel between Herodians and Pharisees, between collaborationists and the resistance, is not the ultimate struggle. The liberation he has come to bring goes beyond political liberation. Jesus stood out against the Zealots and the Pharisees not because he was a Herodian, and not just because he rightly judged that when it came to the final confrontation they would lose and Jerusalem would be worse off than ever, but because they were fighting the wrong fight, fighting in the name of a distortion of the Jewish tradition and, therefore, a distortion of the Word of God.

They were fighting against the forces and idols of paganism in the name of a God they had appropriated to the national tradition, the God of the Law. Jesus has come to show them that this too is an idol, that the real liberation of people lies in the faith that God is he who loves us, he who ultimately and unconditionally loves us (not because we are Jewish, or Christian or revolutionaries, but because we are who we are).

This is the terrifying and destructive love of God which makes us able to *see* who we are, which smashes our own idols, our images of ourselves, and makes us confess our sin. And, in doing so, it liberates us, raises us from the dead to a new and free life in the Spirit of love. The kingdom of which Jesus speaks is not to be achieved just by defeating Roman domination (or by replacing it by the Jewish Law, or by the authority of the Church). The kingdom is fully achieved only when Jesus will hand over the kingdom to God the Father, having done away with every sovereignty, authority and power, so that God may be all in all.

Note

1   *Homelessness: A Fact and a Scandal* (a report published in 1990 by the Department for Christian Social Responsibility and Citizenship of the [Roman Catholic] Bishops' Conference of England and Wales).

25

Life After Death

A lot of Christians are uneasy about the idea of life after death. Why? Mainly for two reasons. The first is that if such an afterlife is seen just in terms of rewards or punishments, it looks like a rather infantile way of persuading people to behave well in this life. The second is that it seems very difficult, if not impossible, to envisage life after death. Pictures of hell seem to have been largely projections of vindictive or sadistic fantasies. And pictures of heaven are just unspeakably boring.

But we need to give up on the pictures. The way to make any kind of adult sense of life after death is to try to enter into the mystery of human death. And the central truth we must start from (and never get very far away from) is that we preach Christ crucified. We preach this because it is our gospel, our good news. It is, strangely, good news that Jesus of Nazareth was tortured to death on the cross. It is good news because we believe that precisely by taking on death, by submitting to death out of loving obedience to the demands of that love he called his 'Father', he took on death and conquered it. In itself, human death is senseless. It is only the cross of Christ that makes ultimate sense of human death, indeed makes even of death a focus of hope. This is because the deepest meaning of the cross is resurrection to eternal life. As St Paul says in his letter to the Corinthians: 'If Christ has not been raised, then our proclamation has been in vain and your faith has been in vain' (1 Cor. 15.14).

If we take this perspective we shall stop thinking of heaven as 'pie in the sky', and we shall stop trying to imagine an afterlife. For of this we know only two things: that it is ours, and that it is to be our eternal life. The first means that it has to be in some way bodily, for, as St Thomas Aquinas says in his commentary on 1 Corinthians, even if my soul is immortal, 'my soul is not me'. The second means that our life, our eternal life, must be now incomprehensible to us. For concerning eternity we know only what it is not, not what it is; for eternal life is God.

But why should I think that human death is in itself senseless? Why do I think that we need the cross to make sense of it? Isn't death the most natural thing in the world?

Well, I think death is indeed natural to all our fellow animals, but not exactly so in our case. Of course lots of other animals find death shocking and grievous. Anyone who has had anything to do with animals socially knows that they can mourn for their companions taken away by death. But in our grief there is something more. When someone we love dies we feel more than shock and deprivation. We feel outraged, resentful. We feel that a kind of injustice has been done.

When an animal dies it is painful for itself and for its companions; but it is indeed quite natural. A dog or cat comes to the end of its life-time as a piece of music comes to its end and completion. Even if it dies prematurely by accident, its end is natural and explicable in the larger scheme of nature. But this is not quite true of us. And this, I think, is because we do not just have a life-time fitting into the rhythms of nature. Rather, we each have a life-story. And that is something more mysterious. Every human life is not just a cycle but an unfinished story which we have been telling.

We have a life-story because by our own decisions we make something of the life we have received. Any cat is indeed the unique individual that every cat is. But that is because of what it has received from nature: its genetic make-up and the various things that have happened to it during its lifetime. But we are unique individuals in a more profound sense. For building upon what we have inherited from our ancestors, and from the tradition in which we have been brought up, we have each made for ourselves, for better or worse, the personality we now have. In this sense we belong uniquely to ourselves.

I oversimplify here, of course. We make our decisions with the help of, and under the influence of, many other people. But they are still our decisions and not simply 'what happens to us.' We are, at least in part, responsible for who we are. So when another animal dies at the hands of nature, nature is simply taking back what she has lent. But when we die at the hands of nature, nature is a usurer taking away more than we received from her. Hence our sense of injustice and outrage. That is why part of our grief and mourning is anger, justified anger at the unfairness of it all. In some way (and it has to do with our life being lived out in language and thought and narrative), we are not just parts of the natural order. We do not just belong to the natural world. We reach beyond it. This is what first of all makes human life mysterious and human death a mystery. And this is why human death is something that needs to be made sense of.

St Paul says that it was through sin that human death came into the world (Rom. 5.12). He seems to mean that we can make some kind of sense of human death by seeing it as a penalty. It is not a very reassuring or comforting sense. But at least it gives human death a meaning: we are condemned criminals, condemned to death, which, therefore, fits into some intelligible pattern – into a story, indeed. I have said that we see death as outrageous because, through our decisions, through personally enacting our life-story, we have made more of ourselves than the life we have on loan from nature. But maybe instead we have made less. Suppose our making of ourselves were really an unmaking. Suppose we have used our freedom not to intensify but to diminish our humanity (that is, to sin). Then it is we who have made a dismal sense of our destruction in death. We, and not nature, are guilty of our own deaths. Our lives have been a prolonged suicide.

Yet Paul does not just view death in these purely human terms. He looks at it in the context of God's love for us. He also has an eye on God's plan that we should not just be freely and fully human by our own decisions (and therefore unworthy of death). For Paul, a crucial fact to be reckoned with is that we are worthy of eternal life, the life which is God himself, because of God's gift of grace. That, says Paul, is God's plan. But our world has rejected this gift of God. We were born into, and live in, a world that, in its basic human structures, has rejected and rejects God's gift and pursues its own substitutes of domination and exploitation – a crucifying world. So our sin is not just a going astray from humanity but a spurning of God's love. This rejection of God's gift has twisted even our humanity, so that we are bent upon becoming worthy of death. Under these conditions of sin, our death becomes the culmination of the unmeaning of our lives. Death has not only taken from us the meaning of our life in society, with our friends and enemies. More fundamentally, we have thrown away the meaning of life with and in God. We have thrown ourselves on the rubbish tip of unmeaning. Death for us is damnation.

Well, it is either damnation or the cross. For the good news is that there was one death which was not a sign of ultimate destruction. There was one man whose death was the culmination of a life of loving obedience to God, obedience to the mission he knew he had been given, the mission of being human, really human, with no thought of dominating and controlling others but simply of giving himself away to them: the mission of being wholly vulnerable to them. It was therefore, of course, a mission that, given what we have made of our world, was bound to culminate in being killed by us.

Here was the first human death that was not a symptom of sin but a sign of loving obedience: a sacrament of response to God's love. And the answer of God was to pour out renewed life upon Jesus, to pour out the Holy Spirit in such abundance that the Spirit not merely raised Jesus from the dead but poured out through the risen Christ upon the rest of humankind. Because of this, if, by faith, we are 'in Christ', our death too can be the culmination of our loving obedience. Our death too can be a conquest of death in resurrection.

But Christians do not just grieve for their dead and go beyond their grief in rejoicing that their death is a union with Christ's death and so with his resurrection. They also pray for their dead because they are our friends, for our tradition has yet more to say about death than this. We do not just rejoice with the dead in their union with Christ's resurrection. We are also in solidarity with them in what may be a difficult and painful transition. They have to lose themselves in Christ in order to be really themselves; and this cannot be an easy thing.

Whenever we sin we not only turn away from God's love; we also turn towards ourselves, get more wrapped up in ourselves. The major evil here, the turning away from God, is, paradoxically, the easiest thing to deal with, for God is so in love with us that we have only to ask for forgiveness to find him eager to restore us to his friendship. The other part, our obsession with ourselves and our own will, is not so easy. For sin is a health hazard. We build up an addiction to our self-flattering illusions about ourselves, a habit that is hard to kick. We can work at it; and that is what penitential practices (designed to make us realistic and humble) are for. All sin involves a kind of self-indulgence; and growing out of this infantile condition, groping towards reality, is a painful business. It involves a kind of practising for death (we sometimes call it 'mortification', 'making ourselves dead'). Most Christians have recognized that people generally die with unfinished business in this respect (not in getting rid of sin, but in abandoning the humourless self-importance in which sin has left us). We have some growing up to do, some self-abandoning, before we can be sufficiently our real selves to be ready for our resurrection into glory.

And in this matter we can help each other. For Christianity is all about coming to God in and through our friendship with each other. When those we love have died we can still be with them and help them with our prayers.

This is what Purgatory is about. We pray for the dead in Purgatory not because we doubt that they are being brought to share in Christ's risen life but to help them in their painful process of being stripped, not of sin and guilt, but of the hangover of sin, of their illusions and addictions.

It is as useless to try to envisage or imagine Purgatory as it is to envisage Heaven. But we ought not to be speculating about an afterlife. What we know is that we have been buried with Christ 'by baptism into death, so that, just as Christ was raised from the dead by the glory of the Father, so we too might walk in newness of life' (Rom. 6.4). And we know that 'if we have been united with him in a death like his, we will certainly be united with him in a resur-rection like his' (Rom. 6.5).

HERBERT McCABE
BIBLIOGRAPHY

The New Creation – first published by Sheed and Ward: London, 1964; reprinted by Continuum: London and New York, 2010.

Law, Love and Language – first published by Sheed and Ward: London and New York, 1968; reprinted by Continuum: London, 2003.

The Teaching of the Catholic Church: A New Catechism of Christian Doctrine – first published by the Catholic Truth Society, 1985 (Foreword by Maurice Couve de Murville, Archbishop of Birmingham); republished by Darton, Longman and Todd: London, 2000 (Foreword by Timothy Radcliffe O.P.).

God Matters – Geoffrey Chapman: London, 1987; subsequently republished by Continuum.

God Still Matters – Continuum: London and New York, 2002 (Foreword by Alasdair MacIntyre; edited and introduced by Brian Davies).

God, Christ and Us – Continuum: London and New York, 2003 (Foreword by Archbishop Rowan Williams; edited and introduced by Brian Davies).

The Good Life: Ethics and the Pursuit of Happiness – Continuum: London and New York, 2005 (edited and introduced by Brian Davies).

Faith Within Reason – Continuum: London and New York, 2007 (Foreword by Denys Turner; edited and introduced by Brian Davies).

On Aquinas – Continuum: London and New York, 2008 (Foreword by Anthony Kenny; edited and introduced by Brian Davies).

God and Evil in the Theology of St Thomas Aquinas – Continuum: London and New York, 2010 (Foreword by Terry Eagleton; edited and introduced by Brian Davies).

INDEX